God and History in the Old Testament

With the help and advice of the following CONTRIBUTORS

T. P. Bronco, Jr.

Patrick J. Clements

Marie E. Darling

Nancy L. Feder

Scott S. Flor

Mark Charles Fox

Chitta Goswami

Paul Grimes

Mark D. Haverland

Jeffrey M. Krasner

Jan Lenkoski

Bill Lindenmuth

James H. Logan, Jr.

Thomas S. Long

Dwight Marvin

William McCown

Arthur S. Milnor

Joseph L. Overlock

Hermann C. Pitts

Deborah Robins

Martha Lois Sasser

Steven W. Schaufele

David L. Siesel

Julie Ann Stern

Hawley Todd, Jr.

W. Christian Vandenberg

James Maurice Wurtz, Jr.

Pamela H. Zachritz

GOD AND HISTORY

IN THE

OLD TESTAMENT

DENIS BALY

HARPER & ROW, PUBLISHERS

NEW YORK, HAGERSTOWN, SAN FRANCISCO,
LONDON

FIRST EDITION

Designed by Sidney Feinberg

Library of Congress Cataloging in Publication Data

Main entry under title:
God and history in the Old Testament.
  Bibliography: p.
  Includes index.
    1. God—Biblical teaching —Addresses, essays,
lectures. 2. Bible. O.T.—Criticism, interpreta-
tion, etc.—Addresses, essays, lectures. I. Baly,
Denis.
BS1192.6.G6 1976   221.6   76-325
ISBN 0-06-060369-0 pbk.

Contents

About This Book

This book is the joint work of twenty-nine people, all of them members of Kenyon College. It took its start from the discovery that modern students, coming to the Old Testament for the first time, are often deeply puzzled by its contents. The culture of the ancient Israelite world to them is strange, distant and irrelevant, and the idea of God well-nigh incomprehensible. The God made known to ancient Israel seems very different from God as they think about him in the modern world. Yet there is remarkably little one can give such people to read on the subject. There are, of course, a number of excellent theologies of the Old Testament, but they presuppose an already considerable knowledge of the Scriptures, while introductory textbooks, which clarify for the beginner the immense wealth of archaeological, historical and textual research, often with great success, can allot very little space to theological questions.

We therefore set out to supply what seemed to us to be a need. We defined our task as follows: to try to put ourselves in the place of the ancient Israelites, and to come to know God as he revealed himself to them. We agreed that we must assume no previous knowledge at all, but that we must not on the other hand confuse ignorance with lack of intelligence. We must be prepared to wrestle with difficult ideas, but at the same time struggle to express them in straightforward language and explain every technical difficulty. We decided also that we must not shrink from the question of the validity of the Old Testament for the world of our own day, even though we knew we could be accused of drawing false parallels, and possibly imposing our own political and sociological views upon the reader. One or two of the Contributors thought it would be wise to omit this question altogether, but the majority were convinced that it must be raised. We do want to insist, however, as we have tried to do in the body of the book itself, that even though we may have stated our ideas emphatically, we are not making *ex cathedra* utterances; we are offering them for serious discussion and debate.

ix

This was our method of working: The first draft of the book was presented in the form of lectures, one every two weeks, throughout the academic year 1974–75. The first four lectures had been prepared in advance, but the others were written in response to advice and criticism from the Contributors. Each lecture was mimeographed and made available at the time it was given. It was discussed for about an hour immediately afterward, and also in small groups during the intervening two weeks, sometimes with the lecturer and sometimes without him. At the succeeding lecture each Contributor returned his annotated copy of the previous one, together with comments on the other reading he or she had been doing. The results of this supplementary reading will be found in the suggestions for further reading at the end of the book.

At the end of the year the first chapter was revised in order that the method of revision might be assessed before the students went home. This revision provided the basis of the present chapters I and II. During the summer vacation the entire book was rewritten in the light of the multitude of suggestions and advice, which affected very nearly every page. As far as possible the results of the discussions were incorporated into the text, but occasionally there had been strong disagreement on the part of one or two Contributors. In such a case the dissent is to be found in the additional notes at the end of the chapter. It was placed there only because of problems of space, and not in order to downgrade it. Majorities are not necessarily right, and these notes represent a serious addition to the text itself.

In the ensuing fall semester all the Contributors read the revised manuscript and offered further comments, as well as helping with the tedious chore of checking the biblical references, etc. Lest we might have developed an "in-group" set of concepts and vocabulary, the manuscript was read by members of the Old Testament introductory class, for whose help we are indeed grateful. In the second part of the semester the book was given its final form.

It had been agreed from the start that *every* comment and criticism, however slight it might seem, should be noted for further consideration. Criticism was to be free and unfettered, with the sole proviso that it should as far as possible be constructive. It might range from a misplaced comma to the flat disagreement with the point of view set forth. Nothing was excluded. However, we did ask all the Contributors not merely to find fault, but to try to assess both what was good and what was bad, and to explain why, and also, if they thought that something had been poorly expressed, to suggest how it might be said better. We tried to be aware all the time that we were engaged together in writing a book, and must always, therefore, take account of the technical problems involved, and that in addition to the problems of content we had embarked upon a sustained exercise in the writing of good English prose.

The Contributors included twenty-six students, plus one faculty member and one alumnus who had asked if they might join us, and whose advice and suggestions were always useful. Of the students six were seniors, four juniors, one a sophomore, and fifteen freshmen, an entirely chance distribution, since the course had been opened to any who were interested. We all agreed that it would have been helpful to have had a more even balance, but the presence of a large number of freshmen was most valuable, for our purpose was to produce a book which would be comprehensible at their level.

We do not at Kenyon make any prior inquiries about religious affiliation, but in the course of the discussion it became clear that the Jewish, Catholic and Protestant traditions were all effectively represented. The range of interests was also wide. Of the majors, declared or proposed, only eight were in Religion. The other fields included Art, Biology, Chemistry, Drama, Economics, English, Music, Political Science and Psychology. There was also a considerable expanse of international experience, for the Contributors included people who had lived for extended periods in Canada, India, Israel, Morocco, Zaire and the countries of Western Europe. I have myself known the Middle East intimately and loved it for very nearly forty years, and although I have taught Old Testament for almost as long, my original training was in Geography, and when I first came to Kenyon I taught in the Political Science Department.

Special thanks are due to Mr. Clayton Carlson, Religious Books Editor of Harper & Row, Dr. Bruce Haywood, Provost of Kenyon College, and Professor Donald Rogan, the present Chairman of the Religion Department, for their constant interest and support, to Professor Eugen Kullmann for reading through the revised manuscript and making many valuable suggestions, and also to Mrs. William Frame and Ms. Marcella Haldeman, for the secretarial help which alone made possible the meeting of repeated deadlines.

In conclusion, we would all agree that the project, considered as a college course, proved well worthwhile. The Contributors have spoken most warmly about it, and they in their turn have earned heartfelt gratitude for the large amount of extra work they willingly undertook. Their comments, though sometimes severe, were always helpful and their contributions have made the book what it is. It has been written by one person, because a book written by a committee is usually a disaster, but it is the product of all twenty-nine of us.

DENIS BALY

Kenyon College, 1975

Abbreviations

ANET   James B. Pritchard, ed. *Ancient Near Eastern Texts Relating to the Old Testament*. Princeton: Princeton University Press, 1955.

IB   *The Interpreter's Bible*. Nashville: Abingdon Press, 1952–7.

ID   *The Interpreter's Dictionary of the Bible*. Nashville: Abingdon Press, 1962.

JB   *The Jerusalem Bible*.

JBL   *Journal of Biblical Literature*

KJV   The King James Version of the Bible (in Britain the Authorized Version).

NEB   *The New English Bible*.

RSV   *The Revised Standard Version of the Bible*.

N.B. Biblical quotations are from the Revised Standard Version of the Bible, copyrighted 1946, 1952, © 1971, 1973 by the Division of Christian Education of the National Council of the Churches of Christ in the U.S.A. and are used by permission. In every case the original form YHWH has been substituted for the translation, "the LORD." Occasionally the original Hebrew word, e.g., *hesed, torah,* has also been given instead of the English translation.

God and History in the Old Testament

PRELIMINARY CONCEPTS

1. In the Beginning—God[1]

The Problem of "God"

This book is an attempt at understanding the concept of God as it is found in the collection of writings commonly known today as the Old Testament. But we start with a disadvantage: the word "God" has already some kind of meaning for us. This is true even for people brought up in an agnostic or atheist home, since the word is part of Western culture. Probably for most people in the West it means at the very least "somebody," however vaguely this "somebody" is conceived. Moreover, this "somebody" is usually thought of by those who believe in him as good and loving, and as the one who can be trusted to protect and comfort them.

Certainly, throughout the Bible "God" is spoken of in strongly personal terms, as speaking, doing, thinking, changing his mind, loving, forgiving and caring.[2] There are frequent prayers and giving of thanks to "God," and the assurance that he can, and does, help men and women.[3] Nevertheless, one cannot go very far in the Bible without becoming aware that "God" can apparently also act cruelly and even, it would seem, irrationally. We are told that he kills men, apparently wantonly;[4] he orders the destruction of a whole people;[5] he tells Moses to speak to Pharaoh, but then hardens Pharaoh's heart so that he shall not listen;[6] he is a "man of war";[7] he does not always give the help he is begged to give;[8] he even puts lies into men's hearts;[9] and he is accused of betrayal and deception.[10]

1. Some, though not all, of those who read the manuscript in its later stages suggested that the first two chapters constitute too long an introduction to the main argument, which does not begin until Chap. 3. However, these first two chapters deal with questions and difficulties raised in the original discussions and the Contributors all agreed that these needed clarification at the beginning. Readers who find such clearing of the ground tedious may move through them swiftly to the third chapter.
2. See, e.g., Exod. 20:1; Ps. 12:5; Isa. 55:8; Amos 7:3, 6; Ps. 103:13.
3. This is the theme of very many psalms. See, e.g., Ps. 121.
4. II Sam. 6:6–7.   5. I Sam. 15:1–3.   6. Exod. 7:3.
7. Exod. 15:3.   8. Ps. 44.   9. I Kings 22:9–23.   10. Jer. 20:7.

Members of the Christian community often claim that for them the problem is solved. In the New Testament, they say, we see the true love of God,[11] and therefore we can leave behind the wrath, anger and cruel judgments of God as he appears in the Old Testament. This certainly sounds attractive, but it will not do. First, in what Christians call the "Old" Testament, the love of God is abundantly bestowed. The Israelites were deeply convinced that their God was "merciful and gracious, slow to anger, and abounding in steadfast love and faithfulness."[12] Furthermore, the wrath and judgment of God are no less apparent in the New Testament.[13] Second, the "New" Testament is written so completely upon the basis of the "Old" that very nearly every verse presupposes its thinking, and presupposes also that that thinking is sound.[14] Third, and this is of immense importance, if the so-called Old Testament does not have real validity in its own right, then Christians would not have known Christ. This may sound to many a shocking statement, but it is inescapable. They could have known him, certainly, but only as Jesus of Nazareth; they could not have known him as "the Christ," i.e., as the Messiah, for this is a thoroughly Old Testament term.[15] They were able to recognize in Jesus of Nazareth "he that should come,"[16] only because the Hebrew Scriptures were there, "written in former days . . . for our instruction."[17]

Therefore, it is a mistake to start with our present concept of God and try to fit the Old Testament God into it. It is always a mistake, in any inquiry, to start with presuppositions, because they obscure the very question that is being studied.[18] We need instead to use the excellent principle of the rabbis, who in their teaching distinguish between *pashut,* the straight meaning of the text, and *derashah,* the interpretation of it. We must begin with *pashut,* with the text itself, and try to find out what it is really saying. But we must remember that what seems to us today to be the "straight meaning" may not be what the writers of the time intended their readers to understand. We must therefore struggle to compre-

11. E.g., Luke 12:32; John 3:16; Rom. 8:38–39; I John 4:16.
12. Exod. 34:6. See also I Kings 8:23; Ps. 136; Isa. 40:9–11; Joel 2:13; etc.
13. E.g., Matt. 22:1–14; 25:31–46; Acts 5:1–11; 13:8–11; Heb. 10:26–31.
14. This is not an exaggeration. Only the three short epistles of John are written without constant reference to the Old Testament. Everywhere else one can go through, verse by verse, noting in nearly all of them some trace of Old Testament thought, very often a direct reference or quotation.
15. The title "Christ" is the English form of the Greek word *Christos,* which is a translation of the Hebrew *meshiach,* i.e., the anointed one.
16. Matt. 11:3; Luke 7:19. See E. Jenni, "Messiah, Jewish," ID, III, 360–65; Sigmund Mowinckel, *He That Cometh* (Oxford: Basil Blackwell, 1956); Helmer Ringgren, *The Messiah in the Old Testament* (London: SCM Press, 1956); Joseph Klausner, *The Messianic Idea in Israel from Its Beginning to the Completion of the Mishnah,* trans. from the 3rd Hebrew ed. by W. F. Stinespring (New York: Macmillan, 1955).
17. Rom. 15:4.   18. See additional notes.

hend, as far as we possibly can, what they were talking about when they spoke of "God." That is the true *pashut,* and we must search for it diligently. This is the whole purpose of this book.

We must go back to the beginning. We cannot *start* with the belief that there is only one God, as if this were self-evident, nor can we begin with the Talmud or with the New Testament understanding. We must go back to the days of the Israelites themselves, when there were many gods and lords. In those days the people were confronted by an actual and serious choice between different "gods," and the consequences of this choice were held to be fateful. The command to the Israelites was unequivocal: "You shall not have any other gods in defiance of me."[19] In the renewal of the covenant ceremony recorded in Joshua 24 the people were solemnly warned how weighty would be the consequences of choosing deliberately to enter into a covenant or agreement with this "god" in place of other "gods." More than three and a half centuries later Elijah put a similar question: "How long will you go limping with two different opinions? If the LORD is God, follow him; but if Baal, then follow him."[20] As late as the time of Jeremiah, i.e., more than two hundred years after the time of Elijah, many of the people in Jerusalem were still choosing to recognize, and even to worship openly, other "gods."[21]

We have an indication of what "serving other gods" meant in ancient Israel from the story of how David, who was being treated by King Saul as an outlaw and had been forced to leave the country, said that this banishment meant he was compelled to "serve other gods."[22] He was saying that he could no longer live as an Israelite, and must go and live instead according to another political and cultural system, that of the Philistines, among whom he had taken refuge.

This gives us a useful starting point. To go and live in a foreign country is to be forced to learn a foreign language, and to think in new terms. It means having to ask about everything—"What is this called?"—because until you have learned the names of things you cannot even buy food, or find the way from one place to another. But names do not stand all by themselves. They are part of the whole complex web of language. Everything is named in terms of its significance for the people who talk

19. Exod. 20:3. The phrase translated here "in defiance of me" is literally in Hebrew "before my face." From what we have learned in recent years about ancient Middle Eastern treaties and covenants, it is evident that all covenants made with a major power for protection laid down that there could be only one Protector. To hedge one's bets and seek for the protection of another great power as well was an act of rebellion. It was defiance of the protecting power and a grave breach of the covenant.
20. I Kings 18:21. For a fuller discussion of this see below, Chap. 7.
21. Jer. 7:16–20.   22. I Sam. 26:19.

this language, and from time to time they insist that things must be called by their right names, or in the modern jargon, "Tell it like it is." This is not just a question of idiom or fashion, but of truth, for words used in a false sense can mislead and deceive. Yet to argue that there are "right" names and "wrong" names is to claim that there is some authority to which one can appeal, some point of reference, by which it can be decided whether a word is being used rightly or wrongly. Almost universally this point of reference is the experience of the community. When a Black person says firmly, "Black is beautiful," he is saying (and he is saying quite rightly) that in the experience of his community the dictionary definition of "black" as meaning "soiled, dirty, evil, wicked, harmful, disgraceful, sad, dismal, gloomy, without hope"[23] is nonsense. Therefore, he says, to use the word as if this were its basic meaning is altogether false and misleading.

All true communal experience goes far back into history. It has been built up over generations and is profound and serious. It is not something which anybody has invented, or constructed artificially. All societies are deeply persuaded that their experience is based upon solid reality; they are sure that a thing is true because for them it has been tried in the fire of hard experience, and cannot now be denied. When they are confronted by something new, which they must incorporate into their world, they give it a name in terms of an already accepted interpretation of the world around them. This interpretation is expressed by the language they use, and is solidly grounded in their experience and upon the reality which they understand to be revealed in that experience.

No community, no society, can continue to exist without this conviction of already established truth, without taking for granted that there is, as it were, something solid, some point at which it is possible to stand securely and to begin to build. When this conviction crumbles, when the members no longer believe in the truth of the "reality" which was thought to undergird all their activity, then society falls to pieces and, as was well said of the later Roman Empire, there is a "failure of nerve." There no longer seems any compelling reason for acting, nor is there any clear sense of purpose, because without a valid point of reference there is no direction at all, no "up" or "down," no "backward" and no "forward."[24]

23. All these meanings of the word "black" are taken from Webster's Dictionary.
24. "For better or for worse, men are social beings. Their 'sociality' includes what they think, or believe they 'know' about the world. Most of what we 'know' we have taken on the authority of others, and it is only as others continue to confirm this 'knowledge' that it continues to be plausible to us. *It is such socially shared, socially taken-for-granted 'knowledge' that allows us to move with a mea-*

When people speak of their "god," therefore, they mean this basic reality, which they believe to be the ultimate and final reality, without which there cannot be life in any sense that the community understands the term. When in ancient Babylon men said that Marduk was "god," or in Assyria that Asshur was "god," they were saying that here was the ultimate reality, and that the world could be properly understood only in these terms.

Obviously, different societies have had very different experiences and will, therefore, with excellent reason argue that the fundamental reality is different from that which other people, building upon other experience, have come to understand. This is why there was dispute about the "gods" in the ancient world. Large-scale societies tend to be pluralistic, or polytheistic, societies, because they must recognize that different sections of the community have different concepts of the world. But even such a society is forced to claim that there is some kind of common experience to which all must pay allegiance, if they are not to merit the name of "traitor" and "disloyal." The argument about amnesty which developed after the American withdrawal from the Vietnam war well illustrates this. Those who saw loyalty to one's country as an absolute duty spoke scornfully of "draft-dodgers" and "deserters," but those who were convinced of a different primary reality spoke, rather, of "conscientious objectors."

Therefore, we must recognize throughout our study that when the ancient Israelites spoke of "God," they were not using the word casually. They were speaking of what they understood to be the ultimate Reality beyond their immediate world, that Reality which gives meaning and significance to everything else, and without which there cannot be meaning at all. We must not assume in advance that they thought of this Reality as nice, or good, or comfortable. That is not what is important about reality. What is important is that it is *real,* that it is the truth about the world, and that it provides a secure and trustworthy basis upon which men and women may live and move and have their being. What the Israelites understood this basis to be will be the subject of our inquiry.

"God" and the "Old Testament"

If names do not exist in isolation, but are always part of a total network of language, which is itself woven around our understanding of ultimate reality, we must use them carefully and with precision. We shall have to define, as we progress in our study, the sense in which the key

---

sure of confidence through everyday life." Peter L. Berger, *A Rumor of Angels* (Garden City, N.Y.: Doubleday, 1969), p. 8 (italics added).

words are being used. Some, however, need clarification at once. One is the term "Old Testament," which derives its meaning from the Christian tradition, that recognizes also a "New Testament." But for many Jewish people, calling their Scriptures the "Old" Testament is displeasing, because it seems to carry the sense of something inferior and secondary. It is true that the term itself comes straight from the concept of the new and old covenants in Jeremiah 31:31–34, but the adverse comparison that Christians have too often drawn between the two Testaments (i.e., the two covenants) has encouraged much misunderstanding. Jewish people speak instead of *Tanak,* but this word itself, together with the three words upon which it is based, *Torah, Nebiim, Ketubim* (Torah, Prophets, Writings), has come to have for them immensely rich connotations which are, of course, entirely foreign to those who do not share their traditions.

Since we are trying to avoid all presuppositions, whether Christian, Jewish, Western, or any other, we would do well to use no descriptive adjective, and to speak instead of the *Testament.* This is a weighty word. It carries with it the ancient sense of "covenant," which is integral to Israelite thought, and also the sense of solid evidence and authority. All these meanings have been part of the deep significance of the material, for good or for ill, for well over two thousand years. It is, moreover, a timeless word, neither "old" nor "new," but incumbent upon us here now. It is a word, therefore, true to the spirit of Deuteronomy, one of the most important of its books, which insists continually that the statutes and the ordinances are not outmoded, but are given to the people "this day."[25]

Another problem is what word to use for the Israelite God, for we shall need continually to distinguish between this "God" and those others whom people around them asserted were "God." The *Testament* often speaks of *Elohim,* which was the general word in Hebrew for God, or gods, but far more often it uses a quite definite name, which is written as YHWH.[26] In English versions this is usually translated as "the LORD," or "the Eternal," but these translations result from later thinking when the idea of one God had become firmly established, and when the sacred name was thought too sacred to mention. For the greater part of the time we shall be considering, however, the name YHWH was in constant use, and indeed among the ordinary people there was at times much

---

25. E.g., Deut. 5:1–3. See also below, Chap. 19.

26. The sacred name is usually spelled in modern English as "Yahweh," since this was probably the pronunciation. However, in the text of this book we have kept the spelling YHWH, because of the traditional Jewish understanding that it should not be pronounced. YHWH occurs some 6,800 times in the *Testament,* as compared with 2,750 for *Elohim.*

doubt about whether he were truly the Lord, or whether power belonged to some other god. We must therefore be careful of equating the term "Lord" too quickly with the God made known to ancient Israel, as if there had never been any doubt about the matter, and would be wise to keep to the ancient name. If these terms YHWH and the *Testament* come as something of a shock to the reader, this will do no harm, because they will help with each occurrence to brush away preconceived ideas.

The Absolutely Other

We now need to explore more carefully what was said earlier about "God" being the ultimate and final Reality. This is not an easy concept to wrestle with because of the meaning which the word "God" has in the everyday speech of the modern world. It is used constantly as if it were the name of somebody, so that when in church or synagogue we hear read to us, "God spake all these words and said . . ."[27] we tend to think immediately of somebody called "God" saying something in an audible voice. But for ancient Israel the *name* was undoubtedly YHWH. *Elohim* or *El,* which we translate "God," was not a name; it was instead a general word for deity. Certainly, the sacred name YHWH and the word "God" became merged in their minds in the period after the Exile, when fully monotheistic Judaism developed, and when they ceased to pronounce the name YHWH, as being too holy for human use. But in the whole of the period before the end of the Exile the problem of "God" was still a very open question.

We have seen that every society works with a commonly accepted understanding of the character of the universe, and the human condition within this universe, an understanding based upon its own experience as it has developed through generation after generation. American society, for instance, has its own way of looking at the world, which is clearly different from the European way of looking at it. One thing which must strike every foreigner coming to live and work in the United States is the strength of the belief that society is necessarily made up of individuals. This belief in the basic importance of the individual is the result of American experience. The same importance is not given to the concept of the individual in the societies of the Old World, except insofar as they have been brought under the influence of American thinking.[28] Moreover, every society works with the conviction that things do not exist in

---

27. Exod. 20:1 (KJV).
28. The emphasis on the individual seems to come from pioneer experience. It is paralleled in Canadian and Australian society.

meaningless isolation. It sees them related to each other in a coherent pattern. This pattern explains and demonstrates the meaning of everything. When something new happens, or is discovered, it is fitted into the pattern and given a name which expresses its meaning, i.e., its relationship to other things in the pattern.

However, behind this pattern there is understood to be some basic and fundamental reality, which holds it all together, and provides the basic principle which relates everything to everything else. In religious terminology we call this source of all meaning "God." In other words, "God" is a word which we use for whatever it is that gives meaning and life to everything, and holds it all together in a coherent whole.

But the difficulty is that we can never say exactly what this Reality is. The one thing that we cannot put into a carefully defined category, and give an exact name to, is the principle which integrates the whole pattern. It is not *part* of the pattern, as everything else is. It is the *basis* and foundation of the pattern. Everything else in the whole vast world can be given some kind of name, but the source of all the names stands alone. In Chinese thought the word for this pattern of the entire universe is *tao,* but Lao Tzu rightly says that "the *Tao* to which you can give a name is not the absolute *Tao.*"[29] Even the name YHWH means no more than "He who is," or "He who is present," or perhaps "He who causes to be." Man can go no further than that in naming "God." The rest is mystery.

We therefore have to use analogies, or models, to explain what is meant by "God."[30] One of the most useful models is that of a person, especially when we are thinking of the activity of "God," or the relation of man to "God" in worship. In fact, it is almost unavoidable when we are concerned with praying, thanksgiving, the need for help, etc. One might very well go much further and say that "person-ness" is ultimate, that it holds everything else together. This has come much to the fore recently, because many people are saying that the final and ultimate question that must be asked about all science and technology (nuclear fission, genetic research, computers, etc.), as well as about economic policy and political activity, is "What is all this going to do to persons?" But this insistence that the ultimate reality, in terms of which everything in the world must be brought under judgment, is personal should never lead us into thinking that "God" is actually "a person," with a proper name, just like all the other persons we meet in daily life.

What we are trying to do here is to discover the model, or the under-

---

29. *Tao Te Ching,* I.
30. See, e.g., Mircea Eliade, *Images and Symbols,* trans. Philip Mairet (London: Harvill Press, 1961), pp. 9–21, and Paul Tillich, *Dynamics of Faith* (New York: Harper & Row, 1957), Chap. III.

standing of "God" which made sense to the ancient Israelites. We are also trying, of course, to discover whether it still makes sense today. It is quite obvious from even a casual reading of the *Testament* that the understanding of "God" in terms of the person model is very important indeed. We meet it constantly. But it is no less evident from the literature of the surrounding peoples that they also used this model, and thought and spoke of their gods in terms of "person-ness." What, then, makes the thinking of the Israelites different, and why were they so conscious of this difference?[31]

It will be the argument of much of this book that they found themselves forced to use another model, which includes the model of person-ness, but far transcends it. They still worked with the model of person-ness, which they found to be entirely valid, but they placed it within a larger context, that of "the other," or "otherness." The context is larger because things and events can be "other" as well as persons.

It is important to use this term, "Absolutely Other," with precision.[32] It is not "Wholly Other," i.e., so completely different that there can be no kind of communication with anything else. It does not mean completely alien. The word "absolutely" is used here to indicate that there is understood to be an absolute distinction between "God" and everything else. Something of what is meant can be seen if we consider different persons at the human level. Between you and me there is an absolute distinction. We each have our own identity. You cannot ever become me, and I cannot become you. Yet you are not alien to me. We have a great deal in common. We can enter into each other's thoughts. This we do largely by means of conversation, and this is probably why the concept of the "word of God" is so important in all three monotheistic religions. Of course, the distinction is vastly greater in the case of "God" than it is in the case of two human beings.

The word "other" does not in the least mean either irrelevant or inferior. On the contrary, if we insist that "otherness" and "God" can be used as closely related words, we are saying that in this sense "other" means what is ultimate, and that it is the basis of all meaning. Nothing at all is excluded from the "otherness" concept, for there is nothing of which we cannot say that it is "other." Light is other than darkness; a chair is other than a table; people are other than things; and so on. We cannot, in fact, define the meaning of anything without speaking of that which is other than the thing we are trying to define. There is good reason, therefore, for saying that with "the other" we come very close to the ultimate and basic principle, and to the secret of the pattern of the universe.

31. See additional notes.   32. See additional notes.

Certainly this does not answer every problem, nor does it provide a complete and satisfactory explanation of what we mean when we speak of "God." All language about "God" is defective and insufficient, because "God" transcends everything we can say about him. All our models, however helpful, have to be complemented, enriched, and corrected by other language and other experience. It is important to grasp, therefore, that "God" is always "other" than what we say he is.

For reasons that we shall discover as we make our exploration of the *Testament,* many of those who formed and shaped Israelite thought found themselves forced to reject as inadequate much of the commonly accepted thinking about "God." When, therefore, they spoke of YHWH, they thought of him as other than the gods of the nations round about, certainly other than man, and other than the world. They could conceive of no image or likeness which it would be proper to use for him.

> You shall not make for yourself a graven image, or any likeness of anything that is in heaven above, or that is in the earth beneath, or that is in the water under the earth.[33]

For them, though he constantly made himself known to them, the "otherness" of YHWH was paramount.

This way of thinking provoked a revolution in thought comparable to the Copernican revolution. The importance of Copernicus is not that he discovered new things, but that he looked at the same old things in a new way. Previously people had looked at the sky and the planets from the viewpoint of the earth. Copernicus, so to speak, stepped right outside the earth, and looked at the planets from the viewpoint of the sun. This new outlook forced people in the end to look at *everything* in a new way.

When we try to discover why there was this breakthrough in Israelite thought, we find the explanation in their history, which is to say, in all the things that happened to them. Their way of thinking is bound to be strange to people who have been born and grown up in the United States, because this country has been throughout its existence wonderfully protected by the ocean from the onslaughts of other countries and other systems. But the Israelites were not protected from this at all. They lived at a crossroads, and foreign armies marched constantly across their soil. Moreover, they were repeatedly thrust into situations in which the foreign society looked as if it were going to swamp them completely.

They could not find in Canaanite thought, or for that matter in Egyptian and Mesopotamian thought, any satisfactory explanation of what was constantly happening to them.[34] This is why the biblical writers

33. Exod. 20:4; see also Isa. 40:25.
34. See additional notes.

are so contemptuous of the "foreign gods." A system of thought built around the concept of "Baal"[35] seemed to them to provide no adequate explanation either for such things as Assyrian imperialism or for their own survival despite the Assyrian conquest.

Obviously, the ordinary Israelites did not make this breakthrough. They found the Baal concept quite sufficient for their daily life, which centered around their farming. They blamed everything else on their rulers, or on the enemy, or they said that their "god" was asleep, and that he had not roused himself to go out with their armies.[36] But the *Testament* is not a record of their thinking. It is the record of people who could not be content with this, people to whom the word of YHWH came, and who therefore did begin to think along new lines. These people stepped right outside the world of their day, and began to look at it from the point of view of "the Other," and of the encounter with the Other. They found that when they looked at the world in this way all sorts of things began to make sense which had not made sense before. Admittedly, this pattern of thought took a long time to develop, because it was neither obvious nor easy, but it never let them down. They never came up against anything which could not be understood in these terms. The idea was capable of infinite expansion, and everything could be seen from this point of view. Therefore, they said in the end that there is indeed only one true "God," and that he is "the Other," but at the same time they never ceased to think of "God" as intensely personal.[37]

ADDITIONAL NOTES TO CHAPTER 1

18. The objection was raised, both by Contributors and by some of those who read the manuscript later, that one cannot begin without any presuppositions at all, and that in fact some of the ideas expressed in the first two chapters are themselves presuppositions. This objection is certainly valid. Nevertheless, the principle is sound that one should always *try* to begin without them and that where they cannot be avoided they should be recognized for what they are: preliminary concepts, tentative and open to correction. As for the possible presuppositions in these first two chapters, we can plead only that they have all been subjected to much criticism and are therefore none of them unexamined preconceptions.

31. George Ernest Wright in *The Old Testament against Its Environment* (Naperville, Ill.: Alec R. Allenson, 1950), p. 25, points out that other nations also used animal and other nature models, which the Israelites did not. But this does not invalidate the fact that they all made great use of the person model.

35. "Baal," which means "lord," was a commonly used Canaanite word for God, or for their gods. What we may call the "Baal concept" always involved using something in the natural world as providing the basis upon which the meaning of everything else could be discerned.

36. Ps. 44:9, 23.

37. This comes out most forcefully in the poems of Isaiah of Babylon, found in Isa. 40–55. See below, Chap. 15.

32. The term *ganz andere* is most familiar to students of religion today from its use by Rudolf Otto in *The Idea of the Holy*. However, he used it in relation to the worldwide phenomenon of religion, in the sense of that "terrifying and fascinating mystery," of which religious man is acutely and uncomfortably aware. In his sense it could equally well be translated "wholly other." However, the term was also used by Karl Barth at about the same time and apparently quite independently, for God as he is made known in the Bible. It is being used in this book very much more in the sense in which Karl Barth used it than in the sense intended by Rudolf Otto, important though that is.

34. It is very important not to isolate the biblical writers from the general Middle Eastern culture of their time, and suggest that they alone thought of their God as active in history. The Hittites, Babylonians and Assyrians undoubtedly spoke of their gods as having caused events to happen, and of these events having been deliberately intended by the god, and taking place in direct response to a divine command. Invasions by some foreign power were spoken of as punishments sent by the god and, more frequently, national victories were ascribed to the god acting on their behalf, or to the king as obeying the god's command. Much of the language used in these texts can be paralleled in the *Testament*. This is well illustrated in Bertil Albrektson, *History and the Gods: An Essay on the Idea of Historical Events as Divine Manifestations in the Ancient Near East and in Israel* (Lund, Sweden: CWK Gleerup, 1967).

Nevertheless, there are important differences. The Israelite prophets alone claimed that God made his will known to them long before the events took place and were therefore unique in foretelling punishment and disaster. We do not find among the surrounding nations any outright conflict with "nature religion," nor any direct challenge to the cyclical view of the world. It is true that the cyclical view was by no means the sole interpretation of history in the other nations, but that it existed unrebuked is undeniable. There is also in the records of other Middle Eastern nations nothing comparable to the Yahwist history. All in all, one must insist that though the Israelites certainly shared with their neighbors some of their understanding of historical events, they were quite distinct in the importance their religious thinking attached to history, both past and present, and even more in their concept of the future.

2. Culture Shock and Ancient Israel

The Strange World of the Israelites

The modern reader, opening the pages of the *Testament* for the first time, steps straight into a foreign country, divided from us both by its character and by distance in time. Today we can cross the intervening space between the United States and Jerusalem in a matter of hours, but even in the modern world we find ourselves in a different environment when we do so. The close relationship of desert and cultivated land, the total absence of rain for five whole months in the year, the widely varied regions and cultures within a small area, the political relationship of little neighboring countries one to another—these, among others, are all things of which most of us have little or no experience, though all of them have characterized the "land of the Bible" throughout the centuries. And so to go there, even today, is to experience what is called "culture shock," to find ourselves in a culture so new to us and so strange that we are taken by surprise, and are often shaken and bewildered. It is to encounter "otherness."

How much the more, then, when we have to go back in time for three or even four thousand years, to a world in which Pharaoh was a power to be reckoned with and not just a name in a book, when a day's journey meant a distance of only a few miles, when animal sacrifice was a part of regular life, when even cities were no more than a quarter of a mile across and often much less, and when wild beasts were a real and present danger to both the farmer and the man upon a journey. In a world so distant from us even such simple words as "father" and "son," "land" and "water," did not mean what they mean for us today. To speak of a "son" meant to emphasize identity, for the function of a son was not to be a separate and recognizable individual, but to be as far as possible the same as his father, to do what he saw his father doing and to continue his work after him. To speak of a "father" was to speak of the source and initiator of life, with all the authority that this implies, a meaning that has well-nigh disappeared from modern Western usage. In that

13

world, constantly threatened by drought and famine, at the mercy of uncertain and erratic rainfall, to speak of "water" is to speak, not of something easily drawn from the tap, but of life itself, for it is recognized by everyone that without water men, women and children all die. When, as can so easily happen, there is no water in the well, and people return with their vessels empty, the very ground, said Jeremiah, is dismayed.[1] To speak of the "land," the *eretz,* however, is to speak, not only of the tiny country itself, but to speak of order and disorder, of the territory of true order and meaning, beyond whose borders lie violence and confusion, where "the nations conspire and the peoples plot in vain."[2]

Nevertheless, these obstacles of time and space, tremendous though they may be, are not impassable barriers. Help may come to us from two quarters. First, the ancient Semitic mind was given to thinking in sternly concrete terms, rather than the abstract speculation of Greek philosophers, and to using down-to-earth language drawn from everyday life. Even such profound thinkers as the writers of the Book of Job and of Isaiah 40–55 speak continually of things one may touch and see and feel, such as the ox and the ass, worms and dirt, the weaver's shuttle, withered grass, prisoners in a dungeon, and the polished arrow in a quiver.[3] This makes for much greater ease of translation, for we are not confronted here with abstractions for which our own language has no equivalent. It is true that we do not today use oxen for plowing, or fight with bows and arrows, and must therefore stop to ask what train of thought these things would have conjured up in the mind of an ancient Israelite, and why the grass, parched by the scorching east wind, was such a vivid symbol to him. Yet they were actual things, and archaeological, geographical and linguistic studies can bring many of them out into the open for us.

We who read the *Testament* today have at our disposal a vast wealth of information. We know what clothes were worn in the time of Abraham, what food was eaten and what vessels were used. We know a great deal about the ancient city of Jerusalem, and have a very good idea of what a man would have seen when he went into the Temple courts. We know infinitely more than was known one hundred years ago about the whole world surrounding the ancient Israelites and the peoples who inhabited that world. We can see, far more exactly than our grandfathers could, the actual situations to which the prophets addressed themselves, and what political choices were open to the rulers whom they counseled.

It is true that we have still a great deal to learn, for there are frustrating gaps in our knowledge. We can still, for instance, only guess at exactly which mountain was known to the Israelites as Sinai, and

1. Jer. 14:2–6.   2. Ps. 2:1.   3. Job 6:5; 7:5, 6; Isa. 40:7; 42:7; 49:2.

where the important sanctuary of Gilgal lay. It is true also that none of these disciplines can prove the Bible either "true" or "untrue," because from beginning to end the writers in the *Testament* are concerned with the activity of that which we call "God," and this activity is not to be disclosed by the pick and shovel of an archaeologist. Nevertheless, this vast labor of research by men and women from many nations has opened for us today a storehouse of knowledge and illuminated many of the darkest caverns. We are at least much more fully aware of the kind of thing the writers had in mind when they spoke of "God" by means of concrete images, and what were the hard political facts which the Prophets described as the work of "God" himself. Certainly, the prime source of our understanding must always be the *Testament* itself, and neither this nor any other book is a substitute for study of the *Testament,* but anyone today who seeks to understand the "God" of ancient Israel must enrich himself with the results of this research, and foolish indeed would be the scholar who set out to write a "biblical theology" without it.

The Crises of Ancient Israel

The second aid to our understanding is at first sight a surprising one: the very obstacles of time and space are themselves an aid. As we have seen, these obstacles are so formidable that they require us to begin again at the very beginning, to take nothing for granted, and to ask about everything, "What does this mean?" We cannot assume that we already know the meaning of anything. This is certainly a daunting task, but it is exactly the task which confronted the Israelites repeatedly in their long history.

Israel stood at the crossroads of the ancient world, and the people were battered by the hammer blows of historical events over which they had little or no control. Foreign armies invaded and occupied her land, alien cultures were thrust upon her, and her people were carried away to distant lands. Unlike those of more secure nations, her inhabitants were therefore thrust again and again into a situation of "culture shock," to such an extent, indeed, that culture shock must be described as a persistent factor in the life and history of ancient Israel. When, therefore, we find ourselves in a foreign environment, whose manners, customs, and "gods" are strange and incomprehensible to us, we find ourselves in the same plight as the Israelites, whose understanding of the world was shaped by repeated encounters of this kind. Plunged into a strange world with altogether different values, many were driven to conclude that what they had taken for granted in the past, and held to be "truth," was true no longer. For these many there seemed to be no alternative but to accept the new culture in its entirety as alone capable of making sense out of the strange world, and consequently to discard the old values as irrelevant, and to worship new "gods."

There were others, of course, who argued that what had been true once could not suddenly become untrue, but they recognized that the old truths must be thought out again in the light of the new situation. It is to the thinking of these people, to their utter readiness to start again from the beginning, willing neither to accept anything nor to reject it without serious thought and question, that we owe the *Testament,* that body of evidence and proclamation which we are here about to study. Consequently, when we ourselves today, upon opening the pages of this *Testament,* likewise encounter massive culture shock, we begin to partake, even though it be only to taste, of the spirit of the *Testament,* and to enter into the mind of the writers.

The Crises of Ancient Israelite History

For the convenience of our study it is possible to list seven crises which have this character of culture shock, and around which a large part of the writings of the *Testament* revolve. They are:

1. The experience of the Exodus, very roughly about 1280 B.C.E.[4] when the people left the cultivated realm of Egypt for what they knew ever afterward as "the great and frightening wilderness."[5] We must begin with this, since the Exodus was the time when the Israelite community took shape as a coherent people, when the covenant with YHWH was made, and when the Law was given.

2. The settlement in the hill country of Canaan, somewhere around 1225 B.C.E. and during the years following, when they came into a country described by a later writer as "not like the land of Egypt."[6]

3. The establishment of the monarchy, something which until then they had rejected as false and "un-Israelite." After an initial failure under Saul, the monarchy was firmly established by David about 1000 B.C.E. and a new lifestyle began to prevail.

(All these events may properly be described as "formative events," and this is the sense in which we shall consider them in the next three chapters.)

4. The encounter with the commercial empires of Phoenicia and Syria during the years around 850 B.C.E. This was the time of Elijah and Elisha.

5. The establishment of Assyrian control over the Middle East,

---

4. After some discussion, it was decided to adopt this form rather than B.C., more familiar to many. The initials may be interpreted as "Before the Common Era," or "Before the Christian Era," as the reader wishes. For A.D. we shall use C.E.

5. Deut. 1:19. "Frightening," or perhaps "dreadful," is a better translation of *norah* than "terrible," which has too broad a meaning in modern English.

6. Deut. 11:10.

beginning with the accession of Tiglath-pileser III of Assyria in 745 B.C.E., and leading to the complete destruction of the northern kingdom of Israel in 722, and the great siege of Jerusalem in 701. This was the period of Amos, Hosea, Micah and Isaiah.

6. The destruction of Jerusalem by the Babylonians in 587 B.C.E., and the beginning of the Exile. The period of Zephaniah, Jeremiah and Ezekiel.

7. The overthrow of Babylon by Cyrus the Great in 539 B.C.E., and the establishment of that "new thing," the vast empire of the Medes and Persians. The great poems of Isaiah 40–55 are entirely concerned with this crisis.

The reader will have noticed, perhaps, that no mention has been made here of Abraham, Isaac and Jacob, of whom also it might be said that they dwelt as aliens in a strange land. This is certainly how the Israelites remembered them,[7] when they collected and preserved the stories about them, but we must remember that these stories as we have them today are told in the light of the Exodus experience and reflect that experience. Of course, this does not in the least deny the importance of the Patriarchal period. Certainly not![8] Yet the *Testament* record makes clear that the Israelites as a people did not truly come to know YHWH, their God, until they encountered him in the grim desolation of the wilderness,[9] and that it was in this experience that they became the "covenant people."[10] Therefore, it is with this experience that we must begin.

The Limits of the Study

The discussions upon which this book is based ranged over a wide field, but in the writing of the book we realized that limits would have to be set. It was decided to base the study upon the Hebrew Scriptures,[11] and to exclude those aspects of the thinking of the *Testament* which involved evidence later than the *Testament* itself. The disclosure of God to the Hebrew people did not, of course, come to an end with the seventh of the crises listed above. Indeed, in our preliminary listing we continued them as follows:

7. Exod. 6:2–4.
8. The Patriarchal period is considered below in Chap. 6.
9. Exod. 3:13–14; 6:2–3.
10. See, e.g., Bright, *A History of Israel,* 2nd ed., pp. 103–139; Noth, *The History of Israel,* pp. 53–137.
11. This meant excluding from our study those books written in Greek, which are known to Protestant Christians as the Apocrypha, but for Catholics are included in the Old Testament.

8. The return from exile and the rebuilding of Jerusalem in very altered circumstances, for Judah was now no more than a tiny part of the Persian Empire and largely without freedom of political action.

9. The encounter with the Greek world and triumphant Greek culture after Alexander the Great had destroyed the Persian Empire in 330 B.C.E.

10. The encounter with the overwhelming political power and military might of Rome. This may be said to begin with Pompey's proud entry into the Temple, and even into the Holy of Holies, in 63 B.C.E., and to have culminated in the Jewish rebellion and the destruction of Jerusalem by the Roman armies in C.E. 70.

We were therefore not able to include within our study such important and fascinating topics as apocalyptic and the development of the Wisdom tradition after the return from the Exile, since these extend far beyond the *Testament*. The subject matter of the book, therefore, is the disclosure of God, and the Hebrew understanding of him, in the period up to, and including, the end of the Exile in Babylon.[12] This is the period usually known as that of "Israelite religion." After the Exile is the beginning of "Judaism."

The Revelation of God

Two further matters need to be considered, for they came up more than once in our discussions. First, is the *Testament* inspired? Is it the revelation of God? This is an important question, but it is not one to which this book can give a definite Yes or No.

In the first place, all the discussions were held, and the book itself has taken shape, within the framework of a course in Religion at a liberal arts college. Such a course imposes its own limitations. It must be what the scholar loves to call "objective." It should stimulate people to think, but it cannot tell people what they must believe. Just as a course in Political Science cannot be used to impose a particular political philosophy upon the students, so a course in Religion may not be used to compel belief. It would be quite improper to flunk students who said, "I know very well that this is what the Bible teaches, but I myself cannot accept it as divine revelation."[13] The question has to remain an open one.

Nevertheless, to maintain a position of aloof, academic objectivity is to misunderstand the subject of religion completely. All religion is concerned with what people believe, and believe wholeheartedly and with passion. To do no more than stand outside and observe its phenomena with the cold eye of the scholar is always to misinterpret it. Of course, one must stand aside and look at even one's own religion with

12. See additional notes.   13. See additional notes.

rigid objectivity, but one must also stand inside and know what it means to believe.

Therefore, anyone who wishes to understand what the biblical writers are saying when they speak of "God" and of his revelation to them must not sit in the seat of the scornful. He must take his place instead *within* the community of ancient Israel, among people fully convinced that "God" manifests himself to men and women and that the writings of the *Testament,* as they gradually took shape among the community, faithfully make known that revelation. To understand what they said was the revelation of "God" to them, one must immerse himself in these words. Yet the reader, just like the student, must be free. He or she must have the completely free choice to say either, "Yes, I myself also believe this to be the revelation of God," or else, "No, I just cannot accept it." There can be no compulsion in religion.

The question also has another connotation: Is the Bible true? Again, the question must be left as an entirely open one, and no interpretation be imposed upon the reader. Yet, no book can be written in a vacuum. Some kind of working hypothesis must be adopted. The position adopted in this book is that the biblical writings are not "inerrant," in the sense of never making any error of scientific, geographical or historical fact. It is surely impossible to hold such a rigid position in a scholarly community today. The biblical documents were, after all, written by men, and men are always fallible. Nevertheless, the historical material in the *Testament* must be taken with great seriousness. It is primary evidence for the history of the time, and no honest historian or archaeologist should treat it as anything else.

But though the *Testament* is written by men, it is concerned throughout with "God." It is concerned with the meaning and significance of the world and of the human condition. It seeks to plunge to the depths and to interpret that ultimate Reality in terms of which all things must be understood. The question of "inerrancy" is secondary in relation to the profundity of this question. In answer to this far more profound question we have been working together with the following understanding:

(*a*) The *Testament* is true in the primary sense that it records the Israelite understanding of "God" with fidelity, and we may rely upon its evidence.

(*b*) The understanding of "God" as made known through the pages of the *Testament* is a valid understanding, which has stood the test of time and is deserving of the most serious consideration. To dismiss as irrelevant writings which have had such power over the minds and hearts of men and women throughout the centuries would be irrational and foolish.

(*c*) The final decision of "faith," of whether to commit oneself to this revelation of "God" as absolute truth must be left to the reader. A book upon this subject can, and should, ask the reader to think carefully and seriously. It cannot require him to believe.

Is the Testament Relevant to the Modern World?

The writers of the varied documents which make up the *Testament* all seem to work with the conviction that what they are saying is not merely for their own time, but for all times. They believe themselves to be making known eternal truth, and it is for this reason that they commit the revelation to writing; they do not wish it to be lost. Their readers evidently shared this conviction, and because they did so, cherished and preserved the books, patiently and faithfully copying them out over many centuries. Writers and readers therefore agree with the words attributed to Moses in the book of Deuteronomy: "I have set before you *this day* life and good, death and evil."[14] If this, then, is the spirit in which the material was both written and preserved, we cannot avoid the question of whether what the *Testament* has to say does indeed apply to our modern technological and scientific age. "The expositor," it has been said, "is surrounded by noises and sounds produced in his own time. While he tries carefully to listen to the past, he has also to respond daringly in terms of the present world."[15]

Here we are admittedly in some difficulty, because it is not easy to avoid preconceptions. But it is not a preconception to say that the writers believed that the truth they were making known applied to all times, and therefore to begin with this hypothesis. If it does not stand up to being used, it will have to be rejected, but it is certainly true to the spirit of the *Testament* to make the experiment of applying its teaching to the very different circumstances of our own day. Consequently, in the course of the book we shall from time to time attempt to do this.

But in doing so we cannot avoid offering certain examples, and these examples may not seem to everyone to be valid, nor the interpretation of them to be correct. Some of the suggestions for consideration may sound like preaching, but this cannot altogether be avoided. All the prophetic material *is* preaching, and to present it in any other terms would be false. So again we have to say that we offer the examples as examples only, matters for honest discussion and debate, not as articles of faith.

14. Deut. 30:15.
15. Markus Barth, *Ephesians: Introduction, Translation, and Commentary on Chapters 1–3* (Garden City, N.Y.: Doubleday, 1974), p. ix.

As was explained in the introduction, this book was first delivered in the form of lectures. These lectures have now been completely rewritten, and given the form of a book, as the result of discussion, and of the criticism and advice of all the Contributors. But before we embark upon our study of the first crisis in Israelite history, it is fitting to repeat the words used at the end of the initial lecture, since they guided all our discussions and should guide also the reading of the book:

> Let me conclude this first session by saying with all the emphasis at my command: A thing is not true because I say so, or because anyone else says so, or even because the Bible says so. We must begin from the beginning. You must make up your minds upon the basis of the evidence. You have your own experience of the world, and it is not mine.

With appropriate changes in the pronouns, this is what we together would say to you, the Reader.

ADDITIONAL NOTES TO CHAPTER 2

12. It has been objected that the P material (see note at end of Chap. 3), the book of Job and many Psalms are postexilic, and therefore limiting the material under consideration to "the period up to, and including, the end of the Exile in Babylon" is artificial. Any such limitation must, of course, be artificial, because nowhere in the *Testament* is there any possibility of a neat and tidy division. Nevertheless, what is proposed here is not unreasonable. Certainly the book of Job was written after the return, but the argument of Chapter 14 is that it is in fact a reflection on the problem posed by the Exile. The P material in its completed form is postexilic, but much of what it contains must be dated back to long before the Exile, and the process of collecting and writing down the material may well have begun during the sojourn in Babylon. The dating of the psalms is still a matter of considerable dispute. Some must certainly belong to the period after the return, but there is now strong evidence for regarding a large number of the psalms (quite possibly the majority) as composed during the monarchy, even though many may have been committed to writing later.

13. A story, well known in Britain, is worth repeating here. It concerns John Keate, headmaster of Eton from 1809 to 1834, and famous both for his concern for the students and for the severity of his punishments. Once in class a boy ventured to say that he could not really believe in the Holy Ghost. Keate explained the doctrine, but the boy still said that he could not believe it. Keate then rounded on him and exclaimed in fury, "Boy, you will believe in the Holy Ghost by five o'clock this afternoon, or I will beat you till you do!"

THE FORMATIVE CRISES

3. The God of Sinai

BACKGROUND READING: The Exodus story is spread over three books of the *Testament* (Exodus, Numbers, Deuteronomy). It would be useful to begin by reading the basic material contained in Exodus 1–20, and Deuteronomy 5–6.

> You have seen what I did to the Egyptians, and how I bore you on eagles' wings and brought you to myself. Now therefore, if you will obey my voice and keep my covenant, you shall be my own possession among all peoples; for all the earth is mine, and you shall be to me a kingdom of priests and a holy nation.
>
> Exodus 19:4–6

The Exodus Experience

The primary formative experience, basic to understanding all else of which the *Testament* speaks, is that vagabond period which we know as the Exodus from Egypt. In this experience the *Bene Israel*,[1] a "mixed multitude" of uprooted people,[2] came face to face with Reality, so absolute that henceforth for them it overrode all other claims to their allegiance. Alone it gave meaning and coherence to the grim situation in which they found themselves. They rightly said thereafter that in this desolation they had found, or rather had been found by, "God."

We must not romanticize the Exodus and we shall not understand it if we do not begin from the fact that "grimness" and "desolation" are indeed the right words to use. We have, alas, *no* direct archaeological evidence of this period in biblical history and though we can identify

---

1. The "children of Israel," i.e., those peoples descended from Jacob, whose other name was Israel (Gen. 32:28). The phrase came to mean the whole community of Israelite people.
2. Exod. 12:38; Num. 11:4.

Kadesh-barnea, evidently an important center for them,[3] we can only
guess at the site of Mount Sinai itself and most of the other places
mentioned.[4] The general area of their wanderings, however, was certainly
that great wasteland which lies between Beersheba to the north and the
cultivated land of Egypt far to the southwest, very much of their time
being spent in and around the Kadesh group of oases.

It would now appear that it was not a straightforward journey, nor
did it lead to an organized conquest, even though the biblical record
as we have it today is told in these terms. This record was written down
much later, when the purposes of God could be seen more clearly. It is,
moreover, composite, woven together from many strands.[5] The pattern
and texture come from the cult, from the gathering of the people together
year after year to retell and relive in communal worship the events which
had first endowed them with meaningful existence. Behind these times
of celebration and rejoicing lay an experience altogether more dusty,
brutal and uncomfortable. They had been no better than refugees, living
as best they might in a savage and hostile environment. The *midbar,*
normally translated in English as the "desert," remained forever in their
thinking as "the great and frightening wilderness,"[6] indeed "a terrible
land."[7]

We must think of different groups of people, some certainly from the
Nile delta, but others no less certainly from the Palestine area, which
then was governed as part of "Egypt," coming together as fugitives in
the wilderness. This is a pattern of movement endlessly repeated in
Palestine history and not yet finished today,[8] whereby those for whom
the existing system has become nothing but meaningless bondage, everyone, that is, "who is in distress, and everyone who is in debt, and everyone who is discontented"[9] take refuge in that trackless solitude which lies
only a short way beyond the farmers' fields. There, in the rocky and
arid wastes, the government writ did not run and the "gods" of the
cultivated lands could exercise no power. There they could be free.

This freedom, however, seemed but empty, for to those who had
come from farming villages the land in which they now found themselves
was a land of drought and death. In later years they vividly remembered
the wretchedness of their plight and how passionately they had rebelled
against those who had brought them from a world of life and food into
one of thirst and starvation. "Why," they said to Moses and Aaron,

---

3. Num. 13:26; 20:1ff.; 32:8; Deut. 1:2, 19; 2:14; 9:23.
4. See additional notes.
5. For an explanation of the different strands see the note at the end of this
chapter.
6. Deut. 1:19; 8:15.   7. Isa. 21:1.   8. See additional notes.
9. I Sam. 22:2.

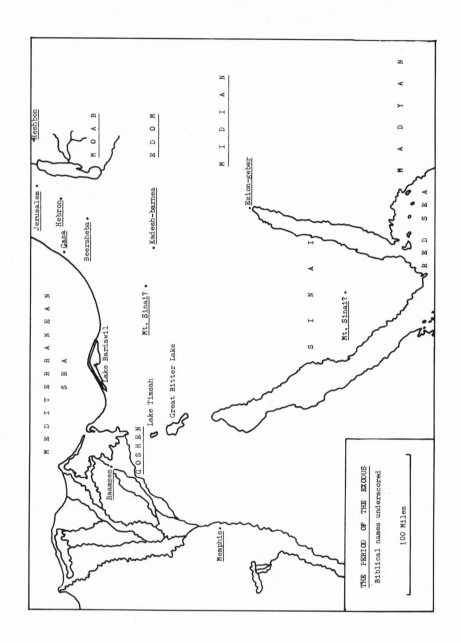

THE PERIOD OF THE EXODUS
Biblical names underscored

100 Miles

MEDITERRANEAN SEA

GOSHEN

Raamses•

Memphis•

Lake Bardawil

Lake Timsah

Great Bitter Lake

Mt. Sinai?

Beersheba•

•Gaza Hebron•

Jerusalem•

Heshbon

M O A B

E D O M

•Kadesh-barnea

M I D I A N

Ezion-geber•

S I N A I

Mt. Sinai?

RED SEA

M A D Y A N

"have you made us come up out of Egypt, to bring us to this evil place? This is not a place for grain, or figs, or vines, or pomegranates; and here there is no water to drink."[10] As they celebrated the Exodus in their worship they recalled also these rebellions.[11]

It is evident that the people were forever after convinced that out of this experience the word "God" had taken on for them a new meaning, and that they must speak of him now under a new name, the name of YHWH.[12] Usually translated as "the LORD," or "the Eternal," this word defies translation. We would probably not be far wrong if we thought of it as meaning "He who is," but in their worship it seems that the people would often ejaculate no more than *Yahu,* that is to say, "O He!" fearing to be more explicit about this dread Reality.[13] From the name itself, therefore, we can learn little, for it does no more than proclaim the tremendous mystery. We must turn instead to the descriptions used of this "God," and in particular to what he is said to have done. Dynamic activity belongs to the very essence of the Reality they experienced, and it is through what they called the *geburoth,* the "strong deeds" of God, that he was most truly revealed.[14]

Something happened. This is the primary fact of the Exodus experience. But it was something for which no word or interpretation could be found in terms of the natural world. The experience was to those who had undergone it in the highest degree "unnatural." These people were not Bedouin or seminomads, accustomed to live and move in the desert. They had dwelt in villages, even though they had perhaps kept sheep and goats which they had pastured in the steppe, and they had belonged, therefore, to a world where all life depended on the careful cultivation and cherishing of the soil. All that lay outside this was for them the land, not of life, but of death.

Their very being had been determined until now by the necessity of coaxing the earth to be fruitful and to produce the hidden food, and for such people the desert offered no hope of life at all. Nature there was their enemy and if nature had its way, their bones would soon lie unburied in some parched ravine.[15] Nevertheless, their experience was that in these arid wastes they had found, not death, but life and they had found it more abundantly. A new and undeniable fact had come into existence, for once they had been Pharaoh's slaves in Egypt, but now

10. Num. 20:5. See also Exod. 14:10–18; 15:22–26; 16:3; 17:1–7; Num. 11:4ff.; 12:2; 14:1–2; 16:3, 12–14, 41; 21:5; Deut. 1:32, 41–43; 9:6–8, 22, 24. To these we should add the idolatry of Exod. 32, especially v. 1; Num. 25:1–5; Deut. 4:3; 9:22–23.
11. Pss. 78:8, 17–20, 32–41; 95:8–11; 106:6–39. See also additional notes.
12. Exod. 3:13–15; 6:2–3.   13. See additional notes.
14. Deut. 3:24; Pss. 20:7; 71:16; 106:2; 145:4, 12; 150:2; Isa. 63:15.
15. See additional notes.

they were free; once they had been no people, but now they were a people. They could not conceive of this as something natural. They knew it to be true only because it had happened. It was not, therefore, to them a fact of nature, but a fact of history.

The difference that this made was fundamental and far-reaching. We shall be exploring its significance throughout the course of this book, and for the moment we must content ourselves with some merely introductory remarks. Nature, in the sense in which it will be used in this book, is all that constitutes your environment. It is the "world" in which you are placed, and this world has a discernible pattern, which can be trusted to recur. History is what happens to you. Natural events are repeatable and predictable events, but historical events are unrepeatable and therefore unpredictable. It is true that nature and history are not altogether separate from each other. They undoubtedly overlap. Yet the essential difference lies in how they are experienced by the human mind.

Thus summer and winter, seedtime and harvest, rain, snow, and sunshine all belong to the natural world, for they are part of an unbroken pattern. Within this pattern we find security. We may safely predict that winter will come, and that it will be cold, that the summer will bring long days and greater heat, and that in due course the harvest will be reaped. Of such things we may be sure. But we cannot say with any certainty at all whether a particular harvest will be rich or pitiable. We cannot say even of this present year whether frost will shrivel the fruit blossoms, or whether drought or hail will damage the wheat. Each particular harvest is an altogether new thing. Until it has been gathered in it is not a fact at all; it is no more than a possibility. History seems to offer no security, since we can never be sure of it. We may certainly foresee the kind of thing that may happen to us, but we cannot say for certain whether or not it will happen. Moreover, there is always the possibility that something entirely unexpected may happen to us. Within nature we know where we stand, but in history we must always wait upon events.

To most people the word "history" connotes the past. It is history as remembered, history as studied. But history as experienced is what happens to men and women, and this is primary history, the raw material of history if you wish. All history has had this character before it has been safely muzzled between the covers of a book. History as studied has already become part of the factual world, always there for you to examine and consider. It does not happen to you. But primary history, the historical event as it occurs, breaks out upon you, confronts you directly and demands an answer. Not merely the grandiose events, but every event has potentially this character. Until it has actually happened it has no part in the secure world of facts. It is indeed not a fact at all—

it is no more than one among a variety of possibilities. But once it has happened, from that very moment, it is completely irrevocable, and it has the power to call in question the whole of your existence, your entire interpretation of the world. It says to you, "What are you going to do *now*?"

We must not imagine, of course, that at this early stage the Israelites thought consciously of what we today would call history. But it is beyond question that they thought of "event," of something happening to them, and of its impact. They were aware of what might be called its explosive, eruptive power, and that they were presented with a choice whether to live in one way or another, a choice to which they were bound to give an answer.

The Mountain and the Sea

We must now turn to discover what other new lines of thought began for the Israelites in the Exodus period, however dimly they may have grasped them at the time, and however much the ideas may have been developed later. Their memories of this period revolved around two climactic events: (*i*) the Deliverance at the Sea, which is the culmination of the "signs and wonders, the mighty hand and the outstretched arm"[16] by which the people were brought out of Egypt, and (*ii*) the Theophany, the manifestation of "God," at the Mountain, variously called "Sinai" and "Horeb."[17] Of the two it is the Mountain which is primary, and the Deliverance at the Sea took place that they might go to the Mountain.

> "Come, I will send you to Pharaoh that you may bring forth my people, the sons of Israel, out of Egypt." But Moses said to God, "Who am I that I should go to Pharaoh, and bring the sons of Israel out of Egypt?" He said, "But I will be with you; and this shall be the sign for you: when you have brought forth the people out of Egypt, you shall serve God upon this mountain."
>
> Exodus 4:10–12[18]

At the mountain, which the people were forbidden to approach lest they perish,[19] we must recognize first the overwhelming sense of otherness, and the sense also of devastating, even terrifying, power. It was certainly not new to think of "god" or "the gods" in this fashion. We find these concepts almost universally in religion.[20] Yet here they take on a new

16. Deut. 7:19.
17. E.g., Exod. 19:11, 18; 24:16; Ps. 68:8 for Sinai, and Exod. 3:1; 17:6; Deut. 4:15; Ps. 106:19 for Horeb.
18. See also Exod. 5:1–3; 7:16; 8:25–27; 10:8–9, 24–26.
19. Exod. 19:20–21.   20. See additional notes.

dimension. Now otherness and power are seen to be at the basis of all meaning, altogether necessary to life and existence. For the first time we have the beginnings of an understanding that "otherness" itself confers identity and significance. Our word "identity" is derived from the Latin *idem* (same) and *identidem* (repeatedly) and reflects, therefore, the conviction that only in belonging to the group, in forming part of what is continually the same, is meaningful existence possible. But these people had fled from a society which thought in these terms, a society to which they found that they could not belong.[21] They could not, of course, do without a society or community, for they had to stay together if they were to survive. But there came into existence in the Exodus a community which is of necessity "other" and turns traitor when it wants to be "like all the nations."[22]

> You know how we dwelt in the land of Egypt, and how we came through the midst of the nations through which you passed; and you have seen their detestable things, their idols of wood and stone, of silver and gold, which were among them. Beware lest there be among you a man or woman or family or tribe, whose heart turns away this day from YHWH our God to go and serve the gods of those nations.
>
> Deuteronomy 29:16–18

This "otherness" is derived from "God," from the source of all meaning, and henceforward all their thinking about God must start from the understanding that YHWH is not what they or the people around them had normally thought of when they used the word "god." YHWH is disclosed on Sinai as other than the gods, and we might go so far as to say that from now on God is not "a god." He is other also than man, and nothing is more evident throughout the *Testament* than the conviction that man is not God and God is not man.

> The Egyptians are men, and not God;
>   and their horses are flesh, and not spirit.
>
> Isaiah 31:3

> I will not execute my fierce anger,
>   I will not again destroy Ephraim;
> for I am God and not man,
>   the Holy One in your midst,
>   and I will not come to destroy.
>
> Hosea 11:9

Although YHWH is spoken of continually in personal terms, to conceive of him as though one could start from the concept of man and arrive at the knowledge of YHWH is altogether false.[23] The mind of God and the mind of man are wholly different, for "YHWH sees not as

21. See additional notes.   22. I Sam. 8:4–8.   23. Ps. 50:21.

man sees; man looks on the outward appearance, but YHWH looks on the heart."[24]

> For my thoughts are not your thoughts,
>   neither are your ways my ways, says YHWH.
> For as the heavens are higher than the earth,
>   so are my ways higher than your ways
>   and my thoughts than your thoughts.
>
> Isaiah 55:8–9

But the conviction goes much further than this. YHWH is other than anything in the whole realm of nature, other than anything that can be perceived, known and studied. From the beginning the command is made that one must never lay hold of something within the world, however vast the world may be, and say of it, "This effectively represents the Reality which gives meaning and significance to everything else." Israelite religion has got to be aniconic, that is, without images. "To whom then will you liken God, or what likeness compare with him?" asked the great prophet of the Exile.[25] There is nothing available which may be used for comparison.

> You shall not make for yourself a graven image, or a likeness, of any-thing [of anything!] that is in the heaven above, or that is in the earth be-neath, or that is in the water under the earth. You shall not bow down to them, or ascribe ultimate value to them.
>
> Exodus 20:4–5; Deuteronomy 5:8–9[26]

This does not mean that the Israelites were at this stage monotheists, for what we call monotheism was not to be accepted until centuries later.[27] Right up to the time of Jeremiah and the destruction of Jerusalem in 587 B.C.E. the people recognized the fact of gods other than YHWH, and sometimes even themselves accepted and worshiped them.[28] What it does mean, though the people were slow to grasp it, is that "God" must henceforward be thought of in terms of true uniqueness, of qualitative difference. He stands absolutely alone, altogether "other."

He stands alone, but he is not in the least remote, for inescapable power accompanied the people every step of the way, a pillar of cloud

24. I Sam. 16:7.   25. Isa. 40:18.
26. Trans. D.B. The thrust of the commandment is that nothing at all shall be used as a representation of YHWH. "Worship," which is the usual translation in the final clause, is a shortened form of "worth-ship," and to worship God is there-fore to ascribe ultimate worth and value to him. It must be admitted that "ascribe ultimate value" is an inadequate translation of the Hebrew 'abad, which has the sense of "to labor, work, serve as a subject, be obedient as a servant, be the slave of," and therefore means "to worship" in all these senses also.
27. See below, Chap. 15.
28. Josh. 24:14–28; Judg. 11:24; I Sam. 26:19; I Kings 11:4; II Kings 1:2; 5:18–19; 16:10–16; 17:16; Ps. 95:3; Jer. 7:16–19; Ezek. 8, etc.

by day and a pillar of fire by night,[29] pulling them forward and thrusting out others to make way for them. This power was undeniable, for they had done nothing to turn back the Egyptians,[30] and in the wilderness without this power they could not have survived. Power, sheer power, was for them a fact, but power of an order altogether other than that of the natural world. Whatever must be said of the Reality which undergirded their experience, it was clear to them that the natural world, which until then had provided their security, must bow down before it. Here, as it were, was power which prevented nature from destroying them, and forbade the desert to act according to its cruel character. Here was power which could make even the arid wasteland bring forth water and food and carve a path through the bewildering sea. The sea and the desert signified for the ancient farmer complete and total chaos, wholly without shape and form and meaning.[31] Whenever they spoke of the sea, it was in terms of chaos that they thought, even though what they called "sea" was only what we would call the "lake" of Galilee, or the marshes of Lake Timsah, for them the "Sea of Reeds," i.e., the "Red Sea" of the Exodus story.[32]

To celebrate the Deliverance at the Sea and the safe passage through the "great and terrible wilderness," as well also to remember the dread Theophany at the Mountain, was to affirm that basic to any serious attempt to make sense out of the world must be recognition of the fact of absolute power. But this is not what men are tempted to call power, for before YHWH governments, armies and the forces of nature were alike helpless.

> Some boast of chariots, and some of horses;
>> but we boast of the name of YHWH, our God.
> They will collapse and fall;
>> but we shall rise and stand upright.
>
> Psalm 20:7–8

> Woe to those who go down to Egypt for help
>> and rely on horses,
> who trust in chariots because they are many,
>> and in horsemen because they are very strong,
> but do not look to the Holy One of Israel.
>
> Isaiah 31:1

29. Exod. 13:21–22; 14:19, 24; 33:9, 10; Num. 12:5; 14:14; Deut. 31:15.
30. Exod. 14:14.
31. See Ps. 107:4–9, 23–32 for parallel pictures of the chaotic desert and sea.
32. Lake Timsah is now part of the Suez Canal, on the edge of the Sinai peninsula. There is no clear certainty about the place of the "Sea of Reeds," which some scholars would place elsewhere, e.g., Lake Bardawil or Lake Manzalah. The term "Red Sea" results from a misunderstanding by the Greek translators, which has been carried over into English.

What is conceived of here is electrifying power, to be approached only with circumspection.[33] This, of course, was not unusual, for other ancient peoples came before their gods in fear and trembling. What is important here is that the divine power is not thought of as wanton,[34] but as charged with meaning, directed and purposeful. The *Testament* does not speak of blind and treacherous fate, or of some mysterious life force, but of there being no true power without an end in view, and it tells, therefore, of how the meaningless chaos of the wasteland was, as it were, galvanized into sense and significance.

But together with power there is mercy. Yet another effect of the Exodus experience was the conviction that no interpretation of the world, and of the human situation, could be valid that did not include as primary the reality of mercy, and the unending mercy of Reality. YHWH is "a God merciful and gracious, slow to anger, and abounding in steadfast love and faithfulness." This is a continually repeated creed.[35] The deep mystery of Sinai was that there they had been spared destruction.

> Who is there of all flesh that has heard the voice
> of the living God speaking out of the midst of fire,
> as we have, and has still lived?
>
> Deuteronomy 5:26

At the sea they had been given freedom and in the desert they had known constant preservation, which they could not persuade themselves that they had in any sense earned. They ought to have died and yet they had lived. Mercy had accompanied them all the way.

> Thou hast guided in thy steadfast love the people
> whom thou hast redeemed,
> thou hast guided them by thy strength to thy holy abode.
>
> Exodus 15:13

This mercy is not something additional, but a necessary part of the quality of Reality, without which there would be no sense or meaning in the world, nor any basis for community. Nor is it something which merely ought to be; it is something which is.

Glory and Holiness

> The glory of YHWH settled on Mount Sinai, and the cloud covered it six days. . . . Now the appearance of the glory of YHWH was like a devouring fire on the top of the mountain in the sight of the people of Israel.
>
> Exodus 24:16–17

33. Exod. 19:10–24; Deut. 5:4–5; I Sam. 5:11; II Sam. 6:6–7.
34. See additional notes.
35. Exod. 34:6; Num. 14:17–19; Deut. 7:9; Ps. 103:8.

Together with otherness and power go glory and holiness. The *Testament* speaks of the glory of YHWH well over a hundred times, and in the Exodus accounts we meet it frequently.[36] The word used is *kabod,* which denotes heaviness. Certainly there is a sense of blazing and blinding light, but integral to the meaning is the sense also of tremendous weight and substance. In a very much lesser degree we might speak today of "a weighty argument" or "a substantial book." By this we would mean that the argument or the book compelled attention because it was full of sound sense and made known the truth. But we might in the same breath use also the metaphor of light and say that it illuminated much that had been dark before. This gives us a hint of the glory of YHWH. In biblical language "to give glory to YHWH"[37] is to speak the truth openly, and no longer to prevaricate and take refuge in falsehood. When the glory of YHWH is manifest all things are to be seen in their true meaning. Here is the searching light of absolute Reality.

The word for "holy" is *qadosh,* which means "separate" or "apart," and therefore belongs closely with the concept of otherness. In all religions that which pertains to "god" is "holy" in this sense, and must be kept carefully separate from things which are in common use. In Islam, for instance, the area of the mosque is *haram,* i.e., forbidden and set apart in perpetuity from the ordinary, and those who go on pilgrimage must put on the *ihram,* special clothing which denotes their separateness from worldly things. It is not surprising, therefore, that we should read of how the feast of unleavened bread is to be a "holy assembly"[38] and the seventh day "a day of solemn rest, a holy sabbath for YHWH."[39] So also the place where the messenger of YHWH appears to Moses is "holy ground," i.e., a place apart,[40] and the priests who minister in the "holy place" of the tabernacle must put on "holy garments."[41] All these ideas would be familiar to other peoples of the ancient Middle East.[42]

Yet once again there is a qualitative difference. First, the entire people are said to be holy, "a kingdom of priests and a holy nation."[43] They are holy because YHWH, their God, the ground of their existence and source of their being, is holy,[44] and they have been separated from the other nations.[45] In one of the rebellions against the leadership,[46] the

36. Exod. 16:7, 10; 24:16–17; 28:2, 40; 29:43; 33:18, 22; 40:34, 35; Lev. 9:6, 23; Num. 14:10, 21, 22; 16:19, 42; 20:6; Deut. 5:14.
37. Josh. 7:19; John 9:24.
38. Exod. 14:16.   39. Exod. 16:23; 20:8.   40. Exod. 3:5.
41. Exod. 35:19. See also Ps. 96:9, where all who came to worship in the Temple must put on holy clothing.
42. On this question see Mircea Eliade, *The Sacred and the Profane* (New York: Harper & Row, 1961).
43. Exod. 19:6.   44. Lev. 19:2; 20:7.   45. Lev. 20:24, 26.
46. Num. 6:1ff.

claim was made that because all the people have been set apart there are therefore no special functions within the community, but this claim was rejected. Holiness is to be understood, not in terms of privileged status or position, but in terms of activity. The actions of the people of YHWH are to be different from those of the people around them, different both in the formal, ritual acts and in what we would call the ethical quality of their day-to-day behavior. This is made clear in what we know as the Holiness Code.[47] Here in the midst of all the ritual prescriptions stands Chapter 19, strongly ethical, deeply concerned for the poor, and saying to the whole people, "You shall love your neighbor as yourself."[48]

It is a grave mistake, of course, to imagine, as some have done, that the other religions of the time were without ethical content. All societies everywhere have been concerned for the plight of the needy and with the behavior of the members of the community toward each other. Yet, Israelite religion is marked by an ethical concern far beyond that of the other nations, and this concern is referred very often directly to the Exodus.[49] This is because of the covenant.

The People of the Covenant

Quite fundamental to Israelite thinking about "God" was the conviction that the relationship was one of covenant, or formal agreement, and that this covenant relationship had been established at Sinai, when they had first come to "know" their God.[50] There is now plenty of evidence to show that this covenant was thought of as parallel to an international agreement of the period made between a major ruler and a country he was taking under his protection. This similarity was maintained throughout the monarchy.[51]

The Israelites were conscious from the first that they were entering into solemn agreement with a great power, who had already demonstrated his strength and his concern. The statement, "I am YHWH, your God, who brought you out of the land of Egypt, out of the house of bondage,"[52] is the clear preamble to the covenant requirements, contained in what we know today as the Ten Commandments. That there was an actual agreement, formally entered into, is essential, and Murray Newman is right to say, "The first thing to be said about this Sinai experience of the Hebrews is that it actually happened. These Old Testament traditions are not referring to an *idea* of a covenant between God and man which could be merely the object of thought and speculation. They testify rather to the

47. Lev. 17–26.   48. Lev. 19:18.   49. E.g., Exod. 23:9; Deut. 16:12.
50. Exod. 19:5; 34:10, 28; Deut. 4:13; 5:2.
51. See additional notes.   52. Exod. 20:2.

occurrence of a real historical event in which a real people and their real God were involved."[53]

The initiative here is that of God. There is not, as in the international treaties, an already existing minor monarchy which could seek the protection of an imperial ruler, such as the king of the Hittites or the king of Assyria. Here the covenant produces the community, and the corporate society of Israel derives its existence from the fact of the covenant, for apart from this covenant there could have been no community at all.[54] Moreover, the covenant is YHWH's covenant and not their possession. It belongs to, and partakes of the quality of, the "Other," that Power which is not part of nature and which alone is capable of maintaining their existence in the wasteland.

In entering into this agreement they had come to terms with that which they must henceforward always recognize to be "God." They had come to terms with absolute and final Reality, whose authority was beyond dispute. But in recognizing that their relationship with ultimate Reality was that of agreement, and not of slavish obedience, they were saying also, however little they understood it at the time, that agreement is fundamental to all true relationship.

Every society is faced with the question of what it is that constitutes the basis of *shalom,* of wholeness and therefore peace and harmony, of what it is that makes community possible. Almost universally in traditional societies it is held to be authority, and the function of the king as the cohesive power, acting on behalf of the god and holding the society together, is understood to be so natural that it is unquestioned. It was exactly this "natural" pattern that the Israelites had discovered to be bondage, and with which they had broken. Hereafter, their distinctness is made evident by the fact that they are a people without a king, held together and maintained in existence, not by authority but by agreement.[55] For any ancient people breach of covenant was seen to be a very serious matter, but for the Israelite people to break covenant was to part company with Reality, to take refuge in a purely fictitious world, which could not endure for a moment the searing wind of truth. Hence comes the wrath of God, the unremitting "jealousy" of YHWH,[56] which cannot but break out against rebellion, against any attempt to live and act on other terms than these. But hence also the profound ethical concern, for if covenant or agreement is the sole basis of meaningful existence, the

53. Murray Newman, *The People of the Covenant* (Nashville: Abingdon Press, 1962), p. 30.

54. See additional notes.

55. The Israelites did, of course, accept monarchy later in their history, but only after much argument. See below, Chap. 5.

56. Exod. 20:5; 34:14; Num. 25:11; Deut. 4:24; 5:9; 6:15; Josh. 24:19; etc.

inner life of the community must be conducted upon this basis. Covenant with God requires also agreement among each other, for what people do to each other is bound up with their concept of Reality.

All these ideas have their roots in the Exodus. It is true that the ideas developed and expanded and that much of what has been quoted here from the Exodus traditions belongs to a later period. They were not fully understood at the time, but there they were, waiting and ready to be used.

The Four Strands of the Pentateuch

It is now fairly generally agreed among scholars that the Pentateuch, i.e., the first five books of the *Testament,* have been built up from four major bodies of written material. Behind each of these lies a long development of oral tradition, during which the stories were carefully remembered and handed down faithfully from one generation to the next. There was also development within each tradition, partly because as a new clan was admitted to the community its memories became part of the common heritage, and partly also because new experiences helped to refine the common understanding of the ancient events. It is customary to refer to these four strands by the initials J, E, D and P.

> J. This comprises traditions of the southern half of the kingdom, i.e., Judah, and was the first to be committed to writing, about 950 B.C.E. The unknown author who was responsible for this is usually known as the *Yahwist.* This tradition uses the divine name YHWH from the beginning, and speaks of the mountain of God as Sinai. According to this tradition the covenant was made with Moses on behalf of the people.
>
> E. This reflects the thinking of the northern half of the country, and was written down about a century later (about 850 B.C.E.). It may possibly reflect an editing of the J material in the light of the northern experience. It prefers the word *Elohim* for God, and maintains that the name YHWH was not revealed until the time of the Exodus. The sacred mountain is called Horeb, and the covenant is described as having been made with all the people.

These two accounts were later combined into one, and sometimes it is difficult to separate them out. This J-E narrative forms the solid core of the Pentateuchal history, though it received later additions and editing.

> D. This is the basis of the book of Deuteronomy, and there is almost no D material in the first four books. It is a restatement of the Exodus tradition in the light of the catastrophe of the Assyrian conquests in the eighth century B.C.E. Later writers belonging to this same tradition

were responsible for editing the historical books of Joshua—II Kings. The authors of Deuteronomy show close affinity with the E tradition and were probably people who had fled from the northern kingdom after its fall in 722 B.C.E. Their work took written form in Jerusalem some time during the seventh century.

P. This represents a tradition which was collected and preserved in priestly circles in Judah, but it was not written down until the Exile, or shortly afterward. Though it was the last to be written, it contains very much ancient material. To this school of thought we owe the first account of creation (Gen. 1:1–2:4a), parts of the flood story, parts of Exodus 1–13, and the detailed regulations for sacrifices and the construction of the Tabernacle. The priestly writers did the final editing of the first four books.

ADDITIONAL NOTES TO CHAPTER 3

4. Three areas have been suggested for Mount Sinai: (*i*) The traditional site at Jebel Musa in the south of the peninsula of Sinai. This tradition, however, dates only from the early Christian period and the archaeological evidence now seems strongly against it. (*ii*) Somewhere in the northwest of Saudi Arabia, close to the Red Sea. This is the only possible area if Mount Sinai is to be identified with an active volcano. The region is still known as Madyan (=Midian), and there is a mountain there known as Jebel Harab. However, it seems too remote. (*iii*) Somewhere not far from Kadesh-barnea. This would seem a reasonable area, but there are no impressive mountains there.

Kadesh-barnea is probably 'Ain Qudeirat about fifty miles south of Beersheba, though some would identify it with 'Ain Qudeis nearby. The "Waters of Strife" at Massah and Meribah were in the same oasis region (Exod. 17:7; Num. 20:13; 27:14; Deut. 32:51; Ps. 95:8; Ezek. 47:19).

Pithom and Raamses (Exod. 1:1) have been identified by many scholars with Tell er-Retabeh and San el-Hagar in the Nile delta, and the land of Goshen (Gen. 45:10; 46:28; Exod. 8:22; 9:26, etc.) with the Wadi Tumeilat region on the edge of the desert nearby.

8. In the years 1936–39, during the Arab revolt against the British government, many of the rebels took refuge in the wilderness east of Jerusalem and in the land across the Jordan. Much of the refugee movement in 1948 and 1967 took place in the same direction.

11. It seems quite unnecessary to claim with Andrew Tunyogi (*The Rebellions of Israel,* Richmond, Va.: John Knox Press, 1969) that the rebellion motif belongs to the ninth century B.C.E. and later. That it was expanded and developed in later years is true, but it was not invented then. It was firmly rooted in the tradition which later writers inherited and preserved.

13. It must be admitted that the use of "reality" and "Reality" is likely to give rise to confusion. When spelled here with a capital letter it has the sense of Deity or "God." The purpose in using this term instead of speaking of "God" is to avoid any suggestion of God as "somebody." We found in our discussions that this sense of a Supreme Being is so firmly established in Western minds that the use of the word "God" almost automatically conveys the idea of "somebody up there."

15. Death from thirst and heat exhaustion can overcome someone in only two days during the summer months in the desert regions. Even today people can lose themselves only a short distance from the cultivated land. A recent case, which attracted a lot of attention in the newspapers, was the death of Bishop Pike in early September 1969. He died, despite a widespread search, only a few miles east of Bethlehem, and not far from a road.

20. "The first affirmation we can make about the Object of Religion is that it is a *highly exceptional* and *extremely impressive 'Other.'* . . . This Object is a departure from all that is usual and familiar; and this again is the consequence of the *Power* it generates" (G. Van der Leeuw, *Religion in Essence and Manifestation: A Study in Phenomenology,* trans. J. E. Turner, New York: Harper & Row, 1963, Vol. I, p. 23, italics in the original).

21. "We touch here upon a fundamental feature of Egyptian kingship, a feature rooted deeply in the Egyptian mentality: the touchstone for all that was really significant was its permanence. That was important which had always been and would never change. . . . Their conviction went deeper than a reverence for traditional values. It derived from an attitude of mind which comprehended the universe as essentially static. Movement and change were not denied to exist, of course; but change, insofar as it was significant, was recurrent change, the life rhythm of a universe which had gone forth, complete and unchanging, from the hands of its creator. . . . Single occurrences, odd events, historical circumstances were ephemeral, superficial disturbances of the regularity of being and for that reason unimportant. . . . What mattered was the nature of Pharaoh's rulership, which was such as to doom every opposition. For his authority was founded not in the social, but in the cosmic order. Kingship, in Egypt, was as old as the world. It dated from the day of creation." (Henri Frankfort, *Ancient Egyptian Religion: An Interpretation,* New York: Harper & Row, 1961, pp. 49–50). The extraordinary number of statues of Rameses II, the Pharaoh of the Exodus, who had a very prolonged reign (1290–24 B.C.E.), probably reflects a great emphasis upon this principle during this very period.

Père de Vaux quotes an interesting parallel to the Exodus story. In the early nineteenth century Muhammad Ali of Egypt settled some Bedouin tribes in the Wadi Tumeilat, and gave them lands, which they cultivated. After his death, his successor tried to impose taxes and conscription on them, but in one night the entire group fled with their herds, leaving their houses open and empty. (*Histoire Ancienne d'Israel des Origines à l'Installation en Canaan,* Paris: Librairie Lecoffre, 1971, p. 352.)

34. The fear that the gods might act in a wanton manner seems to have been particularly strong in ancient Mesopotamia. "Throughout the Mesopotamian texts we hear overtones of anxiety which seem to express a haunting fear that the unaccountable and turbulent powers may at any time bring disaster to human society" (Thorkild Jacobsen, "Mesopotamia," in *Before Philosophy,* ed. Henri Frankfort, Baltimore: Penguin Books, p. 240).

51. The most helpful introductions to this understanding of covenant are George E. Mendenhall, "Covenant Forms in Israelite Tradition," *The Biblical Archaeologist Reader, 3,* ed. Edward F. Campbell, Jr., and David Noel Freedman (Garden City, N.Y.: Doubleday, 1970), pp. 25–53. Delbert R. Hillers, *Covenant: The History of a Biblical Idea* (Baltimore: The Johns Hopkins Press, 1969). See also George Mendenhall's article on "Covenant" in the *Interpreter's Dictionary,* Vol. I.

It is important not to overstate the case. The parallels with international treaties, especially in the more ancient biblical material, are not always as exact as some enthusiasts have claimed, but we must not go to the other extreme and suggest that the people in the wilderness could have had *no* knowledge of treaty documents. They were not, as we have seen, Bedouin, but they need not all have been peasants. Movements of the Exodus type often include a variety of persons, and there might have been at least some men with government experience. Certainly, after the establishment of the monarchy and the beginnings of dealings with other states, the parallel of the YHWH covenant with international treaties becomes more formal and conscious, as the use of such language in the book of Deuteronomy makes clear.

54. Though the southern and northern traditions differ in their assessment of the role of Moses (see Newman, *People of the Covenant,* pp. 39–51), they agree that the covenant is offered to, and accepted by, the people (Exod. 24:4–8, the northern or E tradition; 19:7–8, the southern or J tradition).

4. The Encounter of YHWH with Baal

BACKGROUND READING: Joshua 1–12; 22–24; the book of Judges

The Historical Situation

The second formative period was that of the settlement in Canaan between about 1225 and 1050 B.C.E. Unfortunately, we encounter at once two major obstacles to our understanding: first, the problem of what actually happened, and then, the problem of the undoubted violence of "God" as disclosed in these stories. We must begin with the history.

It is very difficult indeed to reconstruct the period, and quite impossible to write a chronological history of it. The opening chapters of Joshua contain a beautifully schematic and very vivid account of the conquest of the country west of the Jordan under the leadership of one man, Joshua, but archaeological evidence forces us to think of something much more complicated.[1] The biblical account has been coordinated and unified and might perhaps best be described as a "ritualized conquest." The varied traditions have here been brought together in one glorious saga fit for recital in the sanctuary, and intended perhaps for "consecration," for the repeated dedication of the people and the land to YHWH, thought of as the true source of all order.[2]

This does not mean, of course, that the record is unhistorical. Historical memories are behind the stories and historical incidents are certainly included, e.g., the interruption of the river Jordan,[3] and the battle in the valley of Aijalon,[4] but it is impossible now to write what we would today call a history of the period. Nor are we much better off with the book of Judges. It is true that this is much closer to the actual events and gives a lively picture of some important aspects of the period, but the stories, even

1. See additional notes.   2. See additional notes.
3. Josh. 3:7.   4. Josh. 10:1–14.

here, reflect complex traditions,[5] and there is no evidence at all that the compilers of the book in fact arranged the stories in chronological order.

Nevertheless, if for the ancient Israelites "God" was disclosed through historical events, it is of the first importance to gain a clear, and as far as possible accurate, picture of the kind of situation in which the people were entangled, for if we do not do so, we shall be found misinterpreting "God." Of course, any statement on the subject is open to correction in the light of later evidence, but for the moment it would seem that we must envisage nothing in the nature of an organized conquest.[6] Rather, we must think of a largely uncoordinated process, of the existing order of Canaanite society collapsing from within, and of the country being taken over by dissident groups of various kinds. Some of these would have been outsiders, the people of the Exodus stories, who had already taken refuge in the wasteland some time before. But even these did not act together as one coherent group, for their pressures seem to have come from both south and east. Others would certainly have been insiders, mostly discontented villagers, but also some hangers-on in the towns. What these people had in common was that they were all in some sense fugitives and they were landless, having no status in the political state system of the time. They also had in common, of course, the covenant with YHWH, though the village populations would have been included in the covenant later in the period rather than earlier. What is quite definite is that they were not Bedouin, that is to say people belonging by life and tradition to the desert, nor was the situation one of class struggle or race struggle. The Canaanites represent a culture and not a race.[7]

"Common loyalty to a single Overlord, and obligation to a common and simple group of norms created the community, a solidarity which was attractive to all persons suffering under the burden of subjection to a monopoly of power which they had no part in creating and from which they received virtually nothing but tax-collectors. Consequently, entire groups having a clan or 'tribal' organization joined the newly formed community, identified themselves with the oppressed in Egypt, and received deliverance from bondage; the original historical events with which all groups identified themselves took precedence over and eventually excluded the detailed historical traditions of particular groups who had joined later. It is for this reason that the covenant tradition is so overwhelmingly important in biblical tradition, for this was the formal symbol by which solidarity was expressed and made functional. The symbolization of historical events was possible because each group which entered the

5. It is very difficult, for instance, to disentangle exactly what happened in the battle against Sisera described in Chap. 4.

6. See additional notes.

7. See John Gray, *Archaeology and the Old Testament World* (New York: Harper & Row, 1962), Chaps. IV and V.

covenant could and did see the analogy between bondage and Exodus, and their own experience."[8]

The situation of these people was desperately precarious, for the established authorities of the time saw them as outlaws and rebels and accorded them no legal protection. In the course of the period they acquired land, but quite unsystematically and by no one method. Much was obtained by clearing the still unoccupied forests on the highlands;[9] some must have been the result of forcible seizure, where groups found they had the power to do so; and yet other areas became included more peaceably when the inhabitants, either at their own request or because of persuasion, were admitted to the covenant. That there was much violence is evident and it seems to have been inevitable. This was, we must remember, a time of disintegrating political order and social confusion, leading in the end to the triumph of a revolutionary way of thinking. Unfortunately, periods of this kind do not proceed altogether calmly, but are accompanied by painful and brutal explosions. The old order resists the coming of the new. The "haves" do not yield to the "have nots" without a struggle. Violence, or at the very least the urgent tendency to violence, belongs therefore to the very reality of the situation. In this sense it is "of God."[10]

The Problem of Violence

To say that violence in any situation could be "of God" is clearly to say something very shocking indeed. It seems to justify brutality and gloss over all the horrors of war. But this is *not* what is being said here. We are *not* saying that violence can ever be a good and desirable thing, or that those who take to violence are to be called good people. We are also not speaking of God here as "Somebody" sitting up in heaven and deciding in his fury to be ruthless.

"God" is a word—a word which men and women use to express what they believe to be ultimate and final Reality. The question to be asked about Reality is never whether we like it or dislike it, but whether it is true, whether it establishes a solid foundation for understanding the world around us. This ultimate Reality cannot be expressed in a single sentence, nor is it ever exhausted by any symbol, however profound. We are forced to use many different words to express it, and "violence" is such a word.

To say that violence here is "of God" is to say that this violence must be taken with utter seriousness, if the truth about the situation is to be known. It is to say that the crisis cannot be understood if the violence is

8. Mendenhall, "The Hebrew Conquest of Palestine," p. 108.
9. See the story in Josh. 17:14–18.
10. See additional notes.

smoothed over, or disregarded as irrelevant. It is to insist that if we are not to extol violent people, no less are we to explain them away simply as wicked people, and therefore to be excluded. Violence in the kind of crisis we are considering is an integral part of what is happening. No less than the compassion and mercy shown to the suffering, it belongs to the hard facts of the situation. If it is true, as the Israelites believed, that it is through what happens that "God" is most effectively revealed, then violent events no less than peaceful ones confront mankind, and ask the compelling question, "What are you going to do now?"

Of course violence is evil and to be abhorred. Let there be no mistake over that. But Amos insisted that evil could not befall a city if YHWH had not done it.[11] By this he meant the cruel evil of foreign conquest or of civil strife. This violence he said could not happen irrationally. Behind it must always lie solid Reality.

The period of the settlement in Canaan was one in which fighting was very nearly endemic, when the powerful controlled the weak, and justice was of a rough and ready frontier kind. In such a situation the fact of a protecting power is of preeminent importance, because the protection afforded by "law and order" has broken down. In the thinking of those who compiled the stories of the period this protection is bound up with faithful adherence to the covenant, because the protecting Power is YHWH.[12] "The Wars of YHWH"[13] therefore describe the desperation of a people without any legal protector and the Power which thrusts backward those who would overwhelm them. In no sense at all do these stories suggest that violent action is something which men may safely imitate for purposes of their own. "Redress and recompense are mine," says YHWH.[14] The people are protected by their faithfulness to the covenant, and *not* by military methods, even though they live in a situation in which they cannot but be involved in fighting. They are protected, not by their own efforts, but because YHWH fights for them.

> And YHWH said to Gideon, "Go in this might of yours and deliver Israel from the hand of Midian; do not I send you?" And he said to him, "Pray, Lord, how can I deliver Israel? Behold my clan is the weakest in Manasseh, and I am the least in my family." And YHWH said to him, "But I will be with you."
>
> Judges 6:14–15

YHWH and Baal

But what was the fighting about, and why did the people find themselves so often at the mercy of their enemies? This is the subject of the

11. Amos 3:6.   12. Josh. 1:9; 7:7–10; Judg. 2.   13. Num. 21:14.
14. Deut. 32:35. See also additional notes.

book of Judges, and is indeed the problem with which a large part of the *Testament* is concerned. It is the question which Gideon put bluntly to the messenger, "Pray sir, if YHWH is on our side, then why has all this happened to us?"[15] The compilers of Judges answered this question by saying that

> the people of Israel did what was evil in the sight of YHWH and served the Baals; and they forsook YHWH, the God of their fathers, who had brought them out of the land of Egypt; they went after other gods, from among the gods of the peoples who were round about them, and bowed down to them.
>
> Judges 2:11–12

Here we have a recognition of the beginning of that struggle between YHWH and Baal which was to persist until the Exile.

The word *baal,* as we saw at the end of Chapter 1, means "lord" or "owner," and it was used by the Canaanite people when speaking of their gods. Each local sanctuary had its lord, or *baal,* and so in the passage just quoted the writer speaks of the "baals." But the word was also used for the god who was thought to be most powerful, i.e., the great Baal. This was very commonly the storm god, known as *Baal Hadad.* All the baals, whether major gods or gods of local sanctuaries, were identified with some phenomenon in nature: the storm, the crops, the earth, the life-giving water, etc. What we may call the "Baal concept," therefore, is the principle of interpreting everything in terms of the natural world. To this the YHWH concept was unalterably opposed. Since the great Baal Hadad was also thought of in strongly personal terms, one may speak of an encounter, or conflict, between YHWH and Baal, each demanding the submission of the other.

This was not, as has often been claimed, a struggle between desert nomads and settled farmers. Those who dwell in the desert and derive their culture from there are no less in bondage to nature than those who live in better-watered lands. Such people must search diligently in order to find life and the constant subject of conversation when men meet in the tents is, "Where has there been rain?" The immediate and compelling power of nature demands their attention, and any concept of the "Other" seems a contradiction of the facts. "The dwellers in the desert are the hardest in disbelief and hypocrisy, and most disposed not to know the limits of what Allah has revealed to his messenger."[16]

The struggle was also not one between evident right and evident

---

15. Judg. 6:13 (trans. D. B. The word for "happened to us" means literally "found us," a striking example of how the Israelites tended to think of historical events as confronting them directly and demanding an answer.
16. *The Qur'an,* Sura 9:97.

wrong. As the Israelites gradually settled in Canaan and began to farm the land there developed a tension between two conflicting experiences, both of which they had excellent reason to think of as valid. With this tension they lived until it was finally resolved for them in the dark days of the Exile. The pressure to see everything in terms of the natural world was very nearly irresistible, for every villager lived with a sense of quite appalling insecurity. The unpredictable rainfall, totally absent in summer and always erratic in winter, meant that whether there would be food to eat and water to drink was a critical question year by year. To identify oneself with nature, to sink one's whole self in the natural world, to be at one with the fertility of the earth or the life-giving storm, and so to see no difference at all in the being of man and the being of natural things, seemed to offer the only possibility of existence.

It was security that men sought by this identification for it promised to deliver them from the dread fear of the unpredictable, from the ca-tastrophe of change, which spelled to them death and desolation. They urgently wanted the world to remain the same so that they might continue to grow their crops, year after year, in an environment they had come to know and trust. But once embarked upon this line of thought, full as it was of reason and common sense, they became, as we all become, pris-oners of their own complex web of thought. Their language and their thought-forms were derived from the facts of the natural world, and everything which became part of their "world" had now to be interpreted in these terms, for they had no other words to use. Historical events, everything which happened to them, were therefore explained in terms of that cycle of natural events in which they had come to feel at home. His-tory they saw as an endlessly repeated pattern, the "god" continually died and rose again, and all their rituals strove to ensure that no inter-ruption should occur.[17]

But the experience of the Exodus had been of quite another kind. For those who find that they cannot feel at home, because the world that they know allows no place for them, interruption and change become an abso-lute necessity. Such had been the fugitives who had entered into covenant, and had begun to think, however faltering and rebellious their steps, along new lines. For them the existence they had known before seemed out of touch with Reality. Therefore, to return to the old way of thinking and become like other nations was treachery. But as they began to cultivate the land they were forced to ask what they must do if they were to be at ease in that world of villages and farms in which they were carving out a place. They could not believe that they had been intended to remain as

17. See Mircea Eliade, *Cosmos and History: The Myth of the Eternal Return,* trans. Willard R. Trask (New York: Harper & Row, 1959).

fugitives in the wasteland; they had been brought into the land. Yet the only methods available to them seemed to be the methods of Canaanite culture. So very many people of the covenant began to question seriously whether the "God" they had encountered in the wilderness could provide the basis of a workable system in the midst of this different environment.

Others of course—and these are the people whose views are expressed in the *Testament*—insisted that Truth, once encountered and recognized, cannot become untrue. Their argument ran as follows: In the wasteland, "the great and terrible wilderness," something happened to us and just because it was new our bondage was broken and we were able to live as a free people. We had not known this "name" before; we had not known the terms in which the world was properly to be understood. We entered into a solemn covenant to live in accordance with this new event, and it was only on the basis of this covenant that we were able to exist at all. We cannot *now* act as if this had never happened, as if we had not once been fugitives, as if we had not been set free from bondage, as if we had not solemnly covenanted to live according to a new and different system.

The argument they were putting forward was that in the period of the Exodus they had come to know what existentialists today would call *authentic* existence, as opposed to an existence quite out of touch with ultimate Reality, and therefore *inauthentic*. "Man is always in the world, and yet he is quite distinct from it in his way of being. But in his intimate concern with the world, claims Heidegger, *'Dasein* [= Man] can lose himself to the being that meets him in the world, and be taken over by it,' . . . This is what is meant by an inauthentic existence—man becomes merged in the world."[18] If we were to spell Heidegger's word "being" with a capital letter, we should have an admirable description of that against which the followers of YHWH were fighting: To attribute ultimate value to the baals, to the nature gods, meant to lose themselves to the Being, or Beings, that met them in the world and to be taken over by them. To worship these baals meant to be "merged in the world," to see mankind as altogether part of the world, so totally bound up with it that the "commonwealth," the well-being of the whole community, depended upon the closest possible identification with the world of nature.

The choice was a serious one.

Joshua said to the people, "You cannot serve YHWH; for he is a holy God; he is a jealous God; . . . If you forsake YHWH and serve foreign gods, then he will turn and do you harm." . . . And the people said to Joshua, "Nay, but we will serve YHWH." Then Joshua said to the people,

18. John Macquarrie, *An Existentialist Theology: A Comparison of Heidegger and Bultmann* (Harmondsworth, England: Penguin Books, 1973), p. 39. The quotation from Heidegger is from *Sein und Zeit,* p. 76.

"You are witnesses against yourselves that you have chosen YHWH, to serve him."

Joshua 24:19–22

The choice was serious because there was, properly speaking, no possibility of doing both. There were certainly many who tried to do so, and we have evidence that the worship of the baals continued to exist alongside that of YHWH, even in the more austere southern kingdom of Judah. But the question was, "Where is the right place to start?" for one cannot lay the foundation of life in two places at once. If the fundamental and primary experience is conceived to be that of the ongoing, uninterrupted processes of nature, then the historical event takes second place. Catastrophic change is not then thought of as being "of God," and the absolutely new is by definition frightening, if not actually impossible. But if the fundamental experience, the point from which all your thinking begins, is that something happened, out of the blue as it were, then newness is "of God"; it belongs to the very nature of Reality. This was a citadel which the followers of YHWH could not afford to surrender.[19]

It is fascinating to consider whether any other relationship than that of covenant is possible with "God" when he is understood in these terms, though, of course, the question never arose for the Israelites along these lines. It is not possible to construct a comprehensive *system* of thought upon the basis of historical experience, except only upon history as already experienced, history as remembered, since no system can be built upon what cannot be predicted. One can do no more than give an undertaking to live according to certain basic principles in a future which is still left open. The international "suzereinty covenants" of the period, which provided a pattern for the Sinai covenant, were devised as a means of bringing the future within the political pattern and ensuring both protection and obedience in the event of something happening which could not at the time be foreseen. It was probably the extreme precariousness of the future, the very immediate future in the wasteland, which motivated those who first entered into the covenant to accept the protection of this hitherto unknown Power. At that moment in time (the phrase has here real merit) the consequences of making such a covenant, not with a great king but with "God," could not be perceived.

The Holy War

In the light of this, much that to the modern reader is often repellent about YHWH as the Israelites saw him begins to make sense—the jealous God, the chosen people, and the holy war. In part the jealousy they

19. See additional notes.

ascribed to him reflects the antagonisms of people with a revolutionary message against all that has gone before, and their conviction that the old system was meaningless. All revolutionaries seek to export their revolution, for they are persuaded that other people for their own good must be brought within the true order and have the benefit of the revolutionary experience. They tend to see other patterns of order as false and therefore intolerable. It is striking, for instance, to read books, magazine articles and newspapers of World War I and discover how pervasive was the American conviction that their function in entering the war was to eradicate, once and for all, the false order of monarchy and establish in its place the true order of democracy, which they had come to know in their own revolution.

But the "jealousy" of YHWH went deeper than this. Political revolutions are tamed in course of time and the jealousy disappears, but no accommodation between YHWH and Baal ever proved possible. It is essential to the character of YHWH that he is "the Other," standing over against the world, and not to be comprehended in worldly terms, whether the "world" be the world of nature or that whole construct of thought, custom and language within which an established society lives, moves and has its being.

> Of old thou didst lay the foundation of the earth,
>   and the heavens are the work of thy hands.
> They will perish, but thou dost endure;
>   they will all wear out like a garment.
>
> Psalm 102:25–26

It is quite impossible to speak of the "Other," and insist on the contrary that it is not other, but to be identified with something that is already known. The "Other" does not belong anywhere. It comes at you from outside your world, and in this context it is very important that nowhere in the *Testament* is YHWH ever identified with a place. He "bows the heavens and comes down."[20] The "Other" cannot be contained in any construction of man, as Solomon said at the dedication of the Temple:

> O YHWH, who hast set the sun in heaven,
>   but hast chosen to dwell in thick darkness,
> here have I built thee a lofty house,
>   a habitation for thee to occupy for ever . . .
> But can God indeed dwell on earth? Heaven itself, the
> highest heaven, cannot contain thee; how much less this
> house that I have built!
>
> I Kings 8:12–13, 27 (NEB); cf. Isaiah 66: 1–2

20. Ps. 18:9. See also additional notes.

A people committed to the service of such a God cannot but be themselves other, distinct and different, because they have embarked upon a way of life and an understanding of the world which is recognizably not that of the people around them. But they had not gone into the wasteland intending this. They had not gone there in search of a wilderness experience. The new life was not something which they had consciously sought, but something which had happened to them. They had been set apart, chosen from among the nations, despite themselves. Certainly they succumbed to the very human tendency to think that this setting of them apart meant that they were in some way special by nature, but for all this arrogance they were rebuked, for it was a false interpretation.

> It was not because you were more in number than any other people that YHWH set his love upon you and chose you, for you were the fewest of all peoples.
>
> Deuteronomy 7:7[21]

Properly understood, to be "chosen," to discover that one has been set apart by God, is to be laden with a burden almost too heavy to be borne. Those in the *Testament* to whom it happens are appalled and they say, "Send, I pray, some other person."[22] Many, indeed, are found to wish that they were dead.[23]

What then of the holy war? In a vast number of societies the warrior is thought of as sacred, set aside and empowered to preserve the order and harmony of the world from the disorder which threatens it from outside. "Think also of thy duty and do not waver. There is no greater good for a warrior than to fight in a righteous war."[24] *Dulce et decorum est pro patria mori.*[25] Even in the strongly secularized societies of the West death in battle in the defense of freedom is held to have a sacred quality. Hence the war memorials, the cultic significance of Arlington cemetery, and in more than one country the tomb of "the unknown soldier." Such ideas the Israelites evidently shared with the peoples around them. Not only are all the leaders in battle during the time of the judges represented as raised up by God,[26] but in the time of the monarchy we find war being undertaken on the advice of "prophets," that is to say, people with a definite religious function.[27]

21. See also Amos 3:2 and 9:7.
22. Exod. 4:14. See also Judg. 6:5; Jer. 1:5–7.
23. Num. 11:15; I Kings 19:4; Jer. 15:10.
24. *Bhagavad Gita,* 2:31, trans. Juan Mascaro (New York: Penguin Books, 1962). Of course, neither in Hindu nor in any other society was the warrior the only sacred person. There were other sacred duties.
25. It is a sweet and fitting thing to die for one's country (Horace, *Odes,* III, ii. 13).
26. Judg. 2:16; 3:9, 15; 4:6; 6:11–16.
27. I Kings 22:1–12; II Kings 3:9–12.

But to speak of a holy war is to say something much more than this. It indicates belief in a sustained struggle against what is evil and therefore to be destroyed, an attitude clearly portrayed in the command of Samuel to Saul,

> YHWH sent me to anoint you king over his people Israel; now therefore hearken to the words of YHWH. Thus says YHWH of hosts, "I will punish what Amalek did to Israel in opposing them on the way when they came up out of Egypt. Now go and smite Amalek and utterly destroy all that they have; do not spare them, but kill both man and woman, infant and suckling, ox and sheep, camel and ass."
>
> I Samuel 15:1–3

That this concept is to be found in the biblical descriptions of the settlement is beyond question. It is particularly evident in the account of the fall of Jericho[28] and in the book of Deuteronomy.[29] But we have to remember that these books were compiled long after the events which they record. What must be questioned is whether the settlers themselves thought in these terms. Certainly, such an idea owes nothing to Bedouin influence or anything of that kind. It is true that the savagery of at least some of the fighting that did occur may come in part from the desperate experience of the wasteland when the people were without any political authority to defend them, but they were not then or at any other time Bedouin. It is very doubtful whether what we would today call "Bedouin" existed at that period—and in any case, despite popular ideas to the contrary, we have no evidence for Bedouin tribes thinking of war in these terms. Extermination is definitely *not* the purpose of desert fighting, nor is there any understanding at all of a sustained war—far from it, in fact.

In the light of the passage from I Samuel quoted above we cannot deny that the ancient Israelites did try to exterminate at least one of their enemies, whom they believed to be particularly dangerous. But we have no evidence that they sought to destroy any of the others.[30] It would seem then that the concept of a sustained holy war belongs to a later period, to an attempt to understand the meaning of past events rather than an interpretation called forth by the events themselves at the time when they happened. It belongs, therefore, to history as it was remembered and studied and not to the history as it was experienced. It is significant that the holy war concept is to be found very largely in the book of Deuteronomy and in the comments of the people whom we call the Deuteronomic editors, i.e., the men who collected and edited the history of Israel as we have it today in Deuteronomy through II Kings (excluding Ruth). They were

28. Josh. 6–7.
29. Deut. 2:33–35; 3:3–7, 18–22; 7:1–5; 11:22–25; Chap. 20.
30. See additional notes.

trying to find out what had gone wrong in Israelite history and were convinced that the people from the beginning ought to have eradicated more firmly the foreign ideas. Their work is of enormous importance, but they were not themselves soldiers, and it is doubtful whether they ever envisaged an actual war of this kind taking place. In other words, the concept of a holy war must not be ascribed to an understanding of "God" and of "holiness" during the period of the Judges. It belongs to a later period and is not, properly speaking, a concept to be applied to actual warfare.

There can be no doubt that these ideas of the jealous God and so on are open to very considerable abuse, and they have indeed been much abused, though in the last two thousand years more by Christians, who share the Jewish heritage, than by the Jewish people themselves. But the danger inherent in these concepts, and the tragic misuse of them made in later years does not affect the question of whether in their primary form they might perhaps be valid. This is a matter for serious thought.

What is certain is that to the basic concepts of the "Other," of covenant, of the explosive event, and of choice, we owe the intensely personal quality of "God" as he is presented throughout the *Testament*. Admittedly, this was not a new idea, for the Semitic world generally spoke of the gods in personal terms. It is hardly possible to engage in active worship without thinking of speaking to "somebody." But it is remarkable that despite an ever increasing insistence that there must be no image, or likeness, of "God," the language used about him was always outspokenly anthropomorphic. His arm,[31] his hand,[32] his voice,[33] his ear,[34] his eyes[35] are metaphors in constant use. Moreover, he is not only to be addressed; he himself addresses, even accuses, and demands an answer.[36] There is a continual dialogue between God and man[37] of a kind which we do not find in the other Middle Eastern religions of the time. It was apparently impossible for the people of the covenant to speak of the reality of the world except in terms of direct encounter, of question and answer, of "I and Thou," and therefore of commitment and of repentance, of the conscious decision to go back to the beginning and start all over again.

"God" throughout the *Testament* is not man, he is not a person like other persons, he is not even a god like other gods. He must not be thought of as "a person" or "a god." He is not male or female, not black or white, not big or small. Yet not to speak of him in utterly personal terms is not to understand him at all.

31. Isa. 53:1.   32. Deut. 26:8.   33. Ps. 29:3.
34. Ps. 116:2.   35. II Chron. 16:9.   36. Ps. 50:1–21.
37. Gen. 17:18–19; 18:22–23; Exod. 3:1–4, 23; Isa. 6:8–12; Jer. 1; 2:4–8; 12:1–6; 14:13–16; 20:7; Amos 7:1–6; Micah 6:1–8; etc.

ADDITIONAL NOTES TO CHAPTER 4

1. For more detailed information about the history and archaeology of this period, see Yohanan Aharoni, *The Land of the Bible: A Historical Geography,* trans. A. F. Rainey (Philadelphia: The Westminster Press, 1967), pp. 174–253. Albrecht Alt, *Essays on Old Testament History and Religion,* trans. R. A. Wilson (Oxford: Basil Blackwell, 1966), pp. 133–70. John Bright, *A History of Israel* (Philadelphia: The Westminster Press, 2nd ed., 1972), pp. 130–39. A. D. H. Mayes, *Israel in the Period of the Judges* (Naperville, Ill.: Alec R. Allenson, 1974). George E. Mendenhall, "The Hebrew Conquest of Palestine," *Biblical Archaeologist Reader 3,* pp. 100–120; *The Tenth Generation: The Origins of the Biblical Tradition* (Baltimore: The Johns Hopkins Press, 1973). Martin Noth, *The History of Israel,* 2nd ed., trans. Stanley Goodman (New York: Harper & Row, 1960), pp. 141–63. R. de Vaux, O.P., *Histoire Ancienne d'Israel des Origines à l'Installation en Canaan* (Paris: Librairie Lecoffre, 1970), pp. 441–620. Manfred Weippert, *The Settlement of the Israelite Tribes in Palestine,* trans. James D. Martin (Naperville, Ill.: Alec R. Allenson, 1971).

2. One might compare, for instance, what has happened in Jerusalem, where the critical events upon which the Christian community is built have been gathered together into one place (the street of the Via Dolorosa and the Church of the Holy Sepulchre) and within the framework of one week (Holy Week) for the purpose of the corporate and continued identification of the community with the truth they believe to have been disclosed through these events. The actual events were those of a cruel political situation, but they are now seen by the community in terms of unity and triumph. The book of Joshua reflects the same kind of development.

6. The picture of the settlement period presented here is that first put forward by George E. Mendenhall in his article in the *Biblical Archaeologist* (see note 1). It has been criticized by others, e.g., de Vaux and Weippert, but from the point of view of historical geography it is very persuasive.

10. The subject of violence was the subject of lively debate in our discussions. One or two Contributors objected that violence in a revolutionary situation is not actually inevitable. However, it is very difficult to think of any struggle of this kind in history which has not been accompanied by outbreaks of violence, sometimes greater, sometimes less.

Even stronger objection was raised by some to the idea of violence being in any sense "of God," one Contributor going so far as to call it "repulsive." It was argued that God is by definition good, and that one cannot ever speak of violence as good. Violence must therefore be seen as opposition to God on the part of mankind, not as proceeding from him.

14. Mendenhall (*The Tenth Generation,* Chap. III) has rightly pointed out that the Hebrew root N-Q-M, normally translated by some word connected with the English "vengeance," does not mean that at all, but rather vindication, putting right what is wrong in a situation in which the political and judicial system provide no method of legal redress.

19. Some Contributors quite rightly objected that this does not give an altogether fair picture of man's relation to nature or of ultimate Reality being comprehended in terms of the natural world. It would not be accepted, for instance, by Indian or Chinese thinkers. This, however, raises a much larger question than we could cope with in this book, which is concerned with the nature of the Israelite experience, and why the struggle was for them such a critical one. We

had to confine ourselves to the ancient Middle Eastern situation, and not attempt to resolve the problem by transferring it to a quite different historical environment. There can be no doubt that the Middle Eastern cultures of the time were strongly resistant to change.

20. Ps. 18 is also quoted in II Sam. 22, and must be a very early one. It is true that on one occasion God is made known to Jacob as "the God of Bethel" (Gen. 31:13), and that in the Song of Deborah YHWH is spoken of as coming from Seir or Edom (Judg. 5:4; see also the psalm appended to the book of Habakkuk, 3:3), and it may be that at one time YHWH was thought of as belonging to that place where he had first been encountered. However, the idea of YHWH coming from Edom does not necessarily mean that he was to be identified with the region. In any case, such an idea, if it was ever held, soon disappeared.

30. Throughout the book of Judges the stories represent the Israelites as defeating and driving off their enemies, or in the case of the Philistines trying to do so, but never as massacring them. Similarly in the early monarchy the only account of an attempt as wholesale massacre is the passage quoted from I Sam. 15. That even this is exaggerated is clear from Chap. 30, which speaks of David later fighting against the Amalekites.

5. God and the State

BACKGROUND READING: I and II Samuel; I Kings 1–12.

> Then all the elders of Israel gathered together and came to Samuel at Ramah, and said to him, "Behold, you are old and your sons do not walk in your ways; now appoint for us a king to govern us like all the nations."
>
> I Samuel 8:4–5

The Establishment of a State

We come now to the last quarter of the eleventh century B.C.E.[1] and the third of what we have called the "formative crises" in Israelite history. At this time the loose confederation which had existed in the period of the judges was replaced by an organized state with a king at the head of it to maintain order and protect the community from outside attack. The dispute in this crisis concerned the kind of political order which ought to prevail in Israelite society.

The question of the order of the world and society and the understanding of what is meant by "God" are closely bound up with each other. Apart from the "God concept" there is no order at all.[2] Apart from some commonly accepted understanding of ultimate Reality, of the fundamental principle in terms of which everything is to be understood, it is not possible to perceive any coherent pattern in the world, or to establish a society which holds together. What has come to be spoken of as a "just and durable peace" can be built only upon a sound understanding of the nature of the world in which we find ourselves, upon interpreting it in the right terms. If we misunderstand the world, if in some way we misinterpret the political, social and economic facts of which our world is made up,

---

1. The approximate dates of the three first kings are Saul 1020–1000, David 1000–961, Solomon 961–922. After his death the kingdom split in two: the northern kingdom of Israel and the southern kingdom of Judah.
2. See additional notes.

53

confusion and violence will be the result. This is true for all political relationships, whether these are problems of internal organization or are international, i.e., relations with the people beyond our own society.

At the time with which we are concerned the Israelites, who had been settling mainly in the hill country with a minimum of organization and a powerful tradition of sturdy independence, began to realize that this was insufficient. There was clearly much internal disorder and strife.[3] The people manifestly did not live, as they longed to do, "every man under his vine and under his fig tree, with none to make them afraid."[4] Later generations looked back at the reign of Solomon as a time in which they did so live,[5] but of this earlier period the Deuteronomic editors record, "Every man did that which was right in his own eyes," because there was no king.[6]

There was also from outside persistent and increasing pressure from the Philistines. These were a group belonging to what we know as the Sea Peoples who were settling in the southern coast plain at very much the same time as the Israelites were establishing themselves in the hills, and who were steadily moving to encircle the Israelites and gain control of the whole country. The stories of Samson in Judges 13:2-16:31 reflect something of the border struggles, but they record no effective victory in battle, and I Samuel 4 tells of a shattering Israelite defeat. Many people began to say, therefore, that the old methods were no longer working. "Appoint for us a king," they said, "to govern us like all the nations."[7]

In this period we step, quite suddenly, into the realm of what people usually speak of as "history," i.e., historical events as recorded and studied, and as understood in a chronological order. From now on we can write a consecutive "history of Israel," because with the establishment of a state there were properly kept records, and there were also people who thought it worthwhile, not merely to record, but to think about the meaning of the events that were recorded. We are especially fortunate in that the result of their thinking and writing is that we have today evidence for two traditions about the period representing quite different attitudes to the monarchy and what this meant for the covenant with YHWH. One of them is found in what is usually known as the Early Source of the two books of Samuel, and the other in what by comparison is called the Late Source.[8] These names are not entirely helpful, for although the second was committed to writing later than the first, it may not be much later and may well represent a line of thought contemporary with the events

---

3. This is exemplified by the stories in Judges 19–21.
4. Micah 4:4; Zech. 3:10.   5. I Kings 4:25.
6. Judg. 17:6; 21:25. See also additional notes.   7. I Sam. 8:5.
8. For the convenience of the reader the two sources are outlined at the end of this chapter.

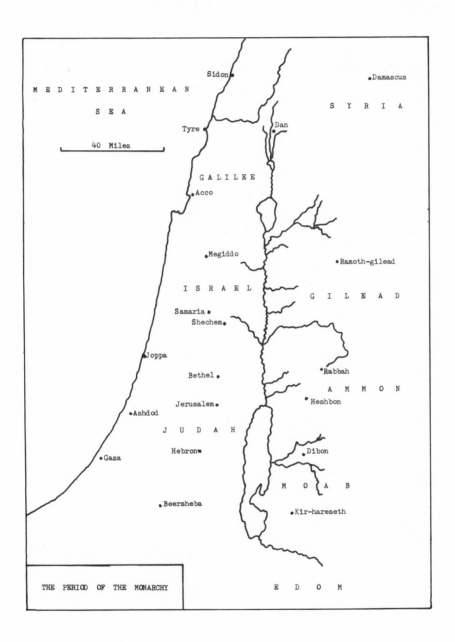

THE PERIOD OF THE MONARCHY

it describes. What is of great importance is that the Early Source was apparently written during the reign of Solomon and the author, therefore, belonged himself to the period and had participated in at least some of its events. It is a quite brilliant piece of writing and it is peculiarly Israelite, for we have no parallel to it from among the more sophisticated surrounding peoples. The kind of thinking it reflects cannot possibly have started from nothing and consequently it provides us with striking evidence that there must have been already at least a group of people who were thinking, as we would say, "historically."

This Early Source speaks of YHWH himself as initiating the monarchy and giving a direct command to Samuel to anoint Saul as King:

> Now the day before Saul came, YHWH had revealed to Samuel: "Tomorrow about this time I will send to you a man from the land of Benjamin, and you shall anoint him to be prince over my people Israel. He shall save my people from the hand of the Philistines; for I have seen the affliction of my people, because their cry has come to me." When Samuel saw Saul, YHWH told him, "Here is the man of whom I spoke to you!"
>
> I Samuel 9:15–17

The Late Source, however, claims that YHWH gave only a grudging consent to the people's demand, which he described as a rebellious rejection of himself as king:

> The thing displeased Samuel when they said, "Give us a king to govern us." And Samuel prayed to YHWH. And YHWH said to Samuel, "Hearken to the voice of the people in all that they say to you; for they have not rejected you, but they have rejected me from being king over them."
>
> I Samuel 8:6–7

Although the institution of monarchy very soon became so securely established that everyone recognized that it must be in some sense "of God," these two attitudes to kingship persisted for centuries. One opinion held that an effective monarchy was directly the will of "God" and that it was therefore wrong to seek to overthrow what "God" had established. In the south of the country, where this point of view prevailed, it was argued that far from monarchy being a rebellious breach of the covenant, it was itself an integral part of the covenant relationship, for YHWH had made an enduring covenant with the house of David.

> O YHWH, I will sing of thy steadfast love for ever.
>
> .   .   .   .   .   .
>
> Thou hast said, "I have made a covenant with my chosen one,
>   I have sworn to David my servant:
> 'I will establish your descendants for ever,
>   and build your throne for all generations.'"
>
> Psalm 89:1–4

Other people—and they seem to have been the majority in the northern part of the country—were altogether more suspicious and more inclined to say about any king, "How can this man save us?"[9] These northerners had little sense of identity with the family of David and did not believe in an enduring covenant between YHWH and the royal house.

> We have no portion in David,
> and we have no inheritance in the son of Jesse.
>
> II Samuel 20:1[10]

After the death of Solomon his son, Rehoboam, came to Shechem, the covenant city,[11] to ask for the people's recognition. He did not, however, receive it and a separate kingdom was established in the north, with Jeroboam I at its head.

The Prophets and the Law

Admittedly this attitude of suspicion did not make for political stability or public harmony, and sometimes it led to actual revolution, notably in the northern kingdom.[12] Nevertheless, to this suspicion about monarchy we owe two developments which probably all would agree to be "of God": the great prophetic movement and the Hebrew concept of *Torah,* usually but inadequately translated as "Law."

In this early period the people who in I Samuel are known as "prophets" and in II Kings as *bene nebiim,* or "sons of the prophets,"[13] were bands of ecstatic visionaries attached probably to the local sanctuaries. Such people were not confined to the Israelite community, for they are mentioned in the writings of other societies,[14] and in the stories of Elijah and Elisha we meet "prophets of Baal."[15] The function of prophets in any society of the time was to be persons through whom the will of the god in a particular situation could be made known. It was given to them to see, in a confusing and difficult situation, through the baffling outward appearance to the inner reality, and so they were also called "seers."[16] Through them the god spoke; reality was disclosed to the people, right action was proclaimed and the society preserved from disaster.

In no community were these prophets merely yes-men. They were quite capable of opposing the policy of a ruler.[17] Nevertheless, their role

9. I Sam. 10:27.
10. See also I Kings 12:16: This was clearly a rallying cry for revolt.
11. Deut. 27:1–26; Josh. 24:1–28; Judg. 9:24, 46 (the sanctuary at Shechem was dedicated to the god, or lord, of the covenant, i.e., *berith*).
12. See additional notes.
13. I Sam. 10:5, 10, 11; 19:20, 24; II Kings 2:3, 5, 7, 15; 4:1, 38; 5:22.
14. See additional notes.   15. I Kings 18:19ff.; II Kings 3:13.
16. I Sam. 9:9.
17. See additional notes.

in society was to help to preserve it, and the majority, therefore, did tend to support the administration and to be strongly conservative in outlook.

> Stand by the roads and look,
> and ask for the ancient paths,
> where the good way is.
>
> Jeremiah 6:16[18]

This conservatism made the prophets of the YHWH sanctuaries staunch defenders of the truths that had been learned in the wasteland, for it was this precarious covenant society they existed to preserve. In the acute, even desperate, crisis of increasing Philistine pressure, some of these prophets must certainly have supported the establishment of monarchy as something demanded by the reality of the situation.[19] Others, with no less justice, saw beyond this immediate crisis to the threat which the authority of a king would pose to a society built upon quite different principles. An organization of society based upon monarchy was exactly what they had fled to the wasteland to escape, and to reinstitute it now, however urgent the need, seemed to them nothing better than a return to Egypt and a denial of the covenant relationship.[20] When the critical events of the time forced them to recognize that there was no alternative to monarchy if the society was to survive, they gave their grudging consent in the name of YHWH. Yet at the same time they felt it their duty to keep a watchful eye upon the monarch and check every tendency for him to become some kind of substitute for YHWH, and take upon himself the role of the "Great King," the protector, the one whose will must prevail. From this constant surveillance there arose in time those great prophets whose teaching we have today enshrined in the *Testament*.

Another markedly conservative group in any society is that body of people whose function it is to administer justice and see that everything is done properly and in order. Justice and law are always that which the members of the society deem to be right and proper, and consequently custom and law go closely hand in hand. The administrators of justice have to ensure that the approved patterns of society are not violated.[21] In the *Testament* justice is called *mishpat,* but the word also means "custom" or "manner of life."[22] The word normally translated as "law" is

18. Jeremiah was certainly not here supporting the administration, of whose policy he was strongly critical, but he was critical because he was convinced that the administration had departed from the traditional ways that ought to be followed.

19. Such a person was the rather shadowy prophet Gad (I Sam. 22:5), called "David's seer" in II Sam. 24:11.

20. See additional notes.   21. See additional notes.

22. E.g., Judg. 18:7, "the custom of the Sidonians"; I Sam. 27:11, "the custom of David"; I Kings 18:28, the custom of the priests of Baal; II Kings 17:33, "the custom of the nations" as opposed to the custom of the followers of YHWH.

torah, but this properly means "teaching" from a verb meaning "to point out the right direction."[23] It also, therefore, carries the sense of the proper ongoing pattern of behavior. It is true that those who administer justice may find that they have to interpret this proper behavior in the light of changed circumstances, as the Supreme Court in the United States has done more than once, but they do not set out to make new laws. They interpret the laws and customs which already exist.

A pattern of behavior for the covenant community had already begun to be established from the time when the community was formed in the wasteland, and the Ten Words, or Commandments, were the requirements which those who accepted the covenant agreed to observe. But with the settlement in Canaan new questions presented themselves and modifications in the pattern of behavior became necessary, much of them based, as we now know, upon long-established patterns, such as the Babylonian Code of Hammurabi.[24] These new patterns did not take written form, however, in Israelite society until later, the earliest collection being what we call today the Covenant Code.[25] This reflects entirely an agricultural way of life, but it makes no mention of the king or of any state institution. Therefore the *mishpat* it embodies is the life of the period of settlement preceding the monarchy. It was probably written down at the time when this pattern of Israelite life was being called in question, i.e., the time of the formation of the monarchy, but before kingship had become established and generally accepted.[26] In other words, it lays down for the guidance of those who must administer the community in the days to come what is, and what is not, "done in Israel."[27]

What is striking about *torah* and *mishpat* as we find them in the *Testament* is that neither of them ever proceeds from the king. Those who had opposed the introduction of kingship into Israelite society had seen from the beginning what form a king's *mishpat* would be likely to take:

> He will take your sons and appoint them to his chariots and to be his horsemen. . . . He will take your daughters to be perfumers and cooks and bakers. He will take the best of your fields and vineyards and olive orchards. . . . He will take the tenth of your flocks and you shall be his slaves.
>
> I Samuel 8:11ff.[28]

The king, therefore, in Israel was not granted authority to initiate *torah* and *mishpat. Torah* was the concern of the priests, who were responsible

---

23. See additional notes. 24. See additional notes.
25. Exod. 20:23–22:33. 26. See additional notes.
27. Judg. 19:30; see also the appeal to past custom in II Sam. 20:18–19 by "one of those who are peaceful and faithful in Israel."
28. In v. 11 the word for the "ways" of the king is *mishpat.*

for giving this teaching and it was given in the name of Moses, who had received it from YHWH. Even *torah* belonging to a much later period is in the *Testament* set within the framework of the Exodus, for only if it is found true to that experience could it constitute "law" for Israel.[29] Thus in the case of Naboth's vineyard[30] even so powerful a ruler as King Ahab had no thought of using his royal authority to dispossess Naboth. Such a thing was certainly not the *mishpat* of Israel. It was his foreign wife, Jezebel, who thought in Canaanite terms, who told him that he was being ridiculous.

Was the Monarchy Syncretistic?

The word "syncretism" means the merging of different religious beliefs. As the monarchy developed in Israel both the southerners, who viewed a strong and secure monarchy as necessary for preserving the covenant relationship, and the northerners who broke away from them at the death of Solomon accused the other of exactly this, of having brought foreign beliefs into the worship of YHWH, and of having therefore accepted other gods.

There was much evidence for both accusations. In the south the Ark of the Covenant had been placed in Solomon's new Temple in Jerusalem, a town which David had captured from the Jebusites[31] and which therefore had a largely foreign population. The Temple itself had been built by Phoenician workmen on the pattern of temples in their own country. It was the only kind of temple they knew how to build and it included inevitably a great deal of Canaanite symbolism.[32] Moreover, Solomon had "multiplied horses for himself"[33] and in many other ways was adopting foreign customs in his administration. Evident for any pilgrim to Jerusalem to see were the shrines to foreign gods which he had allowed to be built on a hill outside the town.[34] These were necessitated by his treaty relationships with foreign powers, for the custom of the time was that an international treaty was guaranteed by the presence in each capital city of the god of the other country. No wonder, then, that many critics thought of these treaties as false covenants, covenants with the forbidden gods.

But foreign, and especially Canaanite, influence was no less apparent in the north. There was no rejection of monarchy, for Jeroboam I had set

---

29. See additional notes.   30. I Kings 21.   31. II Sam. 5:6–9.
32. See additional notes.
33. I Kings 10:26–29; for further explanation see additional notes.
34. I Kings 11:7–8. It is worth noting that these shrines were built on the far side of the Kidron valley, well outside Jerusalem. Solomon was careful not to have them inside the city which his father had captured for YHWH.

up an independent kingdom after his revolt against Rehoboam,[35] and had done so at the urging of a prophet from the old sanctuary of YHWH at Shiloh.[36] Shiloh remained a place where people would come to consult the oracle of YHWH,[37] but it was not hereafter the primary center of his worship in the kingdom. The capital established by Jeroboam was at Shechem, an ancient Canaanite city that had been incorporated into the Israelite community, and the frontiers were sanctified by the building of sanctuaries at Bethel and Dan. These were certainly dedicated to YHWH, but they used for his "throne" the figure of a bull, which was a Canaanite symbol of strength and fertility.[38]

Both the north and the south, then, had by this time completely accepted the need for a king, but in doing so both had taken over into their society much that was essentially foreign. We must ask, therefore, what the role of the king in ancient Israel actually was, and whether this apparently inevitable syncretism was necessarily bad.

The king in Israel is described by three terms: he was *nagid,* a leader appointed by YHWH;[39] he was *'bed YHWH,* the servant of YHWH;[40] and most important of all he was *mashiach YHWH,* the anointed of YHWH.[41] By this act of anointing it was understood that "the Spirit of YHWH came mightily upon him,"[42] and that the power of YHWH was now working directly through him. Yet he was no more than the vassal of the true king, YHWH. It is true that the wise woman of Tekoa said to David, "My lord has wisdom like the wisdom of the messenger of God to know everything that goes on in the country,"[43] but unlike the Egyptian Pharaoh he was *not* thought of as having in himself a divine quality.[44]

In fact, not even the powerful foreign kings had unlimited freedom of action, for all were bound to maintain the accepted custom of the country over which they ruled. Even Pharaoh, from whom all Egyptian law proceeded, was constrained to be the very opposite of willful, and to maintain unchanged the *maat,* or harmonious pattern, which his father and grandfather before him had upheld.[45] But in Israel the "rights and duties of the kingship" were clearly set down in writing, apparently from the beginning, and were kept in the sanctuary of YHWH.[46] The king was quite specifically a king under the covenant and subject to this supreme authority. This was the condition of his right to govern.

35. I Kings 12:20. 36. I Kings 11:29ff. 37. I Kings 14:1–3.
38. "Where there are no oxen the barn is empty; but the strength of a great ox ensures rich crops" (Prov. 14:4, NEB).
39. I Sam 9:16; 10:1; 13:14; 25:30; II Sam. 5:2; 6:21; 7:8; I Kings 14:7; 16:2.
40. II Sam. 3:18; 7:5, 8, 19–29; I Kings 3:6; 8:24–26; 11:13ff.; II Kings 19:34; 20:6.
41. I Sam. 16:6; 24:6; 26:9, 11, 16, 23; II Sam. 1:14, 16; 19:21.
42. I Sam. 16:13.
43. II Sam. 14:20 trans. D. B. 44. See additional notes.
45. See additional notes. 46. I Sam. 10:25.

And when he sits on the throne of his kingdom, he shall write for himself
in a book a copy of this law, from that which is in charge of the Levitical
priests; and it shall be with him, and he shall read in it all the days of his
life, that he may learn to fear YHWH his God, by keeping all the words
of this law and these statutes, and doing them; that his heart may not be
lifted up above his brethren.

Deuteronomy 17:18–20

In the one account of a royal coronation which we have[47] the "testi-
mony" was taken from the Ark and delivered to the king, and king and
people were bound together in one covenant to be obedient to YHWH.[48]
When in the modern United States men and women insist that the Presi-
dent must be under the law, and not take the law into his own hands, they
are proclaiming a principle of government which had its first clear statement in the beginnings of the Israelite monarchy. There kingship was
taken over, with all its majesty and splendor, from the surrounding nations,
but it was made firmly subordinate to the covenant with that "Other"
whom the people had come to know in the wasteland.

Nevertheless, kingship in Israel was certainly syncretistic and it did
incorporate ideas quite foreign to the wasteland experience. It was clearly
a compromise and was acceptable only because the primacy of this
"Other," this peculiar understanding of Reality, was publicly insisted
upon. This compromise was the result of "culture shock," of the encounter
with a foreign society, whose customs were at first rejected and attacked,
but were then gradually accommodated within the *mishpat* of Israel.

It is too easy to read the biblical records casually and see them in
terms of "good guys" and "bad guys," of self-evident right set against
obvious wrong. It cannot be said too often that we must beware continually of such a way of thinking. The adoption of foreign ideas is not
necessarily bad. It could be the purpose of YHWH that they should be
adopted. This is because culture shock, the confrontation with what is
strange and incomprehensible, is itself an event. It is something which
happens to us. It is always an encounter with "otherness." If the Israelite
experience is valid, it is through events, through the happening of new
things, that ultimate, final Reality is made known to men and women. For
this ultimate Reality they used the name YHWH. But we can never say in
advance what demands some new event is going to make. We must wait
until it happens and then try to understand what it means.

When new events crowd in upon a people, pressing them for an
answer, there is bound to be dispute about the direction in which the

47. II Kings 12:9–12, 17–19.
48. Vv. 12 and 17. See also II Sam. 5:3, and for a renewal of the covenant
II Kings 23:3.

events are pointing, about what may be called their intention, just as there was in ancient Israel about whether or not they should have a king. The word of YHWH does not come as a clear-cut command about which no dispute is possible. It is a question and a demand for an answer: "What are you going to do now, and why are you going to do it?" The question is posed by Reality itself, and it cannot be evaded. The answer we give exposes what "god" in fact we worship, what we think of as the final Reality.

One must take care, says Martin Buber, "not to understand this conversation with God . . . as something happening solely alongside or above the everyday. God's speech to men penetrates what happens in the life of each one of us, and all that happens in the world around us, biographical and historical, and makes it for you and me into instruction, message, demand. Happening upon happening, situation upon situation, are enabled and empowered by the personal speech of God to demand of the human person that he take his stand and make his decision. Often we think there is nothing to hear, but long before we have ourselves put wax in our ears."[49]

To refuse to answer when culture shock happens to us, to say that there is no question here because the foreign society is completely false, is a denial of YHWH. It is to insist that the new event is without significance, that it is not "of God." But to surrender wholly to the foreign world, to accept its thinking without question, is no less a denial, because by making such a surrender we say that our past experience, the event from which we began, is nonsense and no longer significant. We must take seriously the question posed by the encounter with what is foreign, and this means taking with equal seriousness the world from which we came and the world into which we are now plunged. We *must* compromise, we *must* draw upon both to find the answer YHWH demands from us. We have no alternative because we cannot wipe either the one or the other out of existence as if it had never happened. In this sense compromise is "of God," and indeed where there is no compromise there cannot be covenant or agreement at all.

Of course, the problem is exceedingly difficult. There is never an immediate solution. We must always, as it were, "wait upon YHWH," and more than one opinion will be put forth in his name. To all these opinions we must listen. And then we must answer.

To grasp this is surely to have the key to understanding the *Testament*. The whole history of ancient Israel was a continual wrestling with this kind of problem, and it was first consciously formulated with the establishment of the monarchy.

49. Martin Buber, *I and Thou*, 2nd. ed., trans. Ronald Gregor Smith (New York: Charles Scribner's Sons, 1958), pp. 136–37.

The Two Sources of the First Book of Samuel

EARLY	LATE
	1:1–28 The birth of Samuel. **2:11–26** The evil conduct of Eli's sons. **3:1–4:1a** The call of Samuel.
4:1b–7:2 The battle of Aphek and the capture of the Ark by the Philistines; the resulting plague and the return of the Ark.	
	7:3–8:22 Samuel as the judge of all Israel; the people demand a king, but this is called rebellion.
9:1–10:16 Saul is chosen secretly as king by Samuel at the direct command of YHWH.	
	10:17–27 Saul chosen publicly as king by casting lots.
11:1–15 Saul saves the people of Jabesh-gilead and is publicly accepted as king.	
	12:1–25 Samuel's farewell address (this has been much edited by the Deuteronomic writers).
13:1–7a; 15b–14:52 The beginning of Saul's campaign against the Philistines and the victory at Michmash.	
	15:1–16:13 Saul fails to destroy the Amalekites and is rejected by YHWH; David is anointed as king secretly by Samuel.
16:14–23 David is appointed to a place in Saul's court. **17:1–11, 32–40, 42–48a, 49, 51–54** The early-source account of the killing of Goliath.	**17:12–31, 41, 48b, 50, 55–58** The late-source account of the killing of Goliath.

18:6–9, 12–16, 20–29
  The early-source account of Saul's
  jealousy of David.

18:1–5, 10–11, 17–19
  The late-source account of Saul's
  jealousy of David.
19:1–10
  Saul tries to kill David.

19:11–17
  David is warned by Michal and
  escapes from Saul.
21:1–9
  David escapes to Nob.

21:10–15
  David escapes to Gath.

22:1–23:13
  David at Adullam; the massacre
  of the priests at Nob; David's
  relief of Keilah.

23:14–24:22
  David spares Saul's life.

25:1b–44
  David, Nabal and Abigail.
26:1–25
  David spares Saul's life.
27:1–28:2
  David as a vassal of the Philistines.
28:3–25
  Saul and the witch of Endor.
29:1–31:13
  The defeat and killing of Saul by the Philistines; David is absent because
  the Philistines did not trust him.

N.B. The following passages are additions to these two narratives:

2:1–10
      The song of Hannah.
2:27–36
      Condemnation of the family of Eli.
13:7b–15a
      Saul is rejected by YHWH because he offered sacrifice wrongfully.
18:12, 30
      The two phrases "because YHWH was with him and had departed
      from Saul" and "a second time" are editorial notes to harmonize
      the two sources.
19:18–24
      Saul behaves like an ecstatic prophet.
20:1–42
      David and Jonathan; another tradition of the break between Saul
      and David.

N.B. The division of the two sources given above is based on that used in *The New
Oxford Annotated Bible with the Apocrypha: Revised Standard Version*, ed.
Herbert G. May and Bruce M. Metzger, New York: Oxford University Press, 1963.

ADDITIONAL NOTES TO CHAPTER 5

2. This perhaps needs some clarification. The Nazi and Communist states both display a quite definite order, firmly enforced, but this order involves a rejection and disavowal of God. What is rejected, however, is that which the Judeo-Christian communities know to be God. There is in Communist Russia, as there was in Nazi Germany, a firm conviction of some other absolute upon which the order of society is based, and to which complete allegiance must be given. There is therefore an undoubted "God concept," even though the word "God" is not used for it.

6. This comment by the Deuteronomists is interpreted by some scholars as meaning that before there was a monarchy life was very much better. Mendenhall, for instance, calls it "a description of self-determination and freedom from interference or harassment by the king's bureaucrats or military autocracy" (*The Tenth Generation*, p. 27). Such an interpretation owes too much to modern ideas of democracy. The situation described in the final chapters of Judges is one which the editors clearly thought to be appalling.

12. There has been a tendency in some quarters to exaggerate this. The northern kingdom certainly began with twenty-five years in which coups d'état were common, and ended with twenty-two similar years. However, in the intervening 130 years there was only one, the revolt of Jehu, and in this period the dynastic principle was accepted. In the southern kingdom of Judah there were also conspiracies and assassinations (II Kings 11:1-3; 12:19-21; 14:17-21). The difference was that in Judah another member of the house of David, usually the next in line to succeed, came to the throne, whereas in the north the assassination of the king led to a usurper seizing power.

14. See Herbert B. Huffman, "Prophecy in the Mari Letters," *Biblical Archaeologist Reader 3*, pp. 199-224; Aubrey R. Johnson, *The Cultic Prophet in Ancient Israel*, 2nd ed. (Cardiff: University of Wales Press, 1962); J. Lindblom, *Prophecy in Ancient Israel* (Philadelphia: Fortress Press, 1962), Chap. 2; Theophile James Meek, *Hebrew Origins*, 3rd ed. (New York: Harper & Row, 1960), Chap. 5; Johannes Pedersen, *Israel: Its Life and Culture*, III-IV (Oxford University Press, 1940), pp. 107-149.

17. It is a mistake to think of prophetic criticism of the ruler as something which happened only in Israelite society. See, e.g., the rebuke of the soothsayer Tiresias to Creon in Sophocles, *Antigone*, 11.988-1090.

20. An interesting parallel is the argument which developed between the northern "liberals" and the southern "conservatives" in America during the sixties. The "liberals" claimed that in order to guarantee freedom and equality to the Black people the power of the federal government must if necessary be strengthened to enforce this. To the "conservatives" this looked like reinstating governmental absolutism and going straight back to George III. For them "freedom" meant freedom for a restaurant owner to do what he liked and serve whom he wished in his own restaurant. Both sides were convinced that they were defending the constitution against the dangerous policies of the other.

21. Some have suggested that this is not true of a monarchy, but a monarchy also depends upon the approval of the governed if it is to avoid revolt.

23. The root *yarah* means to throw, and *horah* to cause to throw and so to point the right direction, and therefore to teach. *Yoreh* means the "first rains," which, thrown down on the earth, cause it to send forth its life. There is consequently a close connection between *torah* and life.

24. The Code of Hammurabi is not a code of law enacted by the king, but a

statement of the accepted custom of the time, and is itself based upon much more ancient custom. See James Pritchard, *Ancient Near Eastern Texts relating to the Old Testament* (Princeton: Princeton University Press, 1955), pp. 1–163, 163–64, 166–77, where the biblical parallels are indicated.

26. Some authorities would argue that the Covenant Code must have been written during the period of the Judges before there was any king, e.g., Ronald E. Clements, *Exodus* (Cambridge, England: The University Press, 1972), p. 128, and Martin Noth, *Exodus,* trans. J. S. Bowden (Philadelphia: The Westminster Press, 1962), p. 175.

29. One might well compare this to the fact that in the United States what is declared "unconstitutional" cannot have the status of law. Here also reference is made to a rejection of monarchy as the basis of order, and to an "exodus" and a "covenant" or union. In modern Hebrew, in fact, the United States is known as *artzoth ha-berith* (the lands of the covenant).

32. See W. F. Stinespring, "Temple, Jerusalem" and G. A. Barrois, "Temples" in ID, IV, pp. 534–68.

33. Cf. Deut. 17:14–17. The accumulation of a strong chariot force seems to have been thought of as something characteristic of the Egyptian Pharaohs, and the account of the delivery of the Israelites at the Reed Sea emphasizes the destruction of the Egyptian chariots (Exod. 14:6–7, 9, 17–18, 23, 25, 26, 28; 15:1, 4, 19, 21). This did not, however, prevent Israelite kings from emulating them, and Assyrian records of the great battle at Qarqar in 850 B.C.E. (not mentioned in the Bible) speak of King Ahab commanding 2,000 chariots, more than any of his allies. (Pritchard, ANET, pp. 277–81.)

44. Roland de Vaux, *The Bible and the Ancient Near East* (New York: Doubleday & Company, 1972), Chap. 9. See also his *Ancient Israel* (New York: McGraw-Hill Book Company, 1961), Vol. II, Chap. 5; John Bright, *The Kingdom of God in Bible and Church* (Nashville: Abingdon Press, 1953), Chap. 1; Georg Fohrer, *History of Israelite Religion* (Nashville: Abingdon Press, 1972), Chaps. 11 and 12; Edmond Jacob, *Theology of the Old Testament* (New York: Harper & Row, 1958), pp. 234–239; Aubrey R. Johnson, *Sacral Kingship in Ancient Israel* (Cardiff: University of Wales Press, 1955); Ludwig Kohler, *Old Testament Theology* (London: Lutterworth Press, 1957), Chap. 5; Pedersen, *Israel,* pp. 33–106; Helmer Ringgren, *Israelite Religion* (Philadelphia: Fortress Press, 1966), pp. 220–38.

45. See Henri Frankfort, *Ancient Egyptian Religion* (New York: Harper Torchbook edition, 1961), pp. 46ff.; John A. Wilson in Frankfort, Jacobsen, Wilson, *Before Philosophy: The Intellectual Adventure of Ancient Man* (Baltimore: Penguin Books, 1949), pp. 91ff. For the role of the Mesopotamian kings see A. Leo Oppenheim, *Ancient Mesopotamia* (Chicago: University of Chicago Press, 1964), pp. 95–109, especially 103.

PAST, PRESENT AND FUTURE

6. The God of the Fathers

BACKGROUND READING: Genesis 12–50, especially 12–13; 15–33; 35; 1–21; 37:1–46:7.

The Traditions of the Patriarchs

This is now a suitable time to look back at the stories of the Patriarchs, of Abraham, of Isaac and of Jacob, for it was during the early part of the monarchy that these stories were first committed to writing. This was done by that profound thinker, known to us today as the Yahwist, whose work is the great body of material which we call "J."[1]

It is probably easiest to understand the pattern of the book of Genesis as we have it today if we remember that *the groundwork is the Yahwist material and the framework that of the Priestly writer*. In other words, the initial collection was the Yahwist history starting with the Garden of Eden story and continuing with stories of all four Patriarchs. About a century later the Elohist account was interwoven with this. It begins to be included in Chapter 15 and is concerned especially with Isaac, Jacob and Joseph. His stories seem to have been collected in the northern part of the country, while those of the Yahwist were drawn from the south. Later the Priestly writer (or writers) set this material within a chronological framework. They did this by adding the introductory account of the creation of the world and then inserting at various points genealogical lists and notes of the age of the Patriarchs to provide definite dates. The only two stories they added to the Patriarchal history were the covenant with Abraham in Chapter 17 and the burial of Sarah in Chapter 23. Before the time of their being written down, all the stories had been handed down orally, recited aloud as part of the cult in the sanctuaries, and also perhaps in the marketplace by some storyteller who had learned the art from his father, or in the tents on a mild summer evening when the hill farmers were camping out to protect the precious vines from the thirsty foxes. They would have been heard with rapt attention by an audience who

1. See the notes at the end of Chap. 3.

followed carefully every word, corrected any alteration, and identified themselves completely with the action as something immediately present to them.

It is difficult to convey to a modern western reader the intensity with which people in a traditional society, unaccustomed to rely upon books, will listen to even the most familiar tale. Although they know the denouement perfectly well, it comes to them each time as a shock, and they greet each moment in the story with cries of wonder, of agreement, or of horror.[2] Since to them it is a real and present experience, it cannot be wantonly altered to suit the occasion. It must remain true to the origin from which it sprang.[3]

Of course, as the years pass the stories tend to become polished, more or less unconsciously, for effective telling. Anachronisms may creep in, though these are remarkably rare.[4] There may also be "wandering stories" which become attached to more than one name, as did in Genesis the story of a man passing off his wife as his sister.[5] Other stories may serve to identify a place and incorporate it fully into the world of which the tellers and the hearers form a part and give it therefore what is understood now to be its "true" significance, i.e., the significance in terms of the Reality which is the basis of their society. Such is the purpose of the stories of how Abraham worshiped YHWH at the Canaanite sanctuaries of Shechem and Bethel[6] and Jacob's vision at Bethel.[7]

We have learned in recent years to treat these stories with great respect as preserving with remarkable accuracy a memory of life as it was lived in the Middle Bronze Age, round about 1900 B.C.E. We have now plenty of archaeological evidence to show how well remembered are the customs of that far distant period, even though they had long since ceased to be familiar customs to Israelite villagers 900 or even 1000 years later.[8] Faithfully preserved through so many centuries, the stories were then, as has been said, collected, arranged, and committed to writing with occasional brief editorial comments, as when it is said that Abraham "believed YHWH and he reckoned it to him as righteousness."[9]

The kind of life these stories disclose to us is that of a pastoral people in the process of becoming sedentary.[10] They were not yet settled, but still dwelt in tents, moving with their herds of sheep and goats in search

2. See additional notes.   3. See additional notes.
4. Such anachronisms in the Patriarchal stories include mention of the Philistines, who did not settle in Palestine until the time of the Israelite take-over of the hill country, and of camels, which first began to be used in large numbers at roughly the same time. The Midianite invasion, described in Judg. 6, was the first large-scale attack by camel owners.
5. Gen. 12:11–20; 20; 26:1–11.   6. Gen. 12:6–8.
7. Gen. 28:10–22. See also additional notes.
8. See additional notes.   9. Gen. 15:6.   10. See additional notes.

of pasture. These movements would have been restricted, for such animals move slowly and cannot go for long without water.

> My lord knows that the children are frail, and that the flocks and herds giving suck are a care to me; and if they are over-driven for one day, all the flocks will die.
>
> Genesis 33:13

They lived, therefore, on the edges of the desert, not in its depths, and were in contact with towns and villages. The stories about Abraham revolve largely about Beersheba on the southern edge of the well-watered land, and those about Jacob belong to the central hills on either side of the Jordan. We should probably think of him as "transhumant," that is moving regularly from the winter grazing in the rift valley[11] to higher pastures in the drought of summer.

The Intent of the Patriarchal Stories

Here we are confronted with two questions. First, what did these writers, especially the Yahwist and the Elohist, see to be the meaning of these traditions and what did they expect people to understand by them? This we can learn from the way they selected and arranged the stories and from the comments they made from time to time. Second, what had come down to them of permanent value from that much earlier age, directing and shaping their thinking? Here the fact that the traditions were in general faithfully preserved is of great importance.

Let us begin with the first question, though space will not permit us to examine each story, or even each strand, in detail. We must be content to recognize certain major themes. First of all there can be no doubt but that those who preserved the stories saw in the experience of their ancestors a reflection and confirmation of their own experience. Their new birth as a coherent people in the wasteland was seen to be a fully valid experience because it was true to the experience of their ancestral fathers. Therefore they recorded that Abraham became a vagabond,[12] forsaking the protection of his family and clan for the restless life of one who was no more than a "stranger and a sojourner" without legal protection or even a place to bury his head;[13] that he "journeyed on, still going toward the Negeb," the drought-bitten wasteland of the south,[14] and that he went

---

11. Penuel, where Jacob wrestled with the angel (Gen. 32:22–32), is in the lower Jabbok valley (modern river Zerqa) not far from where it joins the Jordan.
12. Gen. 12:1–9; Deut. 26:5. The "vagabond Aramean" of the second passage is believed by some scholars to be Jacob rather than Abraham, but the significance of the description remains the same.
13. Gen. 23:3ff.   14. Gen. 12:1–9.

down into Egypt and came out again.[15] To be a true Israelite was to have had this kind of experience.[16]

Second, those who collected and preserved these traditions did so because they saw in them a demonstration of what Isaiah was later to call the "strange work" of God.[17] Looking backward at all that had brought them to the situation of their own day, they could see the dynamism, the thrust and the power, which had brought these events to pass. They saw them as marked by purpose and direction, and yet as having been unpredictable. In no sense at all can men and women set out to make history. They cannot lay hold on anything and say of it, "This shall be the determining factor in the days that are to come." Both Abraham and Hagar were mistaken when they sought to bestow this quality upon Ishmael.[18] What is counted as righteousness,[19] as a firm and level foundation for life is the recognition, and the wholesale acceptance, of this power and purpose as determining the character of events. "It is now said of Abraham that he 'continued to trust' God . . . and of God that He 'deemed' this as the proving true of him."[20] In the stories of Lot the error is always the looking back,[21] the choosing of something because it was "like the land of Egypt,"[22] because of a nostalgia for what is popularly known as the "good old days" or the "old-time religion." On no account was Isaac to be taken back to the land from which he had come.[23]

Yet Isaac must take a wife from the land of his ancestors. The traditions are concerned with both past and future, inheritance and promise, and that which has once been is not to be rejected out of hand as something without value. The stories are preserved because one cannot grasp the fact of the power, or perceive its purpose and direction, without keeping alive the traditions and the heritage as something continually present, something existential, a manifestation of Reality confronting man and demanding an answer. History must be remembered if history as experienced is to be understood.

We make a very great mistake indeed if we imagine that the *primary* purpose of these stories is moral or ethical instruction. Certainly they have been effectively used in this way, but they were not in the first place intended to show us exemplary persons whom we would do well to imitate. When, centuries later, the great prophet of the Exile said to the people, "Look to Abraham your father and to Sarah who bore you,"[24] his entire

15. Gen. 12:10–13:1.   16. See additional notes.
17. Isa. 28:21.   18. Gen. 16; 17:18.
19. Gen. 15:6. See also additional notes.
20. Martin Buber, *Two Types of Faith*, trans. Norman P. Goldhawk (New York: Harper & Row, 1961), p. 44.
21. Gen. 19:26.   22. Gen. 13:10.   23. Gen. 24:1–9.   24. Isa. 51:2.

purpose was to remind his hearers of what had been done through these people, not what they themselves had achieved. Man in the *Testament* is not the example because man is not God. It is because God is holy that the Israelites should be holy,[25] and not because there have been holy men and women. Despite a lot of popular chatter on the subject, the biblical understanding of the universe does not center upon man.[26] It does not assume that one may use mankind as a starting point and derive from this a true interpretation of the world, or discover a proper pattern for human behavior. It insists continually that the world cannot be understood at all except in terms of the activity of the "Other," of that which in its very essence is not man. At no point therefore does the *Testament* offer any man or woman as a model of right behavior, to be accepted without question.[27]

The focus of attention is always the galvanizing power, constantly and even furiously at work, bringing continually into existence, sometimes by means of men and women, but very often also despite human intentions. "As for you," said Joseph, "you meant evil against me, but God meant it for good, to bring it about that many people should be kept alive, as they are today."[28]

The ancient Israelite would have been as deeply shocked as we are, and probably very much more so, by the story of Jacob's deception of his father in Genesis 27. "To mislead a blind man on the road"[29] was one of the abominable acts and a cardinal sin. Moreover, "you shall stand in the presence of a hoary head, and honor the face of an old man."[30] The story, recited in the sanctuary, was a tale to cause men to shudder, to gasp when they heard it. It was not an example of how to behave, nor yet a joke. It was "exalted and serious. The crime against the blind man, the bankruptcy of the whole family—none of that would have caused an ancient reader to laugh."[31] Rather, its purpose was to bring forcibly to mind in the assembly the truth that as with their father Jacob, so also with their own possession of Canaan, the heritage was theirs by gift and not by right. Nor could they ever claim that it *belonged* to them.

The covenant described by the Yahwist in Genesis 15:7-21, certainly one of the oldest traditions at his disposal, laid no prior conditions upon Abraham, who received it in a horror of great darkness, and this is true also of the "everlasting covenant" which the Priestly writer recounts in Genesis 17:

25. Lev. 19:2.   26. See additional notes.
27. See additional notes.   28. Gen. 50:20.
29. Deut. 27:18.   30. Lev. 19:32 (trans. D. B.)
31. Gerhard von Rad, *Genesis: A Commentary*, trans. John H. Marks (Philadelphia: The Westminster Press, 1961), p. 275.

Behold, my covenant is with you, and you shall be the father of a multitude of nations. No longer shall your name be Abram, but your name shall be Abraham, for I have made you the father of a multitude of nations. . . . And I will establish my covenant between me and you and your descendants after you throughout their generations for an everlasting covenant, to be God to you and to your descendants after you.

Genesis 17:4–7

It was an absolute promise, or perhaps more correctly an authoritative appointment to a function, for Abraham was the servant of YHWH.[32] The promise was unconditional in the sense that there was no prior requirement to which Abraham must give his assent, but by no means was it unconditioned and amorphous, leaving him complete freedom of action. It was conditioned, and conditioned absolutely, by its purpose and function. Nobody who had come to "know" YHWH[33] and to interpret the world in terms of his dynamic activity could conceive of an event without the direction and purpose which determined its meaning. The purpose of this covenant was the well-being of the entire world[34] and was not to be narrowly confined within the family of Israel. This theme was there already in the earliest of the written material, that of the Yahwist. Centuries later, in the dark days of the Babylonian Exile, it was brought to magnificent fruition by that prophet whom we call Isaiah of Babylon.[35]

Moreover, the Yahwist insists that the purpose must be the establishment of justice and the maintenance of true order, for it is impossible that he who judges all the earth should do what is not just:

Wilt thou indeed destroy the righteous with the wicked? . . . Far be it from thee to do such a thing, to slay the righteous with the wicked, so that the righteous fare as the wicked! Far be that from thee! Shall not the judge of all the earth do right?

Genesis 18:23–25

The fate of Sodom and Gomorrah was so well known as to be proverbial,[36] and it seemed to the Yahwist that so appalling a disaster could surely not have happened if there had been even no more than ten righteous people there.[37]

To have grasped that men and women are not at the mercy of blind

---

32. Gen. 26:24.

33. The Hebrew word *yada'*, normally translated "know," means much more than this. It denotes close personal relationship, not merely mental knowledge, and is one of the regular "covenant words" used in ancient treaties.

34. Gen. 12:3; 18:18; 28:14.   35. E.g., Isa. 42:1–4, 6.

36. Deut. 29:23; 32:32; Isa. 1:9–10; 13:19; Jer. 23:14; 49:18; 50:40; Lam. 4:6; Amos 4:11.

37. See additional notes.

and capricious fate and that the gods do not kill us for their sport is to have laid hold upon a majestic truth. Nevertheless, it is a dangerous doctrine. On the one hand, those who have come to know this truth must always say, with Thomas Jefferson, "Indeed I tremble for my country when I reflect that God is just,"[38] but on the other hand, it is all too easy to assume that dread and ghastly tragedy falling upon others denotes their wickedness. We cannot say what the end of a thing will be, for we do not know what is still to come. To act upon the understanding that ultimate Reality is disclosed through historical events is to recognize with intense seriousness that we do not live in a static world, whose pattern we already comprehend, but in one which compels us forever to make new assessments. We cannot now pronounce the judgment upon the afflicted because the evidence is not yet all at hand.[39]

The God of the Fathers

When we turn to the disclosure of God that was already part of the inherited traditions, we must again be very selective, since space does not permit a full examination. Chief among these ancient concepts is that of the God of the Fathers.[40] This is an idea more surprising than a first casual reading would suggest. The revelation to Moses was made almost as if there had been three gods, "the God of Abraham, the God of Isaac, and the God of Jacob"[41] and closer study indicates that in fact this may not be far from the truth and that they might once have had three distinct names, *Pahad Yitzhaq, Abir Ya'acob,* and perhaps *Magen Abram* (the Fear of Isaac, the Mighty One of Jacob, and the Shield of Abraham).[42] It is probable that at first these represented traditions of different clans, but as the people came together into one larger community they saw their experience as common to all and the different gods to have been but one. It is evident from the tradition that at one time the fathers had worshiped other gods.[43] When at Mizpah Jacob swore by "the Fear of Isaac" he clearly recognized that "the God of Abraham and the God of Nahor,"

38. *Notes on Virginia,* Query xviii. Manners.
39. See below, Chap. 15.
40. The classic treatment of this concept is by Albrecht Alt, *Essays on Old Testament History and Religion,* trans. R. A. Wilson (New York: Doubleday, 1967), Chap. 1.
41. Exod. 3:6.
42. Gen. 31:42; 49:24. For the possibility of the title *Magen Abram* see Gen. 15:1, and for later use of *Abir Ya'acob* see Ps. 132:2, 5; Isa. 49:26; 60:16. Père de Vaux has challenged the suggestion that these were divine names. He claims that they were descriptions, and that the God of the Father was always anonymous (*Histoire,* p. 259).
43. Gen. 35:1–7; Josh. 24.2, 14–15.

who were to judge between them,[44] were not to be thought of as the same. Each swore by his own god, for the two communities remained sharply separate and did not intermingle their heritage.

The great advantage of such a view is "that it places the figures of the patriarchs from the very first in an organic relationship to the whole religious and cultic practice of the Israelite tribes, and allows it a proper part both in the constant and in the developing features of their religious history. This explains one thing which is otherwise difficult to understand —the fact that these individuals were remembered from the earliest times on."[45] No people can ever incorporate into their thinking an entirely foreign idea, which bears no relation at all to anything in their own experience. It is thus of the utmost value to see how the ancient traditions laid the foundation for the great disclosure of the Exodus, and with what justice it was affirmed that Moses did not lead the people out of Egypt to meet in the desert some novel deity. A "new religion" is a contradiction in terms. Properly speaking, there cannot be a "new God." The ultimate Reality which bestows meaning and significance upon our confusing world must be the same Reality which has undergirded it from the beginning, or it is not real at all. If in the past men and women did not perceive how the world was properly to be interpreted, the fault lay in their perception, not in the nature of Reality.[46]

It is therefore important that the Patriarchal experience is that of personal encounter,[47] and an encounter initiated by God, not by man in search of a god. It is a confrontation "face to face"[48] in which a command is given and a response expected.[49] But it is not a bleak order from above giving the human creature no chance to utter so much as a word. Instead, and perhaps this is most surprising of all, there is argument and debate.[50] It is already grasped, however crudely (as when Jacob entered into an evidently primitive and selfish contract with God at Bethel)[51] that to interpret the world correctly means to recognize both the freedom of human decision and the absoluteness of Reality and therefore the necessity of agreement between these two.

Moreover, reality and order are not seen to be disclosed *primarily* in the visible things of this world. Meaning and significance do not pertain to a particular place. "The god of the clan is not a sky god; neither is he associated with a local sanctuary. He is a god who protects the wandering

---

44. Gen. 31:53. The additional phrase, "the God of their father," is not in the Septuagint, the ancient Greek translation of the Hebrew Scriptures, and seems to be a later comment designed to deny the existence of any other gods.

45. Alt, *Essays on Old Testament,* p. 47.   46. See additional notes.

47. Rowley, *Worship in Ancient Israel,* p. 28.   48. Gen. 32:20.

49. Gen. 12:1–3; 22:1ff.   50. Gen. 15:1–16; 17:18; 24:10–14; 28:18–22; 32:22–32; also 18:16–33, though this has evidently been expanded later.

51. Gen. 28:18–22.

nomads as they travel. . . . They move among forces that are alien and
often hostile . . . but he knows the routes and their dangers and will
guide them safely."[52] They do not need to go to Bethel or Beersheba or
Gilgal to find him; he seeks them out and meets them on the way. If, like
the villager, one may go to a place and be sure that there he will be in
touch with Reality, then Reality belongs to what is familiar and secure,
and makes no demands for change. But what may be called the nonloca-
tion of God, the separation of him from any particular place, from all
identification with the solid earth, means that one confronts Reality each
time as that which is Other. The encounter is a surprise. It may come
upon a man as far away as distant Haran,[53] and he needs the assurance
that even there beyond the Euphrates the God who meets him is the same.
Therefore, it is necessary to say—and it is no false and artificial equa-
tion—that when the people take refuge in the "great and frightening
wilderness," they are met there by "the God of Abraham, the God of
Isaac, and the God of Jacob."

He is the God of the Fathers, or more correctly "the God of your (or
my) father."[54] The identification is with a starting point in time instead
of the security of an established land or place.[55]

Both the temporal and the spatial understanding of Reality have their
dangers. To think of the word primarily in terms of a place, to find one's
identity in the homeland, in "fatherland" or "motherland," is to run all
the risks of enclosure and parochialism. It is to think only too often of the
world outside, beyond the safe frontiers, as being without Reality, a god-
less place where rules no longer apply and disorder prevails. It is to think
of the alien realm as peopled by barbarians and foreign devils, the breed-
ing ground of Communism and all that is "un-American."[56] But to conceive of the world in terms of time, to be identified with a family or tribe
extending through the ages, and to speak of the "father" or the "mother"
of one's people, is often to raise the hideous specter of a "pure race." In
the modern world it causes men and women to discriminate on grounds
of color or blood, and to use the cruel words: white, black, yellow, and
brown. Neither line of thought is protected from corruption and evil. Each
may be guilty of savage exclusion.

52. Georg Fohrer, *History of Israelite Religion*, p. 40.
53. Gen. 31:11–13. This, curiously enough, is the only passage in which God
is spoken of as being the God of a place.
54. Gen. 31:5, 29; 43:23; 49:25; 50:17. Sometimes the name of the father is
mentioned, e.g., "the God of Abraham your father," Gen. 26:24; 28:13; 31:53;
32:9; 46:1.
55. This, of course, is a common way of thinking for a wandering people, who
have no permanent abode but are compelled to move if they are to survive. The
Bakhtiari of Persia, for instance, trace their descent from Bakhtiar, whom they
understand to have been the founder of their people.
56. See additional notes.

Yet there is this difference. Time, as men and women experience it, is open-ended, and the future is without frontiers. It belongs to no one. The spatial world that man inhabits is, on the other hand, enclosed and divided by line. It involves property and possession. The time framework of thought, therefore, provides in principle the greater freedom, the possibility of amendment and reform, the chance of beginning again. Where there is no future there is no hope of change. Indeed there is no hope at all.

Of course, the Patriarchs did not think in these sophisticated terms. They spoke only of the God of our father, and not of any local God. But because they did so they bequeathed a heritage of surpassing value. It was no more than the rudimentary beginning of historical thought, but it delivered both them and those who preserved their memory from bondage to a place.

ADDITIONAL NOTES TO CHAPTER 6

2. I remember once attending a party at the Scots Hospital in Tiberias at which all the staff, both Arab and Western, were present. We played a game of charades in which, to avoid language difficulties, the scenes were well-known Bible stories. In one the letter H was illustrated by the story of Hagar being sent off into the desert by Abraham and Sarah. The Arabs present gasped with shock to think that such a thing should happen and some even burst into tears. To them it was only too real, while to the Westerners it was merely a game.

3. On the question of the historical value of the Patriarchal traditions see Roland De Vaux, *Histoire,* 172–79; Roland De Vaux, *The Bible and the Ancient Near East,* pp. 111–21; G. E. Wright, "History and the Patriarchs," *Expository Times,* 71, 1959–60; pp. 292–96; G. von Rad, "History and the Patriarchs," *ibid,* 72, 1960–61, pp. 213–16. Unfortunately Thomas L. Thompson's important work, *The Historicity of the Patriarchal Narratives* (New York: Walter de Gruyter, 1974), reached us too late to be included. The section on history and the Patriarchs needs revision in view of Thompson's questioning of the historical value of the Genesis narratives.

7. Sacred sites can very seldom be stamped out deliberately, for people persist in coming to worship at them. When therefore another religion, another interpretation of the world takes over, not only the people but also the places they regard as significant must be "converted." Each must be given its significance in terms of the new understanding of the world. Thus, Christian missionaries in pagan Europe as it were "baptized" the land, built churches inside megalithic circles, identified sacred mountains with St. Michael who destroyed the dragon of chaos (Rev. 12:7), and turned the ancient gods into Christian saints. So has Islam identified Jerusalem with Muhammad, and Mecca with Abraham and Ishmael. This is in no sense artificial. The old world cannot just be discarded; it must be shown to be relevant to, and altogether part of, the new and more comprehensive understanding.

A striking example of the persistence of a sacred site may be observed at Ephesus (modern Seljuq) in Turkey. Worship of the Mother Goddess is known in Anatolia from at least 6000 B.C.E. and Ephesus became one of the great centers of this cult, with its famous temple for the goddess Artemis. When the Roman Empire became Christian, the cult was transmuted into the veneration of the

Virgin Mary, who reputedly lived at Ephesus in her old age, and the famous Councils of Ephesus were held in the church that bears her name. The name of Sittna Mariam continued to be held in honor when Turkey became Muslim, and still today village women will come to the ruins of St. Mary's Church to pray for children.

For the significance of this activity during the Patriarchal period see Roland de Vaux, *Ancient Israel* (New York: McGraw-Hill Book Company, 1965), pp. 289–94.

8. See e.g., George Ernest Wright, *Biblical Archaeology*, Chap. III; Cyrus H. Gordon, "Biblical Customs and the Nuzu Tablets," *Biblical Archaeologist Reader,* 2, pp. 21–33.

10. The position adopted here is that put forward by de Vaux, *Histoire*, pp. 213–223. Other suggestions have been that the Patriarchs were merchants traveling with donkey caravans (W. F. Albright, *Archaeology and the Religion of Israel*, pp. 97–101; *Yahweh and the Gods of Canaan*, pp. 64–73; "Midianite Donkey Caravans," in *Translating and Understanding the Old Testament*, ed. Frank and Reed, Nashville: Abingdon Press, pp. 197–205) or that Abraham was a "merchant prince" (C. H. Gordon, "Abraham and the Merchants of Ura," *Journal of Near Eastern Studies*, 17, 1958, pp. 28–31). The most important work on the nomadic people of this period is Jean-Robert Kupper, *Les Nomades en Mesopotamie au temps des rois de Mari* (Paris: Société d'Edition "Les Belles Lettres," 1957).

16. An interesting parallel is Matthew's presenting Jesus as a "true Israelite" because he went down to Egypt and was brought out again. Matt. 2:13–15; the quotation in v. 15 is from Hos. 11:2.

19. The Hebrew word *tsadiq* (righteous) and *tsedaqah* (righteousness) come from the root TS-D-Q, which has the sense of "hard, even, level," i.e., firm ground on which it is possible to build.

26. One must protest strongly against the argument, sometimes expressed by ecologists, that in seeing man as having dominion over nature (Gen. 1:26–28) the Hebrew mind placed man in the center of the universe (see e.g., Lynn White, Jr., "The Historical Roots of Our Ecologic Crisis," *Science,* Vol. 155, 1967, pp. 1203–7). Nothing could be further from the truth.

27. We had considerable discussion over this matter, some Contributors arguing that biblical characters are often "exemplary," and that Moses, David and Solomon, for instance, were thought of in these terms. Hence the attributing of later material to them. The argument put forward in the body of the book is a majority opinion rather than a consensus, though there was fairly general agreement that the *original* purpose of the stories was not to provide examples of human perfection. Christians, it is true, do regard Jesus as a person to be imitated, and this has biblical support (e.g., Phil. 2:5), but they do so because through the man they perceive the ultimate Reality, God (John 14:9). If God is dead, then Jesus ceases to be the true exemplar, and to use him in this way has no biblical support.

37. No traces of these tragic cities have ever been discovered by archaeologists, though they have been long searched for. There is, however, increasing evidence that they may perhaps lie beneath the shallow southern basin of the Dead Sea.

46. So-called "founders of a new religion," i.e., men such as Jesus, Muhammad and the Buddha, always insist that although what they are saying may be new to their hearers, it is not new in essence. See for instance the claim of Jesus that he did not come to destroy the Law and the Prophets (Matt. 5:17–18) and the large part played by Abraham and Moses, and even Adam, in the Qur'an.

56. The conviction that the world beyond the frontiers is meaningless and dis-

orderly is deep-seated and widespread. Lord Frederic Hamilton has an amusing description of the belief of Russian villagers before World War I that outside Holy Russia there were only deaf and dumb people (*The Vanished Pomps of Yesterday,* New York: George H. Doran Company, rev. ed. 1921, pp. 134–37). In my own youth, train coaches entering Germany were always carefully dusted because one was now leaving the "dirty" world outside and entering the realm of cleanliness and order.

7. The Two Mountains

BACKGROUND READING: I Kings 16:8–19:21; 21:1–20, especially chaps. 18 and 19.

The Nature of the Fourth Crisis

The subject of this chapter is the disclosure of "God" on two mountains. One is the thickly wooded Mount Carmel, which juts like a thumb into the sea south of what today we call the Bay of Haifa. The other is the arid Mount Horeb (or Sinai) in the distant wasteland somewhere far beyond Beersheba. The central person on both occasions is Elijah and the stories are to be found in Chapters 18 and 19 of the First Book of Kings. The period is that of the fourth crisis, the encounter with the commercial empires of Syria and Phoenicia in the mid-ninth century B.C.E.

It was a time of turmoil and tension. The precariousness of the food supply throughout the Levant causes all the countries there sooner or later to seek new supplies of food and wealth and to find them in the development of trade. Ancient Israel, the northern of the two kingdoms which had come into existence after Solomon's death, was no exception. In 882 B.C.E. it had been torn apart by violent civil war, and order had been forcibly restored by Omri, at the time an army commander on the Philistine frontier.[1] The biblical record has only stern words for him:

> Omri did what was evil in the sight of YHWH, and did more evil than all who were before him. For he walked in all the way of Jeroboam the son of Nebat, and in the sins which he made Israel to sin, provoking YHWH, the God of Israel, to anger by their idols.
>
> I Kings 16:25–26

Yet we know from Assyrian sources that he was a powerful and effective ruler. Some modern scholars have called him the "northern David," for he followed very much the same policy. He brought to an end the futile strife that had been going on between Judah and Israel since Solomon's

1. I Kings 16:8–14. For this history of the period see Bright, *History*, pp. 236–49; Noth, *History*, pp. 224–45.

death; he built a new capital at Samaria; he expanded once more the
shrunken frontiers; and he reestablished the alliance with Phoenicia, seal-
ing this by the marriage of his son, Ahab, to Jezebel, the daughter of the
king of Tyre.[2] As Syria and Phoenicia were doing to the north of him, he
set out to establish a commercial empire.

The critical problem which developed in Ahab's reign was this: if the
welfare of the country was to be built up by means of commerce, then the
merchants must be able to move freely along the great trade routes of the
Levant, and both they and their goods must be protected from robbers
and all other dangers of the journey. The trade routes themselves, therefore, must be brought under control and the strong arm of the government
be extended to guard and help the caravans. A country which had begun
to depend for its well-being upon commercial activity found any threat to
the free passage of goods a threat to its life. But the extension of power
outwards to ensure this passage brought the countries into collision with
each other, and from these collisions there came tragic and incessant
warfare.

For Israel the chief enemy was the powerful kingdom of Syria with
its capital at Damascus, since each was expanding along the same roads.
With the other great power, Phoenicia, there was no need to quarrel, for
Phoenicia looked to the west and traded across the wide expanses of the
sea. With Phoenicia, therefore, Omri signed a treaty to strengthen himself
for what he saw to be the unavoidable conflict with Syria. As we have seen
already with Solomon,[3] the custom of the time required that a shrine for
Baal Hadad, the god of Tyre, should be built in Samaria[4] and another,
presumably, for YHWH at Tyre, though there is no record of this. The
gods were understood to watch over the agreement and to protect the
rights of one country in the territory of the other. The Phoenicians could
take this in their stride as little more than a formality, for they had been
long established as a trading country, and had come to tolerate foreign
gods and foreign ideas. Moreover, since they were the more sophisticated
partner, the Israelite way of life posed little threat to them.

Israel, however, was a conservative, farming country, which had once
rebelled against the internationalism of Solomon[5] and was still suspicious
of alien ideas. The new wealth of trade unquestionably enriched the country, but it created a new class, that of the rich merchants, ànd deeply
divided the affluent city from the people of the village. The farmer was
confronted with the greatest possible threat to his existence: separation
from the land. The unending war with Syria laid upon him burdens too

---

2. I Kings 16:31. See Ps. 45, which very possibly was composed to celebrate
this marriage; see also additional notes.
3. See above, Chap. 5.   4. I Kings 16:32.   5. I Kings 11:26–12:20.

heavy to be borne. Drafted into the army, he had to leave his fields un-
tilled; taxed to finance some new campaign, he piled up debts to the
wealthy which he could not repay. The new rich with their foreign ideas
saw in the cherished plots nothing but "real estate," to be bought and
sold at will, and could close in upon him and force him to sell, or even
at times cheat him out of a possession that to him was sacred.[6] It was
probably useless for a man to appeal to the king, even if he could get
someone to speak for him at the court,[7] for Ahab, like his father Omri,
was a forceful and dynamic ruler. He had commanded 2,000 chariots,
the largest of the allied contingents, at the great battle of Qarqar, when
the Levant states united to check the growing power of Assyria,[8] and was
clearly intolerant of opposition and complaint.[9]

Then came the drought, three ghastly years in which the always erratic
rainfall fell but fitfully and totalled perhaps only half the normal supply.[10]
Cisterns and wells dried up so that people had to trudge many weary miles
to fill as much as one pot for the family.[11] The situation was desperate.

> As YHWH your God lives, I have nothing baked, only a handful of meal
> in a jar, and a little oil in a cruse; and now I am gathering a couple of
> sticks, that I may go in and prepare for myself and my son, that we may
> eat it, and die.
>
> I Kings 17:12

Marginal farms went out of existence altogether and even those in the better-watered districts produced less than the minimum needed to feed the
family and pay the taxes. No wonder then that once again "everyone who
was in distress, and everyone who was in debt, and everyone who was
discontented"[12] began to flee to the wasteland and hide in the caves.[13]
Such fugitives are seldom tolerant men, for they have lost all that they
once had, and there must surely have been some who were ready to turn
to brigandage as the only means of sustaining life, or even to foment rebellion. Not to see the situation in these terms, and the crisis as being of
this magnitude, is not to understand it.

The dangers of civil strife and the complete collapse of order were
therefore acute, for clearly the country could not stand another year like
the last three. Ahab and Elijah, both of whom were looked up to as
leaders of the people, must have been fully aware of this. But the question
was: Upon what principle does order depend? For Ahab the overriding

---

6. I Kings 21.   7. For an example of this see II Kings 4:13.
8. Pritchard, ANET, pp. 277–81. This important battle is nowhere mentioned
in the Bible, a fact which provides valuable evidence that biblical history is not
just a glorification of ancient Israel.
9. I Kings 18:7–12.   10. See additional notes.
11. Amos 4:7–8; see also additional notes.
12. I Sam. 22:2.   13. I Kings 18:3–4.

necessity was national security and the alliance with Phoenicia not to be questioned, since he saw it as essential to the defense of the country. He seems to have thought of himself as a loyal worshiper of YHWH, for he called all his children by names which included the abbreviated form of the divine name, YH,[14] but he viewed the unruly ecstatics who opposed everything he did as dangerous extremists and nothing but troublemakers. Therefore, when he finally confronted Elijah he said, "So you are the person who is causing all this trouble in Israel!"[15] Elijah's answer was that he had no intention of stirring up trouble in the country, but the present policy of the government was itself disrupting society by its introduction of foreign beliefs, its constant support of the Phoenician merchants and their fellow traders in Israel, and its ruthless suppression of any opposition.

The Contest on Mount Carmel

Once again we do not have here a clear-cut struggle between evident good and bad, but a serious dispute about the terms in which the world was properly to be understood, for Ahab and Elijah each believed himself to be in the right. The immediate and absolute necessity was that of rain, of widespread and torrential storms to fill the empty cisterns and drench the earth with life. It was to plead for rain that the people gathered on the great headland of Carmel, in those days a sacred mountain.

To the Phoenician merchants, then so powerful in Israel, it was sacred to Baal Hadad, the mighty god of the storm, whom they believed to bring the slashing rain, surging in from the sea like a white wall of water, to the coasts and mountain slopes of Lebanon, and to control the winds which sped their ships upon the far-flung trading journeys. Already in Phoenicia there was a marked tendency to exalt Baal Hadad as the supreme power, able both to enrich the terraced fields and to make possible the commerce on which their wealth depended. Phoenician culture, therefore, confronted Israel with an authority to challenge that of YHWH.[16]

A sacred mountain was to all people of that time the "gate of heaven," the very center of the world, where order and meaning were, so to speak, funneled down from the realm of Reality to this actual, factual world beneath.[17] The question at issue, therefore, was the true source of life and

14. Spelled in English either "Jah" or "-iah," as in Ahaziah and Athaliah, the son and daughter of Ahab (I Kings 22:51; II Kings 8:26–27). Names were regarded then, and still are in the Middle East today, as powerful and significant.

15. I Kings 18:17 (trans. D. B.).   16. See additional notes.

17. For the universality of the "sacred mountain" and its significance see, e.g., Mircea Eliade, *Patterns in Comparative Religion* (Cleveland: World Publishing Company, 1963), pp. 99–102, 374–79.

power, or as we might put it in modern terms, which system was the more soundly based, which was fictitious and which was indeed in touch with Reality. At that date, when the pressure was increasing to recognize one god, and therefore one system, as supreme, the urgent battle of the prophets of YHWH was to see that the Israelites did not become submerged by Phoenicia and accept the absolute authority of Baal Hadad, from whose worship there would be little hope of reclaiming them.

The situation was similar to that prevailing in a country like Iran today, where contact with the west and an influx of new wealth have shaken the traditional ways, and where also a strong and energetic ruler is seeking to give the country an honored place in the world and an effective voice in international debates. The ruler is convinced that the stern measures he takes are essential for the good of the country, which he believes would founder without them, and many of the people support him in this. But many also are disturbed, and even rebellious. Their ancient heritage, of inestimable value, seems to them in danger of being drowned forever in the fierce flood of brash new ideas. Both sides can produce excellent reasons for thinking that they are right.

The story of the contest on Carmel is magnificently told and ranks high even in biblical literature, which abounds in vivid and dramatic tales. We see the people, nervously watching in this awesome place as the sacred representatives of the two gods ranged themselves against each other, on the one side the crowded prophets of Baal, and on the other the solitary Elijah.

> Then Elijah came near to all the people, and he said, "How long are you to go on limping between two concepts? If YHWH is the God, follow him; but if Baal is the God, then follow him."
>
> I Kings 18:21[18]

The spokesmen for Baal Hadad were helpless and exhausted because by no device known to them could they produce a devastating event, the searing flame from beyond which consumes all the works of man. It should be remembered that neither they nor Elijah were asking here for the lifegiving rain; they were asking for the most awe-inspiring thing of all, a theophany, an irruption of absolute Reality into the delicately structured world of man's contriving, and this is a fire which can reduce a whole city to smoking ashes. When fire came in response to Elijah's

---

18. Trans. D. B. The normal English translation, "If the LORD is God," is misleading, since to call one of the two "Lord" already suggests that he is true and the other false. But at that time the sacred name YHWH was still used and there was serious debate about which understanding of the world ought to prevail. Many people doubtless thought that they could follow the Baal system in all practical matters, but still invoke the name of YHWH in their worship.

prayer, the people fell flat on their faces and gasped out in terror, "YHWH, he is the God; YHWH, he is the God!"[19]

Insufficient attention has been paid by some commentators to this remarkable fact that what the people were crying out for was rain, but the contest was about fire, and this contest was approved by people whose scorched fields must have caused them to dread the very word "fire."[20] If the question had been which god had the power to satisfy the people's needs, the answer could have been given much more quickly by delivering the longed-for rain at once. But though this was the immediate need, it was not the primary question. The exhausting drought was not an isolated incident. It was the culminating disaster, the consummation of a world gone wrong. In that world no one could see any way of bringing to an end a war which "set on fire their fortresses, slew their young men with the sword, dashed their little ones in pieces, and ripped up the women with child."[21] The war not only bled the people white, but it imposed the alliance with proud Phoenicia and submerged Israel in a way of life which most of its inhabitants abhorred. It is probable that there were many in the government who longed for a way out of the impasse, no less than the people. But they were just as helpless. There did not seem to be a way.

What they all craved, therefore, was what Arnold Toynbee has called a "savior with a time machine,"[22] a power that would deliver them from their bondage to the "here and now," from the weary treadmill of unending years the same. Not until the Exile in Babylon did any prophet of YHWH state clearly that what made the "gods" of the nations into no gods at all was the fact that they could not make anything happen. They could not "save." They were the inspiration of an understanding of the world which saw everything as cyclical, that is to say, in terms of permanence and repetition, and which denied the possibility of any intervention from beyond, of catastrophic change. The essence of these "gods," indeed their virtue in the eyes of their worshipers, was their immobility, the fact that they stayed firmly in the same place.[23] But though the complete statement was not to come for another three hundred years, the initial word is here.

The great Baal Hadad could not disrupt the exhausting cycle, for the whole Baal concept was opposed to sudden change. The function of Baal

19. I Kings 18:39.   20. I Kings 18:24.
21. II Kings 8:12. The description, with the tense of the verbs changed, is that of Elisha, suggesting to Hazael that if he became king of Syria he would continue a war in which far too much of this had already happened. Hazael's answer is a promise that he would not do so. Elisha then sanctioned the revolution and Hazael's seizure of the throne. See the whole passage, II Kings 8:7–15.
22. Arnold J. Toynbee, *A Study of History* (New York: Oxford University Press, 1969), Vol. VI, pp. 213ff.
23. Isa. 41:21–24; 43:9; 45:5–7, 20–23; 26:1–8. See below, Chap. 15.

was to be identified with the pattern of nature and to ensure its continuity, regularly to die with the grain and no less regularly come to life again, annually to reestablish the order of things that already is.[24] Elijah spoke to the God who lives continually,[25] and besought the witness of that dynamic word which is "like a fire . . . a hammer which breaks the rock in pieces"[26] and which does not return to its sender empty.[27]

> O YHWH, God of Abraham, Isaac and Israel, let it be known this day that thou art God in Israel, and that I am thy servant, and that I have done all these things at thy word. Answer me, YHWH, answer me, that this people may know that thou, YHWH, art God.
>
> I Kings 18:36–37

The fire which leaped out of heaven, the vengeance wreaked on the unhappy prophets of Baal, and the blessed moment when the sky "grew black with clouds and wind, and there was a great rain";[28] all these together smashed the unending cycle and demonstrated that there is no necessity that what has always been will therefore continue to be. Eternal Reality is not bound to an unchangeable earthly pattern.

The Still, Small Voice at Horeb

But YHWH is not "a savior with a time machine," nor is it given to men and women to carve their way out of history, and with a sudden swift blow eliminate the facts. Elijah learned this lesson when he discovered that the slaughter of the prophets of Baal, which he had hoped would remove forever those who made life so difficult for the oppressed in Israel, did not achieve this at all. It passed instead the sentence of death upon himself.

> So may the gods do to me, and more also, if I do not make your life like the life of one of them by this time tomorrow.
>
> I Kings 19:2

Such was the curt message of Jezebel, and in urgent flight Elijah sought the distant wasteland, where the chariots of the king could not follow. Back he went to Horeb, back to the "mountain of God."[29]

24. See additional notes.
25. I Kings 18:15. See also Num. 14:21, 28; Deut. 32:40; Judg. 8:19; Ruth 3:13; I Sam. 14:39, 45; 20:3, 21; 25:26, 34; 26:10, 16; 28:10; 29:6; II Sam. 2:27; 4:9; 12:5; 14:11; 15:21; 22:47; I Kings 1:19; 2:24; 17:1, 12; 18:10; 22:14; II Kings 2:2, 4, 6; 3:14; 4:30; 5:16, 20; II Chron. 18:13; Ps. 18:46; Isa. 49:18; Jer. 4:2; 5:2; 12:16; 16:14, 15; 22:24; 23:7, 8; 38:16; 44:16; 46:18; Ezek. 5:11.
26. Jer. 23:29.
27. Isa. 55:11. See also Isa. 45:23; Pss. 33:6; 107:20; 147:15, 18; 148:8; and additional notes.
28. I Kings 18:45.   29. I Kings 19:1–8.

> He . . . went a day's journey into the wilderness, and came and sat down under a broom tree; and he asked that he might die, saying, "It is enough; now, YHWH, take away my life."
>
> I Kings 19:4

In disillusionment and despair he returned to the one secure point that he knew, the one undoubted "gate of heaven": the irrevocable fact that once at this mountain those who had been no people had become a people and order had overcome disorder.

As he hid in the cave, traditionally the selfsame cave where Moses had hid when the glory of YHWH passed by,[30] all the phenomena of the Sinai theophany were repeated—earthquake, wind, fire—but YHWH was not in any of these things. Then came the "still, small voice," or perhaps better "a sound of quiet stillness" (v. 12). The meaning of the encounter with YHWH centers upon the significance of this sound, and it has been much misunderstood. Elijah certainly did not perceive it as a "still, small voice of calm,"[31] rebuking him for the brutal slaughter of the prophets of Baal, for in obedience to what he understood to be the message he returned to stir up bloody revolution in both Syria and Israel. Nor is it sufficient to say that "the meaning of the theophany seems . . . to be an admonition to the prophet to expect, not the supernatural and spectacular inbreaking of Yahweh into history anticipated in the traditional liturgy of the cult with the accompaniments of storm, earthquake and fire (e.g. Ps. 18:12 [13]; Judg. 5:4f.; Hab. 3:3ff; Ps. 68:8 [9]; etc.), but rather an intelligible revelation to find God's direction in the ordinary course of daily life."[32] It is not violence that was rejected, because YHWH remains in the *Testament* uncomfortably violent to the very end,[33] and anyone who takes seriously the disclosure of ultimate Reality through the medium of historical events must take seriously also the fact that only too often violence is an integral part of these events. Furthermore, the *Testament* nowhere suggests that political revolution should belong to "the ordinary course of daily life," and indeed the revolutions that took place in Syria and Israel at Elijah's instigation brought nothing but sorrow and humiliation upon Israel.[34]

We must look instead for a more profound lesson than that YHWH is not in the violent manifestations of nature. He is not "in" nature at all, in the sense of being identified with it. He is not in this sense "in" anything.[35] He is not even "in" the events of the past, even though it had been through these events men that had encountered and discovered him. Elijah

---

30. Exod. 33:17–23.   31. See additional notes.

32. John Gray, *I and II Kings: A Commentary* (Philadelphia: The Westminster Press, 2nd ed., 1970), p. 410.

33. See the closing verses, Mal. 4:5–6.   34. II Kings 10:32–33.

35. See additional notes.

had gone back to his one point of certainty, the indestructible past event, and discovered that YHWH was not "in" that event, despite the repetition of its outward forms. No event can ever be repeated. The apparent repetition is not the same event at all, for it takes place in altered circumstances and these cannot but change its character. The question, "What are you doing here, Elijah?" (v. 13) was a rebuke to him for seeking YHWH in the security of the past, and he was told to pick up his work again, but this time with his eyes fixed wholly on the future.

This is an intellectual breakthrough of incalculable importance, and betokens a revolutionary understanding of historical events. Every society is confronted by the problem of the confusing and immediate present. Decisions, often of far-reaching social and political importance, have to be taken *now*. But in order that the right decisions may be taken it is essential to understand correctly the meaning of the critical situation prevailing at the moment. It was, as we have seen,[36] the function of all seers and prophets to discern this meaning, to see through the misleading outward appearances to the very heart of the matter, to that ultimate Reality which determines the meaning of the crisis. Only when this Reality is known can the frightening situation itself be understood, and appropriate measures be taken.

If we consider, for instance, a present critical situation which is not likely to pass quickly out of date, how are we to describe the stranglehold upon the world's economy now exercised by the oil-producing states of the Middle East? Are we to call it blackmail, savage, vengeful and selfish, or are we to say that it is self-defense, a justified response to Western imperialism? The names we give reveal what we understand to be the basic reality, or realities, of the world and they direct us toward the actions needed to deal with a situation so understood.

Israel was not by any means the only society in antiquity to study the character of historical events in order to understand the world. The surrounding nations of the Levant kept exhaustive records for administrative purposes, and took thought for whether the events so recorded had a message for their own day. On the far side of the globe, the Chinese were developing a far more profound understanding of the past, which they studied exhaustively to determine its meaning for the present. Their knowledge of ancient history was, in Western terms, phenomenal. Nineteen hundred years ago scholars there were aware that there had been a Stone Age, followed by a Bronze Age and then an Iron Age,[37] and at the turn of the eleventh and twelfth centuries of our era Chinese antiquarians

36. See above, Chap. 4.
37. Glyn Daniel, *The First Civilisations: The Archaeology of their Origins* (London: Thames and Hudson, 1968), p. 122.

"laid the foundations of an archaeological method which was superior in objectivity and method to the contemporary and later antiquarianism of the West."[38] However, this remained a concern with *past* events, and past events, insofar as we know them, belong already to what may be called "our world," that enormous body of facts and ideas which is available for us to study. Historical events, it is true, at the moment of their happening have an impact upon man altogether different from the impact made by the permanent phenomena of nature, but once they have happened and have moved back into the past, they are less disturbing.

It is the future which is the domain of the "Absolutely Other," for it is not, and cannot be, part of that world which we know. It is not available to us to study, to dissect and arrange in categories. The reality of the future is beyond question, for we step into it every moment and can never escape it, but it is altogether without any of the things that make up our world. It contains no "things" at all. Nothing there can be said to exist. There are no hard-and-fast facts, only possibilities.

Admittedly, serious and challenging events may already have taken place which for us are still in the future. For instance, our knowledge of what is happening in China is so defective that there could well have taken place there something of which we yet know nothing, but whose results are bound to alter the very fabric of our lives. There could already have occurred events which in course of time are to provoke a nuclear war between Russia and China. But because we do not know them, they form no part of "our world." They do not exist in any terms that we can use. They do not yet constitute "facts" for us. They have no power to challenge us because it is equally possible, as far as we can see, that they may never have occurred. Both the results that they are to produce and the events themselves, even though they may indeed have happened, are for us part of what we would call the future. They remain under the hand of the "Absolutely Other."

Yet, if they have indeed happened, they are irrevocable, utterly real and unchangeable. When at some future date these events, already past in time, come within our knowledge and become part of our world, they may demonstrate that the well-meant political decisions which we are taking now are instead ill-judged and foolish.

For this reason the experience of Elijah at Horeb is the final dethronement of Baal and the world of Nature as being in any sense "God," that is to say, as the *ultimate* determinant of meaning. God is not "in" anything. Nothing has meaning *in itself*. Its own nature does not confer mean-

38. William Watson, *The Chinese Exhibition* (London: Times Newspapers, 1973), p. 12.

ing upon it. Meaning is given to it by that which is "other." This is already apparent in the fact that we cannot speak of the meaning of anything without comparing it with other things. But all the meanings that we ascribe now to things are tentative. They remain open to revision. We cannot say now whether anything that we are doing is good or bad, wise or foolish. We hope that we are doing good, but we cannot say for certain, for we do not know what it is to produce, and what it is to produce is entirely out of our hands.

This recognition that in the final resort it is the future rather than the past which confers meaning upon the baffling present is the foundation of all that we call Hebrew prophecy, and Elijah is rightly named the first of the great prophets of the *Testament*. Here the Absolutely Other is seen in all his fullness and mankind has no alternative but to bow down and worship. There is left for men and women only humility, for they do not create the future which is to determine the meaning of the present. We do not make history. We do no more than respond to history. Every action that we take is a response to something that has already happened. It does not originate with us. Nor can we take any action at all that will bring the future under our control and make history into what we want it to be. We cannot do so because we cannot determine in advance what the other side is going to do in response to the actions that we have taken.

We can do no more than act in trust, directing our actions by our beliefs, and doing as far as we can see the best that we can. But we may be wrong. Here is the tremendous import of what the Bible calls "repentance." We may have to repent even of the good things that we do, because they do not produce the good that we had hoped for. How much the more then may we not do evil in order that good may come, or claim that the end justifies the means, for we must remember that we cannot determine the end. Even Elijah could be wrong and Hosea later said that the revolution he had fostered, fully believing that he was obedient to YHWH, would have to be punished.[39] It is not given to men, even to the great heroes of the *Testament,* to take actions which are predetermined to be right. To know YHWH, to live in covenant with him, is always to act with this understanding.

But no government or people, even those that claim to be godly, ever seems to recognize this. Very nearly all our political actions, whether of force or diplomacy, are designed to bring the future under our control and ensure that those who are on the other side make the responses we intend them to make. We claim that our actions are justified, because we believe them to be right by their inherent nature, and we do not conceive therefore that there could be any need in the future to repent of them. But to behave in this fashion is to deny YHWH altogether.

39. Hos. 1:4.

ADDITIONAL NOTES TO CHAPTER 7

2. It is true that the wording of I Kings 16:31 would suggest that the decision to marry Jezebel was Ahab's own. However, the regular practice was for the father to arrange the marriage of his son, and we have no reason to believe that this did not happen in this case also.

10. For a study of the extreme variability of Palestinian rainfall see Denis Baly, *The Geography of the Bible* (New York: Harper & Row, rev. ed., 1974), Chap. 6, and for a parallel with the time of Elijah see especially pp. 74–75.

11. My colleague, Prof. Badie Nijim, has told me of a year when water was so short at Ramallah (a town not far from the biblical Bethel) that people visiting a friend would take a cup of water with them, because they could not expect their host to have enough to make even one extra cup of coffee. In a newspaper account of the recent droughts south of the Sahara mention was made of a woman who had to walk eighteen miles every day to get only one jar of water for her family. When once on her return she slipped and broke the jar, she had to begin the whole exhausting journey over again.

16. Some scholars believe that the Phoenician Baal was Baal Melkart (the Baal of the City) rather than Baal Hadad. It is not possible to come down authoritatively on one side or the other of the argument, and in any case the basic principle of the argument presented here is not affected.

24. One or two Contributors objected that this understanding of the cyclical view of the universe is not true of all forms of such a view, and that the conclusions drawn are therefore not necessarily valid. However, we are concerned in this book with the world of ancient Israel and not with alternative views which did not belong to that world. There seems little doubt but that the cyclical concepts of the ancient Middle East were directed strongly toward the maintenance of an unchanged, and unchangeable, system.

This was particularly true for ancient Egypt, where "the touchstone for all that was really significant was its permanence. That was important which had always been and would never change" (Frankfort, *Ancient Egyptian Religion,* p. 49). Albrektson, on the other hand, claims that "there is very little foundation for the not uncommon view that history was regarded as cyclic in Mesopotamia" (*History and the Gods,* p. 95), and suggests instead an "undulatory concept," which he likens to that of the Deuteronomist. This is surely going too far. He is quite right to point out that there was a noncyclical view of historical events among the people of Mesopotamia, but such features of Mesopotamian religion as the *Akitu* festival, the weeping for the dying and rising vegetation god, and the careful study of the heavens as revealing the pattern of the universe surely suggest a strongly cyclical view, which in an agricultural society was probably the more powerful. The texts he quotes must be regarded as supplementary to, rather than destructive of, the interpretation put forward in, e.g., Eliade, *Cosmos and History: The Myth of the Eternal Return,* and Voegelin, *Order and History,* Vol. I, *Israel and Revelation.*

27. The most dramatic statement of this is the description of the night of the Passover in the book of Wisdom.

> For while gentle silence enveloped all things,
>   and the night in its swift course was now half gone,
> thy almighty Word leaped from heaven, from the royal throne,
>   into the midst of the land that was doomed,
> a stern warrior, carrying the sharp
>   sword of thy authentic command.

Wisdom 18:14–16

31.
> Let sense be dumb, let flesh retire;
> Speak through the earthquake, wind, and fire,
>   O still small voice of calm!

(Closing words of the popular hymn, "Dear Lord and Father of mankind," written by John Greenleaf Whittier in 1872.) This interpretation of the experience of Elijah is a very common one in sermons.

35. This is another matter on which we had considerable discussion. Some Contributors objected that YHWH was being presented as so transcendent that no place was allowed for his immanence. They argued that he must be manifest in the realm of nature, if nature is his handiwork, and that therefore he must be said to be in nature. We all agreed that the *Testament* steadfastly rejects the idea of YHWH as being identifiable with anything in the natural world. The present wording is an attempt to express our consensus.

8. Signs and Wonders

BACKGROUND READING: II Kings 1:1–8:15; 9:1–37; 13:14–21.

Chariots of Fire

Elijah and his successor Elisha were so highly regarded by many in Israel that at their departing those left behind cried out in despair, "My father, my father! The chariots of Israel and its horsemen!"[1] Those who uttered this cry believed that without such men to guide them the country was defenseless, and they wept and rent their clothes.

Yet the strength Elijah and Elisha had provided was not the defense of military might, and the chariots and horses were chariots and horses of fire. By such chariots Elijah was separated from Elisha[2] and Elisha and his servant were protected from the Syrians who sought to arrest them.[3] Elijah had called down fire upon the sacrifice on Carmel, and fire had gone out from his presence to destroy those who tried to seize him.[4]

Fire had for the ancient Israelites the quality of majesty. They saw in it something akin to absolute Reality, altogether necessary to human existence and yet awesome and strange. In the presence of fire there is mercy and salvation, for wherever it is kindled in the hearth men and women are at once at home and the terrible powers of darkness are banished. But the same fire, transcending in power anything that men can hope to control, can slay a man in a moment of frightful agony. It is both a "coal for warming oneself," a "fire to sit before," and also a searing flame which devours people like stubble.[5] Certainly Elijah had learned on Mount Horeb that fire could at times rage impotently,[6] but throughout the *Testament* fire remains a powerful symbol of YHWH, that is, of the ultimate and final Power which maintains the world, and with which men and women must come to terms, if they are to live and not die.

1. II Kings 2:12; 13:14.   2. II Kings 2:11.   3. II Kings 6:17.
4. II Kings 1:9–16.   5. Isa. 47:14.   6. II Kings 19:12.

93

By fire Sodom and Gomorrah were destroyed.[7] In a flame of fire YHWH appeared to Moses in the bush for the salvation of the Hebrew people,[8] and in fire he descended upon Mount Sinai to make himself known to them.[9] By fire they were led through the cruel wasteland,[10] but by fire also they were destroyed when they rebelled.[11] Fire came down upon the altar at the dedication of the Temple by Solomon,[12] as earlier it is said to have consumed the offerings of those who were faithful to YHWH.[13] Fire and wind are the messengers of YHWH,[14] and in Isaiah's famous vision the Seraphim, or fiery spirits, serve the Lord continually in his Temple.[15] Jeremiah speaks of the word of YHWH as being like a fire[16] and his Glory was disclosed to Ezekiel in "fire flashing forth continually."[17] When the Glory of YHWH left the ruins of the Temple in 587 B.C.E. to be with the exiled people in Babylon,[18] it was believed that the sacred fire had gone with it.[19]

We must therefore understand Elijah and Elisha to have been men set apart, invested with the quality of Reality, sacred and inviolate. So also is Muhammad, the messenger of the One God, always portrayed in Persian miniatures as clothed with flame. Such men were to be approached with reverence and circumspection,[20] and without mockery or abuse,[21] because that which had expressed itself through them is not to be mocked or abused. It is not to be treated lightly, nor is it to be grasped by men for their own possession, as if they could ever be the ultimate arbiters of what is real.

It is true that there is much superstitious awe in this kind of thinking, and a constant danger, that despite the experience of Elijah on Mount Horeb, people may identify the visible symbol with the Reality which it expresses. This is idolatry. Idolatry has been defined by Isaiah of Babylon, that great prophet of the Exile, as imprisonment within an already established set of ideas, from which men cannot set themselves free, because they cannot seriously question the things that represent to them the source of their life. They cannot conceive that the method by which they interpret the world might be tragically at fault.

> No one considers, nor is there knowledge and discernment to say, "Half of it I burned in the fire, I also baked bread on its coals, I roasted flesh and have eaten; and shall I make the residue of it an abomination? Shall I fall down before a block of wood?" He feeds

---

7. Gen. 19:24–28.   8. Exod. 3:2.   9. Exod. 19:18; Deut. 5:4, 22–27.
10. Exod. 13:21–22; Num. 14:14.   11. Num. 11:1–3; 16:35.
12. II Chron. 7:1.   13. Judg. 6:21; 13:20.   14. Ps. 18:8; 104:4.
15. Isa. 6:1–8.   16. Jer. 23:29.   17. Ezek. 1:4, 27.
18. Ezek. 10.   19. See additional notes.   20. II Kings 1:9–15.
21. II Kings 2:23–25.

on ashes; a deluded mind has led him astray, and he cannot deliver
himself or say, "Is there not a lie in my right hand?"

                                                    Isaiah 44:19–20[22]

We commit this kind of idolatry when we elevate the people of the *Testament* into patterns of perfection and accept uncritically the popular idea that Elijah must always be right and the wicked Ahab always wrong.

Yet behind the superstition lies truth. Those who preserved these stories were convinced that what is real cannot be destroyed. Therefore, they believed that Elijah, who for them expressed Reality at a time when, as they were persuaded, the government was trying to impose an artificial system on the country, could not therefore die, as all other men must die. He was swept up into heaven in a whirlwind and a double portion of his spirit rested upon Elisha.[23] The purport of this story is not, as some have claimed, merely a "pious authentification" of Elisha by those of his disciples who wished to see their master raised to as high a place as Elijah had held. It asserts that truth must prevail despite every attempt to suppress it, and despite even the destruction of those men who had boldly proclaimed the truth.

This assertion is one of the great themes of the *Testament*. It is what Isaiah of Jerusalem meant when he proclaimed that the king of Assyria could not destroy the city, and said to him bluntly,

> Whom have you mocked and reviled?
> Against whom have you raised your voice
> and haughtily lifted up your eyes?
> Against the Holy One of Israel!

                                                    Isaiah 37:23

and when he promises the people of Jerusalem,

> You shall be visited by YHWH of Hosts,
>   with thunder and with earthquake and great noise,
>
> .   .   .   .
>
> And the multitude of all the nations that
>   fight against Ariel [i.e., Jerusalem], all that fight against
>   her and her stronghold and distress her,
> shall be like a dream, a vision of the night.

                                                    Isaiah 29:6–7

Isaiah seems to have been convinced that the Assyrians would not capture the city, and so it came to pass.[24] Yet the truth he was proclaiming would still have remained even if his contemporary, Micah, had been

22. The whole passage, Isa. 44:9–20, should be read. See also additional notes.
23. II Kings 2:9–12; see also additional notes.
24. II Kings 19:35–36.

correct and the city had been laid in ruins.[25] Isaiah was insisting that come what might, the Reality which Jerusalem demonstrated to the world could not be stamped out, but was something with which men must always come to terms.[26]

The Problem of Miracles

A similar understanding lies behind the abundant miracles of the Elijah-Elisha stories. Such stories are today a stumbling block, and are often attributed by modern readers to the credulity of what they patronizingly call a less critical age. But the "miraculous" is so much a part of the record of this period that we cannot just erase it and get back to the sober history of our history books. It has to be taken into account by all who want to read the stories with integrity, and cannot be merely explained away or rationalized out of existence.

Of course, miracles are by no means confined to the Bible and can be paralleled in many other religions. Thus stories of the miraculous feeding of a multitude, or of miraculous preservation in time of trouble, are told of Jesus, of Buddha, and of Muhammad, as well as of Elijah and Elisha. But they are seldom told indiscriminately, and in the *Testament* they tend to be confined to only two periods in Israelite history: the time of the Exodus and entry into Canaan and the time of Elijah and Elisha. Most of Israelite history is recounted without any recourse to miracle and the records of the great prophets are remarkably free from them.[27] It is probable, therefore, that we should see miracle stories as belonging to times of intense crisis, and especially to those periods in which it is understood that order has prevailed over disorder. They "mark culminating or turning-points."[28]

Both periods were periods of revolution, and revolutionaries always justify their actions by claiming that the so-called "law and order" of the past had been false and artificial, and must be overthrown if true order is to prevail. Often, indeed, revolutionaries insist that time begins with them and sometimes they establish a new calendar. So we have the Christian calendar, dating from the birth of Christ; the Muslim calendar, beginning with the journey of Muhammad from Mecca to Medina; the attempt by the French revolutionaries in 1798 to establish a new calendar with new names for the months, and even in the United States today the custom of dating certain official documents by both the Christian calendar and the American Revolution.

---

25. Micah 3:12.　　　26. See below, Chap. 13, and also additional notes.
27. See additional notes.
28. Edmond Jacob, *Theology of the Old Testament,* trans. Arthur W. Heathcote and Philip J. Allcock (London: Hodder & Stoughton, 1958), p. 223.

In periods of this kind, people are deeply divided about how the world is to be interpreted, and they argue with urgency and anger about what are the "facts" of the situation. As the crisis develops, the dissident minority, whom the majority condemn as dangerous subversives, are brought to the brink of despair. Not only are they the minority, but they lack the material weapons to enforce the opinions they believe so passionately to be right. All power is in the hands of the government, who are in their terms "the wicked," and who do not hesitate to use this power. The army, the police, the judges, the king's ministers, the teachers in the schools are all apparently at the beck and call of those in power, and their pay and position depend upon the continuation of the system. No help, it would seem, can be looked for there. In the end, of course, it may be possible— in fact it *must* be possible, if the minority are as right as they are convinced they are—to win over some of the opponents, and convince them of the justice of the cause. Perhaps they could even persuade some important army officer, such as Jehu, that he would make a better king, who would clean up the country. But for the moment all is frustration.

Of course, it would be absurd to argue that all minorities who think like this are in fact justified. "True believers" can often be very dangerous indeed. But occasionally this kind of minority stands for something fundamentally sound, something altogether worth dying for, and so solid that in the end it wins through and becomes the basis of a new political and social system. The minority then becomes the majority, but in what terms are they to recount their experience, and explain the total reversal of their fortunes? Only it would seem, in "impossible" terms, for the theoretically impossible has in fact happened. By all the rules, so to speak, they ought to have been wiped out of existence, for everything was against them. Only right was on their side, but of what value is right against all the forces of those who insist that "right" is "wrong"? The minority had seen only too often a man like Naboth lose his land because he could not stand up against the power and wealth of the other side, even though in principle he had every right to the land;[29] they had seen men thrown into prison, sold into slavery, and even put to death without any redress.

It takes tremendous faith not to become cynical about right always prevailing when one finds oneself living on, year after year, through a situation of this kind. It seems impossible that men could survive it, and even more impossible that the situation could be reversed. But somehow power is given to carry on, and then the "impossible" happens, and in face of all the arguments that until then had been accepted as evidence the right is established. "This is the Lord's doing, and it is marvelous in our eyes."[30] To those who have survived this experience, who have lived when they had thought again and again that they would die, there is nothing

29. I Kings 21:1–14.   30. Ps. 118:23.

left to say but, "It is a miracle that we are here today. We cannot explain it. If it had depended on us alone, we should not be here at all."

We should remind ourselves that until the revolution of Jehu in 842 B.C.E. those who opposed the Phoenician alliance were still people on the run, hiding from the authorities in the caves and the wasteland.[31] The wonder tales about Elisha, which have given so much difficulty to the commentators, belong therefore to memories of how the YHWH loyalists had survived in these difficult days. They had found themselves then constantly on the verge of starvation,[32] or of being sold into slavery when in their distress they had incurred debts which they could not pay.[33] Those had been days when a very small amount of food had sufficed for an uncomfortably large number of people, possibly because other fugitives had taken refuge with them.[34] Yet they had managed to survive through it all, and afterward they remembered Elisha as one who had been a tower of strength in very critical times.

Consequently,. either removing the quality of miracle from the stories, or else not looking beyond the literal meaning, is wholly to misunderstand the experience, and to lose sight of what it costs to be faithful to the truth. If there is quite literally abundant bread in the desert,[35] or an inexhaustible supply of oil during a famine,[36] then the desert is no longer a wasteland and starvation ceases to be starvation. It is the sheer, brutal suffering in famine, and the hardship and the desolate loneliness under oppression that these miracle stories insist on, for without these things there would be no wonder at all in the event.[37]

Miracles and History

The very word "miracle" is, of course, an offense to the historian, because it introduces into the material that he is studying an element which he is not equipped to assess. He may write a scholarly history of the prolonged struggle between Syria and Israel in the mid-ninth century B.C.E., but he cannot, *insofar as he is a historian,* determine whether or not "God" had been active in the events of that period, because what we call "God" cannot be verified or disproved by the means used to verify or disprove other historical statements. Consequently, historians tend to reject any suggestion that God intervened, interrupting thereby the processes of history.

We must therefore ask whether theologians are justified in speaking, as they often do, of "God" *intervening* in history. Is this a fallacious concept? The answer is, Yes, it is fallacious. This is a very brash statement, because it seems to fly in the face, not only of a great deal of scholarly opinion,

31. I Kings 18:4.   32. II Kings 4:38.   33. II Kings 4:1ff.
34. II Kings 4:42–44.   35. Exod. 16:9–21.   36. I Kings 17:8–16.
37. See additional notes.

but even more important, of evidence from the *Testament* itself. Many of the Psalms of Lament, which plead for YHWH's help, seem to assume that sometimes he acts and sometimes he does not.

> We have heard with our ears, O God,
>   our fathers have told us,
> what deeds thou didst perform in their days,
>   in the days of old.
>
> .   .   .   .   .   .
>
> But now thou hast cast us off and abased us,
>   and hast not gone out with our armies.
>
> .   .   .   .   .   .
>
> Rouse thyself! Why sleepest thou, O Lord?
> Awake! Do not cast us off for ever!
>
> Psalm 44:1, 9, 23

> Contend, O Lord, with those who contend with me;
>   fight against those who fight against me!
> Take hold of shield and buckler,
>   and rise for my help!
>
> .   .   .   .   .   .
>
> How long, O Lord, wilt thou look on?
>   Rescue me from their ravages!
>
> Psalm 35:1–2, 17

Moreover, the historical records speak more positively of direct intervention. Exodus 14, which is composed from all three strands, J, E and P, describes the crossing of the Red Sea in terms of the angel of YHWH stepping in, as it were, to check and reverse the events that were taking place. The siege of Jerusalem in 701 B.C.E. is said to have been brought to an end by the action of YHWH on a single night.[38]

That in the *Testament* YHWH's activity is conceived in these terms is undeniable. But we must not stop there. On the one hand, Isaiah of Babylon roundly rebuked those who said in the language of the laments, "My way is hid from the Lord, and my right is disregarded by my God" or "YHWH has forsaken me, my Lord has forgotten me."[39] He insisted that "the Creator of the ends of the earth does not faint or grow weary."[40] At no time does YHWH relax, and therefore to speak of times of his action and times of his inaction, however temporary, is false.

On the other hand, we must be careful to distinguish between the activity of YHWH and human response to that activity. For the *Testament* "the essential mark of a miracle does not lie in its 'miraculous' character,

38. II Kings 19:35.
39. Isa. 40:27ff.; 49:14ff. For a detailed study of Second Isaiah's rejection of the language of the Israelite laments, see Claus Westermann, *Isaiah 40–66,* trans. David M. G. Stalker (Philadelphia: The Westminster Press, 1969).
40. Isa. 40:28.

but in the power of revelation that it contains, . . . So the scope of the miracle is determined by its significance as a sign."[41] Indeed, a miracle is not a miracle unless someone perceives it to be a miracle.[42] The selfsame events that many would describe as no more than ordinary events are by others seen as charged with meaning, and so they properly call them "miracles."

In order to preserve what has earlier been called the explosive, eruptive character of historical events, it is certainly helpful to use language which suggests direct intervention and interruption. But what is interrupted is not the process of history, with its continuing pattern of cause and effect. The interruption occurs in what James Robinson has called "the dimension in which man actually exists, his 'world,' the stance or outlook from which he acts, his understanding of his existence behind what he does, the way he meets his basic problems and the answer his life implies to the human dilemma."[43] It is the "world" of man, the whole complicated structure of thought in terms of which he perceives and interprets things, that is pierced by the activity of "God," for it is to man that God speaks and from man that an answer is demanded.

So far in this book we have spoken of "God" as absolute and final Reality. This was in order to rid ourselves of all superficial notions of "God" as being, as it were, "somebody up there," somebody or something a little less than ultimate, and not altogether real. But if the absolute and final Reality is indeed that of which the ancient Israelites spoke when they used the name YHWH, then Reality is neither abstract nor neutral. The ultimate and final Reality is in this understanding overwhelmingly personal. To say and to believe that "YHWH is the God," the only real Reality there is, is to insist that the world is to be understood, finally and in the last resort, only in terms of what we might, perhaps, call "personness." It is to be understood in terms of speaking one to another, of dialogue and debate, of encounter and confrontation, of direct question or demand and no less direct an answer. It is in historical events, in things that happen, that the confrontation occurs. But it is the answer and not the question which is the responsibility of man. In Karl Barth's famous phrase, "God is always the subject of the sentence."

For the series of historical events recorded in the *Testament,* scholars in recent years have used the term *Heilsgeschichte,* sometimes translated

41. Jacob, *Theology of Old Testament,* p. 224.
42. Jacques Ellul, *The Politics of God and the Politics of Man,* trans. and ed. Geoffrey W. Bromley (Grand Rapids: Wm. B. Eerdmans, 1972), p. 62.
43. James M. Robinson, *A New Quest of the Historical Jesus* (London: SCM Press, 1959), pp. 28ff. It should be noted, however, that in the same passage Dr. Robinson speaks of history as "distinctively human, creative, unique, purposeful," which seems to be at variance with the understanding in the *Testament* that history is primarily the work of God.

"Salvation History,"[44] and this term has now become a common one in discussions of biblical theology. When used in the sense of those events which were remembered because men had seen in them the activity of YHWH working out his purpose for his people the term *Heilsgeschichte* is a valuable one. But it has also been used to mean that these events had somehow a peculiar quality which made them different from other events. Used in this sense, as it often is, the term *Heilsgeschichte* is dangerous and misleading. It argues that there are two kinds of history: ordinary history, which is studied by the historians, and "sacred history," containing only those events in which God has been active and which are therefore the fundamentally significant events. Looked at in this way, events of the second kind are regarded as excluded from the realm of historical study.

Now, we have already seen that the historian, *qua* historian, does not have the tools to decide whether or not "God" has been active in any event at all. The most that he can say is that people have believed this or that event to be the revelation of "God." There he must stop.[45] However, this is a very different thing from saying that some events are so sacred that he must not lay his hands upon them. When we define certain events as "sacred events," and seek by this means to preserve them from the prying eyes of the historian, we are saying inevitably that other events, i.e., the great majority of historical events, do not have this quality. They are in these terms non–sacred events, which are not "of God," and do not in consequence make known to men the ultimate source of his life and being. Alan Richardson has rightly called this method of interpretation a "disengagement from history."[46]

It is therefore necessary to insist that either all history is "of God" or that no history is. It is entirely false to suggest that some events are the result of his intervention and that other events have nothing to do with him. This is to make "God" less than God. It is to suggest that there is a whole category of things, whose meaning is unrelated to what in principle is the ultimate source of all meaning. If we are to take seriously the argument that "God," i.e., the ultimate source of all meaning and significance in the universe, is made known primarily through historical events, we must recognize that the nature of *all* events is to disclose him. Whether men and women perceive this disclosure in all events is quite another matter. Usually, it would seem, they do not. They tend to be quite unaware of any disclosure of ultimate Reality until the events become frightening catastrophes. Amos, the first of the prophets whose teachings we have in written form, saw clearly that all events have in principle the power to

44. See additional notes.   45. See additional notes.
46. Alan Richardson, *History, Sacred and Profane: Bampton Lectures for 1962* (London: SCM Press, 1964), Chap. 4.

confront man and demand an answer from him, and that therefore all events disclose YHWH to mankind. He blamed the people of his day for not having seen in such events as a drought, a plague of locusts, and a pestilence, the confrontation with YHWH.[47] These were all events of what we might be tempted to call "ordinary history," because they were far from infrequent in the Israelite farmer's experience. But the people had failed to recognize the disclosure, and so he warned them that there would shortly come upon them a disaster of such magnitude that they would be left in no doubt at all.[48]

If we wish to enter into, and understand, what the ancient Israelites meant when they said, "YHWH is 'God,' " we must try to avoid two errors, both connected with the studying of history.

The first error is to suppose that there really are two categories, a major category containing all the events which are properly included in history books, and another, highly selective, category of events we call "interventions of God." This will lead us into thinking that all the things we read about in the newspapers, both good and bad news, are separate from the things that are "of God." We shall certainly tend to think that normal events belong to the major category and that "interventions" are therefore abnormal events. But this will lead us to conclude, as probably many people do conclude, that normal events take place apart from "God," who is to be looked for in the sacred and special category. This may seem to some a possible way of thinking about history, but we make a grave mistake if we imagine that this is the intention of the *Testament*.

The second error is related to the first. It is to suppose that "history" is a study only of the past. We tend to forget, because it is not comfortable to remember, that the essence of historical things is explosive. They are things that happen. It is this "happening" quality which is important, and which makes them different from the other things that we study. We certainly cannot study them until after the explosion has taken place, but by that time they are no longer happening. In becoming available for us to study, they have become like all other things, part of our "world."

It would be foolish indeed to claim that the study of past events, of things that once happened, is not of enormous importance. Such a study throws a flood of light on the confusing things that are happening to us now. We could not understand all that makes up our world if we did not strive to acquire this learning. But we slip very easily into thinking that the

47. Amos 4:6-11.
48. Amos 4:12. The disaster he had in mind was that of foreign invasion and conquest, which he believed to be inevitable. He never gave a name to the probable conqueror, for Assyria had not yet shown itself the terrifying power that it was to become a few years later.

total meaning lies there, if only we had eyes to see it. We tend continually to assume that if we could assemble all the facts leading up to the Vietnam war, or the Middle East crisis, or the present uncertain economic situation, we should then comprehend the meaning of these disturbing crises and know what actions to take in order to deal with them effectively. We are consequently provoked when the actions that we do take, upon the best available evidence and with the very best intentions, do not resolve the crisis or provide solutions to our problems.

In the thinking of the *Testament,* the error into which we fall when we do this is to forget that our "world," i.e., the whole structure of facts and ideas available to us for study and for "great argument about it and about,"[49] consists of what may properly be called "things," even if these "things" are the most rarefied concepts. Therefore, in the thinking of the *Testament,* to assume that all the things collected in the history books can provide the fundamental basis of meaning is a breach of the Covenant. It is to forget YHWH, and say, once again, that *things,* whether they be things "in the heaven above, or the earth beneath, or the water under the earth"[50] are the primary disclosers of ultimate Reality.

In terms of the *Testament,* the primary determinant of meaning for human existence is not that there is a whole world of things available for us to study and to use. To take YHWH seriously is to recognize wholeheartedly that before we can ever study what is past, we are confronted *now,* in the present. It is to recognize that we stand always upon the knife-edge between past and future and that our whole society has a life to live at this very moment, a life which even now is taking us into a future which we cannot predetermine or manipulate. This for the *Testament* is the starting point for all understanding of the world, and to begin here, conscious that hour by hour we have to live, not upon our own terms, but in encounter with the Other—this is to know YHWH and to worship him.

But this Other is not remote and inaccessible. "The word is very near you; it is in your mouth and in your heart, so that you can do it."[51] The Other confronts us through every event, great or small, and is continually in our midst. To "love YHWH with all your heart, with all your being, and with all your might"[52] and to "love your neighbor as yourself,"[53]— the neighbor you meet at every turn—these are the same commandment.[54]

---

49.   Myself when young did eagerly frequent
         Doctor and Saint, and heard great Argument
         About it and about: but evermore
         Came out by the same Door where in I went.
                    Edward Fitzgerald, *The Rubaiyat of Omar Khayyam*

50. Exod. 20:4.   51. Deut. 30:14.   52. Deut. 6:5.
53. Lev. 19:18.   54. See additional notes.

ADDITIONAL NOTES TO CHAPTER 8

19. A most interesting passage in II Maccabees, one of the books of the Apocrypha, tells of how this fire was miraculously preserved and of "the feast of the fire given when Nehemiah, who built the Temple and the altar, offered sacrifices" (II Macc. 1:18–36). For the sacred fire in the *Testament* see Julian Morgenstern, *The Fire upon the Altar* (Chicago: Quadrangle Books, 1963).

22. One Contributor commented: "Isn't this a highly interpretive condensation of Isaiah's comments? The passage 44:9–20 seems to be saying that there is a kind of spiritual blindness which results when men, by their own manipulations and efforts with the materials at hand, create their own gods to order. The inability to question the source of their life seems to be only a symptom of this larger problem of self-created gods and not the main problem itself." But surely all spiritual blindness is the result of imprisonment within an already established set of ideas, and these ideas themselves are human constructs, which men and women make by their own manipulations and efforts with the materials at hand. Almost universally men and women start from the "world" that surrounds them and utilize something out of it to act as a symbol of "God," i.e., the ultimate and true source of life. Neither the Babylonian spokesmen nor Isaiah were so crass as to suggest that the statues of Bel and Nebo were themselves the source of life.

23. The Israelites of that period did not believe in any effective life after death (see below, Chap. 11), and therefore could not use the language which later generations might have used to express the idea that death does not mark the end. We ourselves are also limited by the language we use, and much of modern interpretation of this passage fails to grasp the tremendous and essentially death-defeating power which the word *ruach* (spirit) represents (Ezek. 37:1–14). The word "spirit" does not have this connotation in modern usage.

26. It is very difficult to ascertain exactly what Isaiah did think would happen to Jerusalem and how literally he intended his oracles to be taken by his hearers. Probably he believed that it would not in fact be captured, though he was well aware of its desperate weakness (Isa. 1:5–9; 22:1–14). Recent arguments that all the oracles proclaiming the defeat of Assyria and the delivery of Jerusalem are *ex post facto* and were added to the book at a later date seem to raise just as many difficulties as they seek to solve. See below, Chap. 13.

27. There is one biblical miracle story about one of the writing prophets (Isa. 38:1–8), although we know that in later tradition such stories did develop about all the great heroes of the *Testament* (see Louis Ginzberg, *Legends of the Bible,* New York: The Jewish Publication Society of America, 1956). The book of Jonah is based upon such a legend and was written to teach an important lesson about the proper attitude to foreigners. Miracles, of course, play an important part in the book of Daniel, but these stories belong to the time of the Maccabees (second century B.C.E.) and were designed to strengthen the people in their desperate struggles against those who wished to suppress the Jewish religion altogether.

36. It is false to imagine that the language of "miracle" and the "impossible" belongs only to a precritical era. Father Luke Grollenberg, who lived through the ghastly years of the Nazi occupation of Holland, has written of the wonder tales which developed among the Dutch at that time (Luke H. Grollenberg, *Interpretation of the Bible,* trans. Jeanne C. Schoelen Mooijne and Richard Rutherford, C.S.C., New York: Paulist Press, 1966, pp. 6–7). In my own youth in Britain during World War I, I was told the story of the "angels of Mons" who held back the first

German advance on Paris, and more recently have heard educated Israelis make such statements as, "There were no roads in Palestine before 1948," or "The British maps of Palestine were all wrong." As statements of literal fact these were, of course, ridiculous, but they represented the conviction that with the establishment of the State true order had at last replaced the prolonged disorder of the preceding years. They reflected the inability of the speakers to reconcile in their minds the existence of symbols of an orderly political and social structure (roads, maps, etc.) with a period that was identified in their minds with confusion and disorder. Similarly, the Russians often claim that all inventions which have contributed to the order of the modern world, such as electric light and the telephone, are Communist inventions. In their thinking "Communism" and "order" are synonymous terms, and to attribute any of the sources of order to a realm outside the Communist world would be for them a profound contradiction. Thus, even in the sophisticated societies of the modern world, there is a tendency to make statements which cannot be literally correct in order to express what is understood to be an inner truth of profound significance. There is a valuable brief discussion of this in "Symbol and Myth in Modern Rationalistic Societies" by Gregor Sebba (Thomas J. J. Altizer, William A. Beardslee and J. Harvey Young (eds.), *Truth, Myth and Symbol*, Englewood Cliffs, N.J.: Prentice Hall, 1962, pp. 141–68).

43. The term *Heilsgeschichte* was first used by Christian theologians and in their thinking, therefore, culminates in the event of Jesus Christ. It remains, however, apart from this a valid term for the material we are studying.

44. "We must not let ourselves be carried, however, from a recognition of the historian's limitations to a depreciation of the importance of his ruthlessly critical methodology. We should have no quarrel with him, nor should we accuse him of skepticism when in dealing with the Biblical record he confines himself to what is humanly describable. . . . All we can ask of him is that he leave the door open to the credibility of divine action in history" (James D. Smart, *The Strange Silence of the Bible in the Church: A Study in Hermeneutics*, Philadelphia: Westminster Press, 1972, p. 110).

53. The whole question of miracle caused a lot of discussion and the second half of this chapter is an attempt to express the results of this. One or two, however, would wish for a statement which more strongly emphasized miracle as actual miracle, and a summary of their argument, as expressed by one Contributor, is given here:

In defining miracle, we must begin by recognizing that YHWH is the Reality behind every event. It is false, therefore, to equate miracle and the phrase "an act of God," as though this phrase would distinguish miracle from other events. All acts are acts of God, but if miracle is synonymous with the word "event," it is of little use as a special term. To define miracle as an event in which men recognize by faith that God is acting is inadequate, for it suggests that the distinctive character of miracle is not the divine action but the human reaction. It is clear that the *Testament* considers miracle as a YHWH-centered event, YHWH acting in a special way.

We may, perhaps, use the analogy of language. An event is a word spoken by God to man, but these events cannot be random, for true randomness conveys no meaning. Nor can they all have the same significance, for all events cannot be the same word. There must be elements of both repetition and distinctiveness for the pattern of events to transmit meaning from YHWH to man.

Miracle in this analogy is a special kind of word, communicating a special meaning. Its significance lies both in man's interpretation and in the "intention" of

YHWH, just as the meaning of a word is not merely what the listener decides to hear. If we wish to understand how the Israelites thought, we must believe, as they did, that YHWH really stands behind miracles in a special way and proclaim with them, "God worked mightily here!"

But what constitutes "miracle"? A miracle reveals both the saving nature of YHWH and also his supremacy over the natural world. The two meanings are related because it is the very intrusion of YHWH as "the Other" into the natural world which *is* salvation. Such events (e.g., creation events) proclaim that man is saved from the endless cycle of the natural and is in the hands of the supernatural, YHWH. All events, of course, reveal something of YHWH's saving nature, but miracles do so in a special way. Most events take place within the natural system of cause and effect. They are tied to the past through a chain of connected causes, and they are tied to the future through the effects they produce—effects which lead on to further causes and effects. A miracle is an event which is tied to the future, but is not tied to the past as a "natural" event is. Its cause lies outside the natural order, in a direct link with "the Other." (See C. S. Lewis, *Miracles: A Preliminary Study*, London: Geoffrey Bles, 1947, Chap. VIII.)

THE UNDERSTANDING
OF CREATION

9. Maker of Heaven and Earth

BACKGROUND READING: Genesis 1–11.

My help comes from YHWH,
maker of heaven and earth.

Psalm 121:2

The fifth of the crises listed in the second chapter was the establishment of the Assyrian empire during the eighth century B.C.E. and the bringing of the whole world known to the Israelites under one imperial authority. The response to this crisis is to be found in what for many people is the heart of the *Testament:* the teaching of the Hebrew prophets. However, we must postpone our study of this teaching until Chapter 13. First, we need to examine three concepts which form an important part of the background of the prophetic message: the understanding of "God" (*a*) as Creator, (*b*) as expressed in the worship of ancient Israel, (*c*) as contained in the teaching of the "Wise." It is with the first of these concepts that this chapter and the next are concerned.

The General Climate of Opinion

We must begin with what may seem at first to be obvious: the reminder that ancient Israel formed only a very small part of the Middle Eastern world of the time, and that this world had had an enormously long history. The biblical story of Abraham, with whom the history of the Israelites begins, ranges from distant Ur of the Chaldees, close to the Persian Gulf, to Egypt and the Nile. Moreover, in coming to Palestine Abraham entered a country which even then was of tremendous antiquity. Five thousand years before his day there had been at Jericho a fortified town, with evidently a well-developed social organization and means of communication with both the Red Sea and the distant plateau of what is now

Turkey.[1] We must therefore conceive of a widespread floating mass of ideas about the world, some of them very ancient.

This thinking was not in general what we would call speculative, nor did it usually take the form of objective study and examination. Instead, it portrayed the world as experienced by man.[2] The primary concern was always with the world as it is, and as constituting the realm of human activity. When people of the ancient Middle East spoke of origins and creation, their interest was not in questions of scientific cause and effect. Nor were they concerned with the problem of the physical world, or with existence and nonexistence. For them to speak of the origin of something was to speak of its nature in relation to man, and to tell the story of creation was to give an account of what the world in which man lives is like. The story was not intended to give a factual explanation of how the world came into existence, or to define why it has the character it does, but to show *the right way of understanding the world,* so that men and women might know how to live and act within it. For them the primary question was always the question of order and disorder.

The "world" meant to them everything that constituted order and meaning. The alternative to this was chaos and meaninglessness. The "world," therefore, in this sense of the word, included the gods, because the absence of the gods would be chaos. *Enuma Elish,* the great Babylonian myth which contains the account of creation on which, in large measure, the account in Genesis 1 is based, speaks of the primordial chaos as that time "when none of the gods had been brought into being."[3] When people recounted the myths of creation they were not looking backward in time to the beginning of things,[4] but looking at the totality of the world and seeing how all the parts were held together in one coherent whole; and in reenacting the myth with each New Year, they were laying again the foundations of their world. "Myth belonged originally to the context of survival, an expression therefore of one's understanding of existence. . . . Reflection on Creation meant to rehearse (i.e., to repeat by narrative) in the present world and in man's dangerous situation, the beginning, when what is now came to be. Relationship with the beginning meant relationship with the basis of the world."[5]

To this wealth of varied experience, and the expression of it in myth and ritual, the Israelite people were heirs. They accepted without any

1. Kathleen Kenyon, *Archaeology in the Holy Land* (New York: Frederick A. Praeger, 1960), p. 44. James Mellaart, *Earliest Civilizations of The Near East* (London: Thames and Hudson, 1965), p. 36.

2. See additional notes.

3. *Enuma Elish,* I,7, in Alexander Heidel, *The Babylonian Genesis* (Chicago: The University of Chicago Press, Phoenix ed., 1963), p. 18.

4. See additional notes.

5. Claus Westermann, *Creation,* trans. John J. Scullion, S.J. (Philadelphia: Fortress Press, 1974), pp. 12–13.

question, since there was no alternative concept available, what is loosely called today the "three-storied universe," with heaven above, earth in the middle and the waters beneath, but how this came to be they interpreted in the light of their own experience. "Three-storied universe" is, however, a misleading term, for the Israelites did not think geometrically of three dimensions in the way that we do.[6] Heaven and earth represented for them the realm of order, heaven being the realm of true, or absolute, order, and earth the realm of threatened order. The earth was always the dry land, and especially the inhabited land of agriculture. The seas, or the deep, always meant the realm of chaos, disorder and meaninglessness, and so did the barren and unruly desert.

Therefore, creation of heaven and earth meant for them, as it did for the surrounding peoples, the separation out of meaningful existence from the chaos of meaninglessness. In the opening verses of Genesis we learn that light was separated from darkness (v. 4), and heaven, the realm of absolute order, was separated from the waters of chaos (vv. 6-8). The picture here is not of a "three-storied universe," but a concept of absolute order surrounded, as it were, by chaos. When the ancient Israelites spoke of "above," when they looked "up," they conceived of this as looking *into,* toward the center, i.e., in the direction of greater and greater solidity and reality. The sky, in which were placed the sun and moon, to keep order during the day and night (v. 16), was only the visible part of the realm of heaven. Of a still greater quality of solid reality was the "heaven of heavens," but even this is not to be thought of as suitable for YHWH, who altogether transcends even the utmost heaven in quality.[7] To look "down," therefore, meant to peer with horror into the deep, the menacing abyss of chaos. When at the time of the Flood, the earth (but not the heaven) dissolved again into chaos, the terrible waters poured in upon mankind from every side.[8] It is, of course, not easy for somebody brought up in the modern Western world to think of "up" and "down," and "above" and "below," in this manner. Yet it is important to try to do so, if we are to understand what the writers of the *Testament* were talking about when they spoke of what we would call "creation," and when they tried to give an account of how it came to pass.

Creation in the Testament

It is customary, at least in introductory books, to concentrate on the first two chapters of Genesis as providing the two biblical accounts of

6. See additional notes.
7. I Kings 8:27. The literal translation "heaven of heavens" of the KJV is better here than the RSV "highest heaven," which inevitably suggests to the modern reader one heaven on top of another.
8. Gen. 7:11.

Creation. This is a mistake. In the first place, Genesis 1–2 form only the introduction to a much longer body of material (Gen. 1–11) in which are interwoven two accounts, J and P,[9] of how the world came to be as it is. What might perhaps be called the essence of the world, its fundamental nature and character, cannot be correctly perceived until there has been demonstrated the division of the earth, the spreading abroad of the nations, and the utter confusion of their speech.[10]

In the second place Creation, as presented in the *Testament,* cannot be understood apart from a study of the Psalms, which take for granted the fact of Creation and praise YHWH as the Creator,

> The earth is YHWH's and the fulness thereof,
>   the world and they that dwell therein;
> for he has founded it upon the seas,
>   and established it upon the floods.
>
> Psalm 24:1–2 KJV[11]

The Genesis accounts were not written to convince the Israelites that Creation had happened and to persuade them to believe in it. They were attempts to express in words an already accepted understanding of the world.

Third, during the more than two centuries after 750 B.C.E. the understanding of the significance of Creation continually deepened. This new understanding did not come easily, nor when it came was it readily accepted. It was forced upon the people by historical events, which brought the terrible flood of meaninglessness surging in upon them in a series of tidal waves, each succeeding wave seeming more appalling than those that had gone before. The first was the "overflowing scourge" of Assyrian imperial power,[12] which in the last half of the eighth century flooded all Israel and Judah, leaving only Jerusalem like a desolate hut in a field,[13] and poured like a deluge into the land of Egypt. The second was the onslaught of Assyria's successor, Babylon, in the early years of the sixth century, so cruel a storm that even the city which had escaped the Assyrian fury was overwhelmed. "Vast as the sea" was the ruin of Jerusalem[14] once described as "the joy of all the earth."[15] The third was the tragedy of the Exile itself, best understood in modern terms as a refugee situation, in which people of Judah began pitifully to pick up the pieces and build once

9. See explanatory note at the end of Chap. 3.
10. Gen. 10:25, 32; 11:9.
11. Cf. Pss. 33:6–9; 65:5–13; 74:12–17, etc.
12. Isa. 28:18.   13. Isa. 1:8.   14. Lam. 2:13.
15. Ps. 48:2. Lam. 2:13–17 portrays the complete reversal of the situation described in Ps. 48:1–6. In both the sight of Jerusalem amazes the foreign onlookers, but whereas in the days of her greatness even kings slunk back in terror, in the days of her desolation the amazement produces nothing but derision.

more some sort of a life in a foreign, incomprehensible land.[16] The fourth, in 539 B.C.E., was the total overthrow of Babylon and the Babylonian empire by Cyrus, the "bird of prey from the east."[17] His attack was not that of an already known kingdom, terrible though this would have been, but an even more horrifying penetration of the known world by someone from "beyond," not merely from beyond the towering Zagros Mountains which border Mesopotamia (though this was true), but from outside what was understood to be the orderly earth. Cyrus was for them a barbarian, a denizen of the meaningless wasteland of the Iranian plateau.

In these four terrible periods the troubled seas of chaos and disorder almost overwhelmed the Israelite people, and for many called in question the truth of Creation, since order seemed to have been annulled. But for some among them, even though they were probably only a minority, the very fury of the storms demonstrated the indestructible nature of the Creation, and proclaimed ever more vigorously the glory of the Creator. This is the view found in the writings of these centuries: in the Prophets (notably in Isaiah 40–55) and in the book of Job. We need, perhaps, to remind ourselves again at this point that the *Testament* does not set out to record popular Israelite religion and beliefs, of which it is often critical. Throughout our study, therefore, we are concerned with the understanding of those who taught the people—prophets, priests, and wise men[18]—and even among them only with the ideas of the more profound thinkers, whose teaching in the end prevailed.

The Special Character of the Israelite Experience: Existence in Time

The Israelite people shared with many of their neighbors a foreboding sense of constantly threatening disorder. *Enuma Elish,* for instance, which represents Babylonian thinking, portrays creation as a conflict with the dragon of chaos, which was overthrown, but not destroyed, so that the conflict had to be reenacted every New Year to ensure that the order of the world should be maintained. A similar understanding is to be found in the Ugaritic writings. It appears also as a poetic metaphor in the *Testament,*

> Thou didst divide the sea by thy might;
>> thou didst break the heads of the dragons on the waters.
> Thou didst crush the heads of Leviathan.

Psalm 74:13–14[19]

But in the *Testament* it is no more than a poetic metaphor and the belief in a cosmic struggle annually renewed is altogether rejected. In Psalm

16. See Ps. 137.   17. Isa. 46:11; see also additional notes.
18. Jer. 18:18.   19. See also Isa. 27:1.

104:26 Leviathan is no longer a dragon, but a sportive sea beast. Elsewhere Rahab, another name of the dragon of chaos,[20] is transferred to the power of Egypt which had been overthrown at the beginning of the Exodus,

> Was it not thou that didst cut Rahab in pieces,
>   that didst pierce the dragon?
> .   .   .   .   .   .
> That didst make the depths of the sea
>   a way for the redeemed to pass over?
>
> Isaiah 51:9–10

> For Egypt's help is worthless and empty,
>   therefore I have called her
>   "Rahab that sits still."
>
> Isaiah 30:7

For ancient Israel the question of disorder did not involve a cosmic struggle, but an immediate and actual threat, and she perceived it in two forms: in the desert and sea, between which she was squeezed into a very narrow space, and in the nations which beset her on every side. The second constituted the greater danger, for not only did she have, as does the modern state of Israel today, an apparently insoluble problem of "secure boundaries," but she lay athwart the one road which led from Egypt to Syria and Mesopotamia. She was thus caught in an endless power struggle over who should control the Fertile Crescent,[21] and she said rightly,

> Sorely have they afflicted me from my youth;
> .   .   .   .   .   .
> The plowers plowed upon my back;
>   they made long their furrows.
>
> Psalm 129:2–3

In Israelite fears this power struggle overrode even the constriction between desert and sea and the desperate insecurity of the rainfall, for when she considered both "the roaring of the seas" and "the tumult of the peoples,"[22] it was the latter that affrighted her most. She could, as it were, live with the ever-present disorder of the natural world, alarming though this might be, but the disorder of temporal events, all that was gathered up in the phrase "the nations," threatened to destroy her completely. Here had to be the main thrust of her intellectual enquiry, and this was a major factor in causing the thinking of very much of the *Testament*

20. Job 26:12; Ps. 89:10.
21. See additional notes.
22. Ps. 65:8.

to be built on the assumption that "existence in time has a priority over the existence of material things."[23]

The significance of the days of Creation in the P account (Gen. 1:1–2:4a) is not the question of whether the universe was literally made in seven days, but that time provides the framework. Immediately after light is created, it is separated from the darkness, and there is produced evening and morning: one day.[24] From that moment on, as it were, the clock begins to tick; hour succeeds to hour, and day to day. Time has been created, and in the writer's understanding the necessary condition for all activity, and the basis of all further creation, now exists. It is not until time has been made that the heaven and the earth are given their separate existence, and time is the framework for all that follows thereafter. "These are the generations [the *toldoth*] of the heavens and the earth when they were created,"[25] to be succeeded by the *toldoth* of man, all those "begats," in which the reader of Genesis so easily founders. For the writers of the *Testament* no meaningful existence was possible unless conducted within the framework of time and history. So the way is prepared for Abraham by the "generations" of heaven and earth, of Adam,[26] of Noah,[27] and of Shem.[28] The surrounding nations did not think in these terms, and in *Enuma Elish* time was already there when the gods were created.[29]

Another factor contributing to this conviction that time is the primary condition of existence was the Israelite understanding that the complete separation of order from disorder in human society, and the promulgation of true pattern of relationships, took place at a definite point in history and not in the mythological realm. The full covenant relationship was brought into existence, and *Torah* was given to man, in the period of the Exodus, and not before.[30]

The Creator and the Creation

Three points need to be made here:

(*a*) The Israelite experience convinced them that order does not come into existence naturally. They rejected altogether, not only creation by conflict, but also any belief in Creation through generation and birth, though these ideas were not foreign to Middle Eastern thought.[31] For them order was something which must first be *established,* and then

---

23. Westermann, *Creation*, p. 43.   24. Gen. 1:5.
25. Gen. 2:4.   26. Gen. 5:1.   27. Gen. 6:9.
28. Gen. 11:10ff. The framework of Israelite existence was given by listing the *toldoth* of the foreign nations: the sons of Noah (10:1ff.), Ishmael (25:12ff.), and Esau (36:1ff.).
29. *Enuma Elish,* 1:13, 38. See additional notes.
30. See additional notes.   31. See additional notes.

continually be *cherished* and *maintained*. It may be shaped and fashioned as in Genesis 2, or produced by direct command as in Genesis 1, but creation is always emphatically act or deed, and it is the result of definite intention or will. In their thinking it could not happen otherwise. There was consequently a recognizable and necessary distinction between Creator and that which is created. The created world derived its entire character and life and meaning from the Creator, and yet it was not in any sense the same. According to the *Testament*, therefore, the created world does not directly manifest the Creator, and man cannot by studying the creation perceive the Creator. All that he can perceive is the Creator's handiwork.

Although the analogy must not be pushed too far, the distinction is similar to that which exists between an author and a character in one of his books, which, of course, is his creation. Thus, we may say correctly that Macbeth believed, "for mine own good all causes must give way," because he said so, but this provides no evidence for what his creator, Shakespeare, believed. The Creation does not *manifest* the Creator.[32] What the play does do, because it is the creation of Shakespeare, is to demonstrate the greatness of the author as a dramatic writer. So it is in Israelite thinking about the created world. It does not manifest the character of the Creator, but it proclaims his greatness.

> The heavens are telling the glory of God;
>   and the firmament proclaims his handiwork.
>
> Psalm 19:1

> Praise him, sun and moon,
>   praise him, all you shining stars!
> Praise him, you highest heavens,
>   and you waters above the heavens!
> Let them praise the name of YHWH!
>   For he commanded and they were created.
>
> Psalm 148:3–5

(b) Creation is not understood by the writers of the *Testament* as something which happened in the long distant past and is now over and done with. YHWH is thought of as forever Creator, and as making each thing which exists,

> For thou didst form my inward parts,
>   thou didst knit me together in my mother's womb.
>
> Psalm 139:13

All created things are therefore dependent upon the continuing power of YHWH to bring them into being and to maintain them in existence,

---

32. See additional notes.

These all look to thee,
   to give them their food in due season
When thou givest to them, they gather it up;
   when thou openest thy hand, they are filled with good things.
When thou hidest thy face, they are dismayed;
   when thou takest away their breath, they die
   and return to their dust.
When thou sendest forth thy Spirit, they are created;
   and thou renewest the face of the ground.

Psalm 104:27–30[33]

No created thing has life in itself, nor can it maintain itself in existence. Moreover, if the Creator has power to bring into existence, he has also—and this must never be forgotten—the power to bring existence to an end. Just as the potter may squash down the clay pot he is making, and make another, so, "O house of Israel, can I not do with you as this potter has done? says YHWH. Behold, like the clay in the potter's hand, so are you in my hand."[34]

Though in the earlier period the concept was that creation takes place out of something already there (Gen. 2:7), the idea which prevailed was that YHWH creates by sheer command.

By the word of YHWH the heavens were made,
   and all their host by the breath of his mouth.

.   .   .   .

For he spoke, and it came to be;
   he commanded, and it stood forth.

Psalm 33:6–9

This "word" is neither a sound nor only an idea; it is a direct command immediately producing the thing commanded.[35]

My word that goes forth from my mouth
   . . . shall not return to me empty,
but it shall accomplish that which I purpose,
   and prosper in the thing for which I sent it.

Isaiah 55:11

It is, moreover, irresistible power: "Is not my word like fire, says YHWH, and like a hammer which breaks the rock in pieces?"[36]

This compelling, galvanizing, power of YHWH, continually at work, is often spoken of as *ruach,* a word which means "spirit, breath, and wind." It may range from the gentlest zephyr to a howling gale, but always under control, bringing order where there is disorder and life

---

33. See additional notes.   34. Jer. 18:6.
35. The Hebrew word *dabar* means both "word" and "thing."
36. Jer. 23:29.

in place of death. When we are told in Genesis 1:2 that the *ruach* of God moved over the face of the waters, we must think of a raging tempest of confusion compelled by the command of YHWH to smother its fury and come to order:

> Thou didst rule the raging of the sea;
> when its waves rise, thou stillest them.
>
> Psalm 89:9; see also 93:3–4

And when in the desolation of the Exile the people said, "Our bones are dried up, and our hope is lost," the prophet was told to summon the tremendous desert wind to breathe life into the dead bones.[37]

(*c*) Finally, we need to realize that for the Israelites every act of creation is an act of salvation;[38] it is always the granting of a place of safety to those imprisoned in a realm of disorder. To create is to save, and though the wrath of YHWH is real, and to be feared, at no time does he cease to be the One who saves. We may see this in those psalms which place side by side the Creation and the Exodus. Psalm 95 speaks of YHWH as Creator in verses 1–7 and then immediately calls upon the people to recall their rebellions in the wasteland of the Exodus (7b–11). So also in Psalm 135:6–9:

> Whatever YHWH pleases he does,
> in heaven and on earth,
> in the seas and all deeps.
> He it is who makes the clouds to rise at the end of the earth,
> who makes lightnings for the rain
> and brings forth the wind from his storehouses.
> He it was who smote the first-born of Egypt,
> both man and beast;
> who in thy midst, O Egypt,
> sent signs and wonders
> against Pharaoh and all his servants.

This is spelled out with great clarity in Psalm 136:1–22.

To understand Creation as the *Testament* speaks of it, therefore, is to view the entire world as having been made by the Other, and as being in no sense the source of its own life. It is to think of Creation and Salvation as belonging to the same activity. It is also to think of them as being not just something which happened once, but as constituting the whole of history; established securely in the past,[39] at work always at this very moment,[40] and still to be made anew in the future.[41] Creation is in the *Testament* the condition of existence.

---

37. Ezek. 37:1–14. In this famous Vision of the Valley of Dry Bones there is a continual interplay on the three meanings of the word *ruach*.
38. See additional notes.
39. Pss. 93:2; 96:10.   40. Ps. 147:2–20.   41. Isa. 11:6–9.

ADDITIONAL NOTES TO CHAPTER 9

2. See e.g., H. and H. A. Frankfort, J. A. Wilson, T. Jacobsen, *Before Philosophy: The Intellectual Adventure of Ancient Man* (Baltimore: Penguin Books, 1949); S. H. Hooke, *Middle Eastern Mythology* (Baltimore: Penguin Books, 1963); E. O. James, *Myth and Ritual in the Ancient Near East* (London: Thames & Hudson, 1958); A. N. Kramer (ed.), *Mythologies of the Ancient World* (Garden City, N.Y.: Doubleday, 1961).

4. Some Contributors with good reason objected that the people *were* looking backward to the beginning of things. This is perfectly true, but the time element did not play a prominent part in their thinking about creation. Obviously they thought of creation as having taken place earlier than their own day, but they were not asking the question, "How long ago did it happen?" nor were they trying to establish a chain of events which could help to explain the present order.

6. Speaking of the problem of entering "more fully into the consciousness of our [medieval] ancestors by realizing how such a universe must have affected those who believed in it," C. S. Lewis says, "The recipe for such realization is not the study of books. You must go out on a starry night and walk about for half an hour trying to see the sky in terms of old cosmology. Remember that you now have an absolute Up and Down. The earth is really the centre, really the lowest place; movement to it from whatever direction is a downward movement. As a modern, you located the stars at a great distance. For distance you must now substitute that very special, and far less abstract, sort of distance which we call height; height which speaks immediately to our muscles and nerves" (*The Discarded Image*, Cambridge: University Press, 1964, p. 98). Certainly the ancient Israelites were aware of physical height, but a high mountain meant to them essentially a sacred mountain, i.e., one in closer touch with ultimate Reality. So one has the delightful picture in Ps. 68: 15–16 of the great mountain of Bashan (modern Jebel Druze) gazing enviously at the height of Mount Zion, which physically, of course, is much lower.

17. This translation is adopted by RSV, NEB and JB. KJV has "a ravenous bird." No translation, however, can capture the terror which the single Hebrew word, *'ait,* is meant to convey. It comes from a root meaning "to give a shrill screech," which petrifies the unhappy hearer. If we want to grasp something of what the exiles, and also the Babylonians, thought was happening to them, we must think perhaps of the vicious noise of a plane diving out of the clouds to bomb a helpless village. This may sound like an exaggeration, but it is not. It is important to remember that there had been no real kingdom of Persia before the time of Cyrus, and therefore nothing akin to what the inhabitants of the Fertile Crescent would have understood to be an ordered society. The terror that overcame them was the terror of the unknown.

21. I remember during World War II in Palestine being awakened by the noise of tanks and armored cars of the British army moving northward from Egypt to invade Syria and drive out the Vichy French. I could not help reflecting, as I watched them, that I was seeing yet again in our own day the oldest, and one of the most constantly repeated, military movements in history.

29. The word *Enuma* means "on the day that." The J writer in the *Testament* begins his account of the creation of man with the same phrase (Gen. 2:4), but it leads immediately to a history of mankind, developed in Gen. 4:17ff. The framework of his thought is no less historical than that of the P writer. *Enuma Elish* does not have a historical pattern, and the days and months established in tablet V are strictly cyclical.

30. The point was made by some Contributors that the true pattern of relationship was established at Creation, and that the giving of the covenant relationship was a subsequent act of grace necessitated by man's rebellion. This is valid if one is thinking of man in the abstract, as "male and female," but the pattern of actual society, i.e., of practical human relationships within a community, was not established at Creation.

31. The belief in Creation through generation and birth seems to have been more widespread in ancient Egypt, where the experience was that the sun and the Nile together produce life (Henri Frankfort, *Ancient Egyptian Religion,* New York: Harper & Row, 1961, pp. 21, 52–53).

32. This idea is very well developed in Dorothy Sayers' interesting book about creation, *The Mind of the Maker* (New York: Harcourt, Brace, 1941). There was considerable discussion on this point and some Contributors insisted that a book must in some sense reveal the character of its author, even if only indirectly. This is true of a book, since there the creator is a human person just as we are and his characters are men and women. But at this point the analogy breaks down, because God is not human, and there is not therefore a similar continuity. Even with a human creator we can do no more than glean some understanding (possibly incorrect) by studying the thing which he has created. The creator is not *manifest,* i.e., demonstrated with absolute clarity, in the creation.

33. Psalm 104 is based upon the Egyptian *Hymn to Aton* (see Pritchard, ANET, pp. 369–71), but has been transformed according to Israelite experience. The *Hymn to Aton* breathes throughout a spirit of permanence, a sense of what always happens, but the psalm records also dramatic acts in time (vv. 5–9).

38. One Contributor commented, "I am afraid I cannot accept this. I agree that most creation is a saving act, but if every act of creation is an act of salvation, then the disorder and chaos must never have been made. They must have been preexistent since they obviously are not an act of salvation. Also saving for the Hebrews in Egypt was at the same time destruction for Pharaoh's army. For every saving act for Israel some other people lost." This raises two valid points. However, in Israelite thought disorder and chaos were not something that was made, for YHWH did not create chaos (Isa. 45:18). Chaos is not a thing but a state or condition. It is the absence of order and coherence. Certainly also the saving of the Hebrews meant destruction for the Egyptians, a fact to which the rabbis later gave serious thought. However, in Israelite understanding the Egyptian system was not a system of coherent order, but of a meaningless oppression. They did not see their being saved from this as having *caused* the death of the Egyptians.

10. God, the Creator, and Man, the Created

Man, the Creature of YHWH

"And God saw everything that he had made, and behold, it was very good" (Gen. 1:31). That is to say, "as it should be, suitable to its purpose, effective and efficient,"[1] a first-class piece of work in fact, in which all the parts are properly related to each other and perform the function for which they were designed. Holding a special position within this complex pattern of Creation stands man, of whom it is said that God deliberated before he made him.[2]

There is an ambivalent attitude to man in the *Testament*. Twice in the Psalms we find the question, "What is man that thou art mindful of him, and the son of man that thou dost care for him?" and two answers are given. Psalm 8, which reflects the thinking of Genesis 1, says, "Thou has made him a little less than God, and dost crown him with glory and honor" (v. 5), but Psalm 144 says that "Man is like a breath, his days are like a passing shadow" (v. 4).

In the thinking of the *Testament* man is no more than a created being, and he partakes to the full of what it means to be created, which is to be limited and mortal, and not to have as his own possession the gift and power of life. Between YHWH and man there is an immeasurable distinction, for man is not God, and God is not man:

> God is not a man, as I am,
> that I should answer him.

> Job 9:32

> The Egyptians are men, and not God
> > Isaiah 31:3

---

1. This is the primary meaning of the word "good," as defined by Webster.
2. Gen. 1:26. This, of course, is the P account. In the J account only the creation of man is described. The rest of creation is assumed.

> I am God and not man,
>   the Holy One in your midst.
>
> Hosea 11:9

The perspectives of YHWH and of man are therefore different, for they do not stand in the same situation, and 'YHWH sees not as man sees."[3]

> For my thoughts are not your thoughts,
>   neither are your ways my ways, says YHWH.
>
> Isaiah 55:8

YHWH sees with the totality of understanding of the Creator, from whom nothing is hid, since it is all his own work, but man sees always with limited vision. He is one with the created world, finite and mortal.

> Behold, thou has made my days a few handbreadths,
>   and my lifetime is as nothing in thy sight.
> Surely every man stands as a mere breath!
> Surely man goes about as a shadow!
> .   .   .   .
> For I am thy passing guest,
>   a sojourner, like all my fathers.
>
> Psalm 39:5-6, 12

> Man cannot abide in his pomp,
>   he is like the beasts that perish.
>
> Psalm 49:12, 20

> As for man, his days are like grass,
>   he flourishes like a flower of the field;
> for the wind passes over it, and it is gone,
>   and its place knows it no more.
>
> Psalm 103:15-16

For the fate of the sons of man and the fate of beasts is the same; as one dies, so dies the other. They have all the same breath, and man has no advantage over the beasts.

Ecclesiastes 3:19[4]

Yet it is said that "God created man in his own image."[5] This is a statement paralleled nowhere else in the *Testament,* and it must not be taken out of its context, which is that of the creation story. Certainly "image" cannot here mean physical form, as if YHWH were thought of as having the appearance of a man. The ascribing of *any* likeness to

---

3. I Sam. 16:7.
4. Among the many passages which speak of the mortality and frailty of man see, e.g., Gen. 18:27; Job 7:7; 14:1-2; Pss. 62:9; 90:3-6; 119:19; 146:3-4; Isa. 2:22; 40:6-8.
5. Gen. 1:27.

YHWH had already been ruled out by the terms of the covenant,[6] and all the evidence we have suggests that this was taken seriously in Israel. It is inconceivable that the P writer, in the mid-sixth century B.C.E. should reject this weight of Israelite opinion, and revert to a pre-covenant concept. Moreover, the Israelites thought of man as a total living entity, and seem to have had, in fact, no word for "body."[7] They could speak of a dead body, or corpse, or they could speak of "flesh," the substance of all living animals as distinct from God. They could also speak of different parts of the body, of the heart as representing the essence of man, and especially man as a thinking being,[8] of the bowels as representing his emotions,[9] as well as the face, eye, hand, ear, tongue, etc. to express various psychological concepts.[10] What they could not do, because to them it would have been an artificial division, was to separate man out into such component parts as body, mind, and spirit.

The word "image" tends to suggest to the modern mind something static, but for the Israelites almost all words had an active connotation. Their interest in anything was in what it *did,* in its function rather than its essence. What an image does is to represent, and to act on behalf of, the one whose likeness it is. The condemnation of any kind of image for YHWH was not on the grounds that nothing can be made which looks like God, but because nothing that man contrives could ever simulate the activity of God. When in the later period all images of gods (and not merely images of YHWH) were condemned, it was not the appearance that was derided; it was the inability to act.[11] If the image cannot act, so in their thinking the one which it represents cannot act either.[12]

The image, or likeness of God presented in the first chapter of Genesis is of the "One who Creates," which, as we have already seen, means the One who produces order and meaning in place of disorder and meaninglessness, and who, moreover, cherishes and maintains the order which he has established. The activity required of man as the "image" of God is to be fruitful, to subdue the earth and to have dominion over other

6. Exod. 20:4. The purpose of this is to prohibit images and likeness of YHWH, since the worship of other gods is already ruled out by the previous commandment.

7. See additional notes.

8. Gen. 6:5; 8:21; Exod. 8:19; 31:6; Deut. 29:19; I Kings 3:9; Ps. 33:11, etc. N.B. It would be best for readers who do not know Hebrew to look up these passages, and those in the two following footnotes, in the KJV, which gives a more literal translation. The RSV and other recent translations tend to paraphrase in order to convey the meaning.

9. Pss. 26:2; 73:21; Song 5:4; Jer. 4:19; Lam. 1:20; 2:11, etc.

10. E.g., Prov. 21:29; Ps. 10:7-8; Prov. 18:15; Prov. 12:19.

11. Pss. 115:2-8; 135:15-18; Isa. 41:7, where the sting of Isaiah's scorn is the immobility of the image.

12. Isa. 41:21-24. One might paraphrase the challenge somewhat crudely in modern terms as, "Don't just stand there; do something."

living things.[13] This command has been greatly misunderstood in recent years, for "subdue" certainly does *not* mean ruthless exploitation for man's own purposes, nor does it make man the center of the world. Man's function is to foster the life already given by God, to develop order in an otherwise disorderly situation, and to cherish and maintain that order, just as a wise governor of a province subdues all disorder and by his dominion cultivates and preserves order among the people.

It is extraordinarily difficult for the modern mind to comprehend how frightened man was in the ancient Middle East of wild nature, and what excellent reason he had to be frightened. Men were very few in number compared with animals, and cultivated land was still only a fraction of the total area. At the time of the Israelite takeover there were perhaps 50,000 people in the whole country west of the Jordan and in the early monarchy only 200,000, living in about 500 towns and villages.[14] Even as late as 750 B.C.E. Amos could speak of lions and bears as animals one might meet outside the village,[15] and in 722, when the Assyrians devastated Samaria and transferred large sections of the population, wild beasts overran the land.[16]

The word "subdue" must be read in this context. From the Israelites' first entry into the country after the Exodus, when they settled in the still untamed forests, the prime necessity was to bring the land within the realm of peaceful cultivation, and to preserve this realm by diligent husbandry. This they did faithfully. Together with the cutting down of trees came the first careful terracing of the hills.[17]

The ideal relationship with the rest of creation was in fact that of covenant, or agreement, and this was earnestly looked for as one of the blessings still to be granted by YHWH in the days to come:

> You shall be in league with the stones of the field,
>   and the beasts of the field shall be at peace with you.
>
> Job 5:23[18]

I will make with them a covenant of peace and banish wild beasts from the land, so that they may dwell securely in the wasteland and sleep in the woods.

Ezekiel 34:25[19]

---

13. Gen. 1:28.
14. See additional notes.   15. Amos 5:19.
16. II Kings 17:24ff; cf. I Kings 13:23–25. See also Baly, *Geography*, Chap. 9.
17. R. Zon, "Agricultural Terraces in the Judean Mountains," *Israel Exploration Journal*, 16, 1966, pp. 111–22.
18. "League" here is in Hebrew *berith*, the word normally translated as "covenant." It might be better to translate this phrase, "You shall have a covenant with the stones of the field."
19. "Wasteland" is *midbar*, as elsewhere in this book. RSV has "wilderness."

I will make for you a covenant on that day with the beasts of the field, the birds of the air, and the creeping things of the ground; and I will abolish the bow, the sword, and war from the land; and I will make you lie down in safety.

Hosea 2:18

Man was never intended to be the proud ruler of conquered and enslaved territory. He is *adam,* taken from the *adamah,*[20] or as we might put it in English, he is human, taken from the humus, and therefore he must act with humility. "You are dust, and to dust you shall return."[21]

> Put not your trust in princes,
>   in a son of man, in whom there is no help.
> When his breath departs he returns to his earth;
>   on that very day his plans perish.

Psalm 146:3–4

The Israelite understanding of the world was not only active and dynamic; it was also strongly collective and communal. Just as they did not divide out the body into its component parts, so they did not normally think in terms of separate individuals.[22] When they spoke of "man," they thought not so much of "a man," as of all men and women, and their minds moved easily to and fro between the individual and the community of which he was a part. This led to the concept referred to by scholars as the "corporate personality,"[23] which plays an important part in the language of the Psalms.

The Israelites could not help, of course, recognizing that there were different languages, and separate, even antagonistic, nations. This they ascribed to man's arrogance and his willful determination to give himself a status which he did not properly possess.[24] Properly understood, as they saw it, all men were related, and should have remained in the covenant relationship with God which had been established after the flood.[25] The "Table of Nations" in Genesis 10, omitted by the casual reader of the Bible, is an important part of the creation story, because it demonstrates the community of all mankind as integral to the fact of creation. It is "an ambitious undertaking, the first of its kind known from anywhere."[26] designed to show that the very function of mankind,

---

20. Gen. 2:7. See also additional notes.   21. Gen. 2:19; cf. Eccl. 3:20.

22. The concept of the individual was developed more strongly in the Exile, especially by Ezekiel, e.g., Chap. 18.

23. See e.g., H. Wheeler Robinson, *Inspiration and Revelation in the Old Testament* (New York: Oxford University Press, 1946), pp. 70ff. In very many of the so-called "individual psalms" the singular "I" stands for the whole community. This is especially true of the laments.

24. Gen. 11:1–9.   25. Gen. 9:8–17.

26. E. A. Speiser, "Man, ethnic division of," *ID,* III, pp. 235–42. A very helpful study of Gen. 10.

as created by God, is to be in harmony, and violence among men therefore a denial of man's true nature. The ultimate purpose of the Creator
is to restore this community, which was shattered by the tragedy of Babel.
Abraham is called out of his country so that "all the families of the earth
shall be blessed,"[27] and this remains the true function of the "chosen
people":

> In that day Israel will be the third with Egypt and Assyria, a blessing in
> the midst of the earth, whom YHWH of Hosts has blessed, saying, "Blessed
> be Egypt my people, and Assyria the work of my hands, and Israel my
> heritage."
>
> Isaiah 19:24–25

> I have given you as a covenant to the people,
>   a light to the nations,
>   to open the eyes that are blind,
> to bring out the prisoners from the dungeon,
>   from the prison those who sit in darkness.
>
> Isaiah 42:6–7[28]

> Out of Zion shall go forth *Torah,*
>   and the word of YHWH from Jerusalem.
>
> .   .   .   .
>
> Nation shall not lift up sword against nation,
>   neither shall they learn war any more.
>
> Isaiah 2:2–4; Micah 4:1–4

God addresses Man

The wealth of meaning in the sentence, "God created man in his own
image," is by no means exhausted by what has been said above. "The
creation of man in God's image is directed to something happening between God and man. The Creator created a creature that corresponds
to him, to whom he can speak, and who can hear him. . . . Mankind
is created to stand before God."[29] There is face-to-face encounter, the
meeting of "I" and "Thou."

In this I-Thou relation of God and man, Creator with the created
being, the first word is spoken always by the Creator, who enters into
this relation in the very act of creation:

---

27. The KJV is probably better than the RSV "shall bless themselves," though
both are possible, and both may in fact be intended.

28. The whole passage, Isa. 42:1–7, should be read, for it is placed in the context of Creation (v. 5). The "Servant" here is probably corporate, i.e., Israel, as in
41:8–9, since he is to speak to the "nations" (v. 1).

29. Westerman, *Creation,* p. 56.

> YHWH called me from the womb,
>> from the body of my mother he named my name.
>>> Isaiah 49:1

> Before I formed you in the womb I knew you,
>> and before you were born I consecrated you;
>> I appointed you a prophet to the nations.
>>> Jeremiah 1:5

Throughout the *Testament* man is understood to be the created being, which is to say that he owes his nature, his whole meaning, and his function and purpose to that which is not himself. Therefore, he must be spoken to before he can know what is required of him by his Creator. "Earthling, stand upon your feet, and I will speak with you";[30] "Whom shall I send, and who will go for us?"[31]—these are the primary words. It is to the question and the command that man responds.

But in what sense can it be said that YHWH addresses man?[32] All ancient Israelites were convinced that God addressed man directly, but at the same time they recognized that this Word of YHWH, though unquestionably given, was mysterious and difficult to interpret. It was for the ordinary Israelite a "dark saying,"[33] needing men of vision and deep understanding to make the meaning clear. In ancient Israel three groups of people existed to expound to the community the teaching of YHWH. These were: the priests to interpret *Torah,* i.e., the true pattern of life and the relation of man to God; the wise elders to deal with disputes, and to train the young in the proper manner of day-to-day behavior; and the prophets to make known the true meaning of a particular situation, and therefore to show what ought to be done.[34]

One of the biggest problems for the ancient Israelites, as also for those today who wish to understand their thinking, was the distinction between the Word of YHWH and its interpretation. To have received the Word of YHWH was to have stood in his council[35] and to have been altogether attuned to his activity and purposes. It was to have felt a fire aflame in the very bones,[36] and taking possession of one's whole being. But this awesome Word had to be given audible shape in human words and expressed in terms which common folk could understand. What they heard was not the direct command of YHWH, but the words of their teachers, who evidently did not all say the same thing. Whom, therefore, were they to believe? The book of Deuteronomy twice offers advice to

30. Ezek. 1:1. The translation of *ben-adam* (son of man) in this context is not my own. I owe it (and much else besides) to my colleague, Prof. Eugen Kullmann.
31. Isa. 6:8.   32. See additional notes.   33. Ps. 78:2.
34. Jer. 18:18, where the plotters say that even if Jeremiah is killed, all the regular teaching will still go on. Also Ezek. 7:26.
35. Jer. 23:22.   36. Jer. 20:9.

those who were puzzled about this, but each time leaves much room for argument about whether the prophet had spoken the Word of YHWH faithfully.[37]

We need to remember that the prophets whose teachings we have today in the *Testament* are only a handful out of all the many prophets who spoke in the name of YHWH throughout the four centuries of the monarchy. We know the names of only a few others, such as Uriah,[38] but there must have been a very large number, for prophets were an important part of Israelite society. To the ordinary citizen they were all "prophets of YHWH," but they did not all give the same message. The majority, it would seem, spoke in opposition to such men as Micah, Isaiah and Jeremiah, and yet were sincerely convinced that they were saying what YHWH had told them to say. This led sometimes to hot arguments, and even quarrels, between opposing prophets, each stating emphatically, "Thus says YHWH."[39]

What has been preserved for us today is the teaching of those who were vindicated by YHWH, manifesting himself through events. They were shown to have made known the truth because that of which they spoke had truly come to pass. This was an important criterion of the authentic prophet of YHWH, and in the end the only one which left no room for doubt.[40] Yet at the same time when the prophets spoke, the truth of what they said was far from clear, for there could be a long delay between the proclamation and the fulfillment, so long that sometimes the doubters would say in derision, "Let YHWH make haste, let him speed his work that we may see it." [41]

Those who were proved to have been wrong have come to be known as the "false prophets," and probably quite a number of them were just as self-seeking and dishonest as Micah accused them of being.[42] But it would be going quite beyond the evidence to suggest that all of them, or even that most of them, were so corrupt. It is more likely that they were conditioned by their society, as all people tend to be, and consequently really could not think in terms which transcended the society. They were false because their minds were out of tune with the "Other," and they could not, therefore, "stand in the council of YHWH," which is not, and cannot be, contained within the framework of any society or any cultural pattern, however vast. They were not, however, necessarily false in the sense of being insincere. They may well have been men of wide learning and profound conviction.

---

37. Deut. 13:1–5; 18:21–22. See additional notes.   38. Jer. 26:20.
39. See the quarrel between Zedekiah and Micaiah in I Kings 22:1–28, and between Hananiah and Jeremiah in Jer. 28.
40. Deut. 18:22; Jer. 28:9. See also additional notes.
41. Isa. 5:10; cf. Ezek. 12:22.   42. Micah 3:5–7, 11.

The problem was an acute one because the word sought from the prophet did not apply merely to general principles. Whether spoken in the sanctuary, the market place, or the council of the king, the Word of YHWH through the prophet spoke always to a specific situation, though the people at large might not perceive how critical it was,[43] and it called for decision and practical action. When King Zedekiah questioned Jeremiah secretly, and asked, "Is there any word from YHWH?" he was seeking political and military advice, as such other kings as Ahab, Jehoshaphat and Hezekiah had done before him.[44]

It was in the midst of a critical situation that YHWH encountered man face to face, calling upon people to repent, to rethink their entire attitude and policy. It was laid upon the prophet to make this message clear. Nothing that has been said so far should be allowed to suggest that prophets were mere political commentators. They were far, far more, for they were called upon to make known the truth. Anything might provide the searing moment of revelation: a vision of the night,[45] the sight of an almond tree in blossom, or a pot boiling over,[46] a plague of locusts,[47] the sack of a Philistine city,[48] or the thoughtless rejoicing of the people when Jerusalem was saved from the Assyrians.[49] Because in the providence of YHWH Israel stood at the crossroads of the world, their situation was one of constant tension, and the encounter with YHWH came repeatedly upon the people. Only too often they failed to heed the encounter, and said to the prophets, "Let us hear no more of the Holy One of Israel."[50] Amos warned the people of the northern kingdom that the result of such blindness would be that when at last in their desperation they longed to know the truth, the Word would no more reach them, not because it was not sent, but because there was no one left capable of recognizing it.[51]

The question is important because of the dread possibility of confrontation by YHWH in our own day. If—and it is a big "if"—we do indeed wish to enter into the experience of the Israelites, and have like them the Word of YHWH proclaimed to us, we must surely divest ourselves of all persuasion that we already know what it means, and of any thought that it could not come to us as "other" than what we know. We must enter into their doubt and perplexity, taking our place with men and women who were wholly convinced of the reality of YHWH, and

43. Amos spoke in a time of prosperity and expansion, when the people saw no crisis at all. For this he was expelled from the sanctuary (7:10–12). By contrast, the situation of Isa. 7:1–9 was one of terror and imminent disaster.
44. Jer. 37:16–17; I Kings 22:6; II Kings 3:11; 19:1–7.
45. Job 4:12ff.   46. Jer. 1:11–14.   47. Amos 7:1–3.
48. Isa. 20:1–6.   49. Isa. 22:1–14.
50. Isa. 30:11; cf. Jer. 26:7–9; Micah 2:6.
51. Amos 8:11–12; cf. Isa. 29:9–12.

of the fact of his Word, but were repeatedly blind to its coming, and uncertain about how to interpret it.

The Response of Man to God

The response of man, the created being, to YHWH, the Creator, is worship and obedience, which, properly understood, are the same thing. Worship in the usual sense of the word, i.e., the whole ritual of prayer, praise, thanksgiving and sacrifice, we shall consider in the next chapter. For the moment we are concerned with the response of man outside the sanctuary.

This is also nonetheless worship, for the word means "worthship," i.e., the recognition of the true value of things, and consequently the ascribing of ultimate value to YHWH alone.

> Not unto us, YHWH, not unto us,
> > but to thy name give glory,
> > for the sake of thy steadfast love and thy faithfulness.
> >   Psalm 115:1

In this connection we should recollect that the ancient Israelite town was crowded within a protecting wall; the houses were tiny and the streets no more than narrow alleys. Only two areas were available for communal activity: the sanctuary, or "open square before the house of God,"[52] and the area around the town gate. An open space was needed inside the gate for the purpose of defense, and this served as a market place. Outside the gate was also the market, for there the farmers from nearby villages offered their produce for sale, and animals were bought and sold.[53] At the gate were seats for the wise elders, who would meet for consultation and debate, and to give advice to those who needed it. Some would act as judges in disputes, and so the gate was also the court of law.[54] Job speaks of having performed this function in the days before tragedy came upon him:

> When I went out to the gate of the city,
> > when I prepared my seat in the square,
> the young men saw me and withdrew,
> > and the aged rose and stood.

>   .   .   .   .

52. Ezra 10:9.
53. Animals set aside for sacrificial purposes were apparently sold in the sanctuary area itself.
54. Markets easily became the place of judgment, for so many disputes arose over buying and selling. Our word "forensic" for legal matters comes from the Latin *forum*, or market place, and the word "category" comes from the Greek, from bringing a matter down (*kata*) to the market place (*agora*) for a decision.

I put on righteousness, and it clothed me;
   my justice was like a robe and a turban,
I was eyes to the blind,
   and feet to the lame.
I was a father to the poor,
   and I searched out the cause of him whom I did not know.

Job 29:7–16

The prophetic teaching in the *Testament* is insistent that the activity in the gate and in the sanctuary must correspond. The prophets attacked the worship of their day because the people failed to see any connection between the two. In his "Temple sermon" Jeremiah accused the worshipers of trusting in lying words, and repeating unthinkingly, "The Temple of YHWH, the Temple of YHWH, the Temple of YHWH!" "Will you steal," he asked, "murder, commit adultery, swear falsely, burn incense to Baal, and go after other gods that you have not known, and *then* come and stand before me in this house, which is called by my name, and say, 'We have been saved'—only to go on doing all these horrible things?"[55]

"I hate, I despise your feasts," proclaimed YHWH through the prophet Amos, "and I take no delight in your solemn assemblies," because of the corruption of justice:

I know how many are your transgressions,
   and how great are your sins—
you who afflict the righteous, who take a bribe,
   and turn aside the needy in the gate.

Amos 5:21, 12

The responsibility of man before the Creator is to recognize his created status, and his place within the covenant. The sins which Jeremiah listed in his Temple sermon were all breaches of the covenant, and so were the sins which Hosea attributed to the people of the northern kingdom:

Hear the word of YHWH, O people of Israel;
   for YHWH has a controversy with the inhabitants of the land.
There is no faithfulness or kindness,
   and no knowledge of God in the land;
there is swearing, lying, killing,
   stealing, and committing adultery;
   they break all bounds and murder follows murder.

Hosea 4:1–2[56]

55. Jer. 7:4, 9–10 (trans. D. B.). See also Isa. 1:12–17; 5:7; Hos. 6:6; Amos 5:14–15; Micah 6:8.
56. These passages should be compared with the requirements of the covenant in the Ten Commandments (Exod. 20).

The sin of man was pride, claiming for himself status and power that he should not rightly have:

> May YHWH cut off all flattering lips,
>   the tongue that makes great boasts,
> those who say, "With our tongue we will prevail."
>
> Psalm 12:3–4

> Rise up, O judge of the earth;
>   render to the proud their deserts!
> YHWH, how long shall the wicked,
>   how long shall the wicked exult?
> They pour out arrogant words,
>   they boast, all the evildoers.
>
> Psalm 94:2–4[57]

The nations should know themselves to be but men,[58] and the Prince of Tyre is condemned—

> Because your heart is proud,
>   and you have said, "I am a god;
> I sit in the seat of the gods,
>   in the heart of the seas,"
> yet you are but a man, and not a god,
>   though you consider yourself as wise as a god.
>
> Ezekiel 28:2

Of course, the rebuke of pride, dishonesty, murder and adultery is in no way peculiar to Israelite religion. Almost all religions, in fact, condemn them wholeheartedly. The only point being made here is that within the framework of Israelite understanding it was related to Creation and covenant.

This is already apparent in the creation stories, where the fundamental error of man is to use himself as the criterion, and to interpret the world in terms of himself instead of the Creator. Adam and Eve ate the fruit of the tree because it was "a delight to the eyes" and "to be desired";[59] Cain killed his brother Abel because his own offering was not accorded the recognition he believed was his due;[60] and the men of Shinar sought to attain to the heavens, and acquire a name for themselves.[61] The story of Adam and Eve in Genesis 3 is usually spoken of as the "fall" of man, but this term comes from a period after the *Testament*. It would be much better to speak of his separation—he became a dis-

57. See also Prov. 3:5–8; Isa. 2:12–19; 5:15–16, 21; Jer. 9:23–24; 13:15.
58. Ps. 9:20.
59. Gen. 3:6. Strictly speaking, of course, it is of Eve that this is said. However, the conclusion of the story makes clear that both were equally to blame.
60. Gen. 4:5.   61. Gen. 11:4.

placed person. Adam and Eve were driven out of the garden; Cain was driven into the wilderness, and the builders of the tower of Babel were scattered abroad over the whole earth. The result of human arrogance, which denies the fact of creation, is the shattering of relationship and of the pattern of the created world. Man is now set over against the Creator, over against his fellow men, and over against the earth itself, with which he must wrestle to get his food.[62]

The magnitude of this separation is enormous. The *Testament* sees the arrogance and willfulness of man as threatening to throw the order of the world again into chaos, for it is as if a great rift has appeared in the harmony of creation. It was the wickedness of man, and the continual evil of "every imagination of the thoughts of his heart" that brought about the Flood.[63] This thinking is continued by the prophets. Because the people "trust in oppression and perverseness, and rely on them," said Isaiah, the whole structure of their kingdom would be smashed so ruthlessly that nothing would be left but useless fragments.[64]

Hosea, in the passage already quoted (4:1–3), insisted that as a result of the wickedness of man:

> the land mourns,
> and all who dwell in it languish,
> and also the beasts of the field,
> and the birds of the air;
> and even the fish of the sea are taken away.[65]

The magnitude of the separation emphasizes also the greatness of the covenant, and why the breach of the covenant is so serious, for the covenant is the reestablishing of communication, and the saving, therefore, of the whole threatened creation. Where there is already harmony, there is no need of covenant or contract. Covenant is the coming together, and the making of an agreement, by parties previously apart from each other. A covenant is a treaty. It is the making of peace, and the restoration of order.

ADDITIONAL NOTES TO CHAPTER 10

7. We have used the expression "do not seem to have had" advisedly, because the evidence is not altogether clear. The normal word *geviyah* for "body" is used only for a corpse right up to the end of the monarchy, with the possible exception of Gen. 47:18, where the reference is clearly to bodies that are as good as dead. In I Sam. 31:10, 12 it is used for the dead body of Saul, as is *guphah* in I Chron. 10:12. The first clear use of *geviyah* for a living human body is in Neh. 9:37. Since the

62. Gen. 3:17–19.   63. Gen. 6:5.   64. Isa. 30:8–14.
65. For other passages portraying the wickedness of man as threatening the order of creation, see e.g., Isa. 24:1–3; Jer. 12:4; Amos 8:9.

number of examples is very small, we may have fallen into the trap of an "argument from silence," but it remains true that there is in the *Testament* no direct evidence for a word which means exactly what we would mean by the word "body."

13. The usual English translation of *'ir* by "city" is very misleading. The normal settlement covered about two and a half acres, and held some 500 people. Megiddo, one of the larger towns, had at the time of Solomon about 2,600 people living within its walls, which enclosed thirteen acres. In the great period of the monarchy there were only two true cities, Jerusalem and Samaria, and neither of these was large. Before Jerusalem was captured by David it held about 2,500 people, in the early monarchy perhaps as many as 5,000 and in the later monarchy about 7,500. John Wilkinson ("Ancient Jerusalem: Its Water Supply and Population," *Palestine Exploration Quarterly*, 1974, pp. 33–51) suggests that the last figure could have been as much as 10,660, but not more.

20. *Adam* is the general word for "mankind," and also the name of the first man in Gen. 2. The etymology is uncertain and the derivation from *adamah* (earth) or *adom* (red) is now rejected by many scholars, though, of course, this does not alter the fact that the Israelites saw a close relationship between the words *adam* and *adamah*. An individual man is usually spoken of as *ben-adam* (son of man).

32. The rest of this section reflects our discussions of what is a very complex problem and does not, of course, exhaust it. Some Contributors questioned the emphasis upon the difficulty of understanding the Word of YHWH, and wished for a much stronger statement of its clarity to those who truly heard it.

37. Each time the principle is quite clear, but the practical application of the principle in specific cases would have been much less evident. Doubtless no prophet claiming to speak in the name of YHWH ever said in so many words, "Go and worship Baal." He would have been more likely to say, "If you bring sacrifices to YHWH's Temple, he will deliver the city," and few people would have thought of this as directing them toward other gods. But according to such prophets as Hosea, Isaiah and Jeremiah this kind of oracle demonstrated essentially Baalist thinking.

40. It is not intended to suggest that the prophets were merely "vindicated by events," as if it just happened to turn out that way. In the kind of situation to which the prophets spoke the decisions taken on the basis of their oracles were bound to have momentous consequences. Therefore, when a bitter dispute arose about whether an oracle was true or false, the final argument was always, "In the end you will have to realize that I am telling you the truth because the events of which I am speaking will in fact happen to you." So Isaiah insisted that his oracles must be written down and kept so that in course of time the people would grasp the truth of what he had been saying (Isa. 8:16ff.). On this question see below, Chap. 14.

WORSHIP AND OBEDIENCE

11. The Dead Do Not Praise YHWH

BACKGROUND READING: The book of Psalms.[1]

The Praises of Israel

We come now to the understanding of YHWH as it was expressed in Israelite worship, and for this our best source is the book of Psalms. This is the longest book in the *Testament,* and it is also the one which most strongly resists any kind of selective reading. It would be quite false to suggest that one psalm provides a better illustration of Israelite worship than another. Hence in this chapter we must allow much greater space for direct quotation and permit, as far as possible, the whole body of psalms to speak for themselves. We may profitably begin with the following:

> The dead do not praise YHWH,
>   nor do any that go down into silence.
>
> Psalm 115:17

> Sheol[2] cannot thank thee,
>   death cannot praise thee;
> those who go down to the pit cannot hope
>   for thy faithfulness.
> The living, the living, he thanks thee,
>   as I do this day.
>
> Isaiah 38:18–19

Here we may notice three important points. The first is that "only there, where death is, is there no praise. Where there is life, there is praise. The possibility that there could also be life in which there was

---

1. For those coming to the Psalms for the first time it might be helpful to begin with the collection of short psalms, 120–134, known as the "Songs of Ascent." Most of the main themes are to be found there.
2. I.e., the realm of the dead.

133

no praise, life that did *not* praise God, does not enter the picture here. As death is characterized in that there is no longer any praise there, so praise belongs to life."[3] For the psalmists, life belonged together with the praise of YHWH, who is the source of all light and life,[4] and so to cease to praise him would be to cease truly to live, and to descend into the realm of meaningless death.

The second point is the importance of the phrase "this day," which distinguishes the worship of Israel from that of the surrounding nations. All nations accorded praise to their gods, for to worship a god is to praise him. But their praise was largely either in general terms or in terms of the constantly repeated pattern, of life given by the sun day after day and reborn each returning spring. The Israelites alone praised their God so frequently for acts and events in history.[5]

Third, the quotation from the Psalm of Hezekiah in Isaiah 38:9–20 shows that in the *Testament* psalms are by no means confined to the Psalter, i.e., the book of Psalms. The songs in which the ancient Israelites made known the glory of YHWH or besought his help sprang from the ongoing life of the people, and must not be thought of as only the ritual acts of the sanctuary.[6] Out of their life came their praises. We must therefore not draw any hard-and-fast line between the sanctuary and the world outside, between the sacred and the profane,[7] nor must we separate out into exclusive categories the people who performed the service of YHWH in the sanctuary.

In the Psalms YHWH is addressed as "teacher":

3. Claus Westermann, *The Praise of God in the Psalms,* trans. Keith R. Crim (London: Epworth Press, 1965), p. 159. See also Pss. 6:5; 30:9; 88:10–11; 119:175.

4. Pss. 16:11; 18:28; 27:1; 36:9; 119:105; 147:2–20; 148.

5. There is a helpful comparison of the Babylonian, Egyptian and Israelite psalms in Westermann, *Praise of God,* Chap. 2. See also Charles Gordon Cumming, *The Assyrian and Hebrew Hymns of Praise* (New York: AMS Press, 1966).

6. For psalms outside the Psalter see e.g., Exod. 15; Num. 10:35–36; Deut. 32:1–43; Judg. 5:1–31; I Sam. 2:1–10; II Sam. 22 (= Ps. 18); 23:1–7; Jonah 2:1–9; Hab. 3.

7. Pss. 15 and 24:3–6 speak of the purity needed by those who enter the sanctuary to worship. There was certainly a distinction from the world outside, but it was not an absolute one. The sanctuary was a large open space, in which stood the "house," i.e., the building set aside for YHWH. Although primarily intended as an area for ceremonial worship, the sanctuary provided space for other activities as well, e.g., meetings between people (Neh. 6:10), teaching, etc. This tradition of the sanctuary as primarily an enclosed space, of which only part is a building, persists in the Middle East today in the Muslim mosque. The mosque is intended primarily for prayer, but the open space serves also for meeting, study, conversation, etc. The Muslim schoolboy will go there to study for an examination, for he often does not have the space at home. The situation in ancient Israel must have been rather similar.

> I bless YHWH who gives me counsel;
> in the night also my heart instructs me.
>
> Psalm 16:7

> Make me to know thy ways, YHWH;
> teach me thy paths.
> Lead me in thy truth, and teach me,
> for thou art the God of my salvation.
>
> Psalm 25:4–5

> So teach us to number our days,
> that we may garner a heart of wisdom.
>
> Psalm 90:12 (D. B.)

> Teach me, YHWH, the way of thy statutes;
> and I will keep it to the end.
> Give me understanding, that I may keep thy law,
> and observe it with my whole heart.
>
> Psalm 119:33–34; cf. vv. 66 and 99–102

This teaching was given, as we have seen in the last chapter, through the priest, the prophet and the wise elder. Although the prophet and the elder certainly spoke in the market at the gate, all three taught within the sanctuary, and both priest and prophet had an important role in the ritual worship. The priest offered sacrifice and the prophet announced the oracle of YHWH. We need also to remember how small was even the city of Jerusalem, and that all the leading people in the community almost certainly knew each other personally. They met together constantly and they shared a common heritage. They could, of course, disagree with each other vehemently, but their teaching, however diverse, was all part of one spectrum, and their disagreements only extreme positions on it. That the teaching of the three groups is not to be seen as separate, but as part of one whole fabric, is shown by the fact that the words of all three are to be found in the Psalter, as well of course as the words of the worshipers.[8] For the purpose of careful study it is necessary to separate and analyze, but for sympathetic understanding we must try to look at the entirety.

The same applies to the problem of the date of the psalms. We do not understand them if we do not perceive them as dynamic and living—

---

8. The word of the priest is to be seen, for instance, in the blessing of the people (Pss. 134; 20:1–5), and in the summons to sacrifice (Ps. 76:11). The words of the Wise are to be found in such didactic psalms as 37, 49, and 127, with their close parallels to the book of Proverbs. Ps. 128 contains both proverbial wisdom and the priestly blessing. Ps. 50 is decidedly prophetic, and should be compared with, e.g., Micah 6:1–8.

endowed with such vitality that the words often leap out of the page, and, though written two and a half millennia ago, still used today in the worship of synagogue and church. This vital, living quality was there at the beginning. The psalms were embedded in the activity of the people and had sprouted from their brief cries of praise when they saw the mighty acts of YHWH.[9] These praises continued to grow and blossom for nearly a thousand years. Some psalms, e.g., Psalm 18, may go back to the very beginning of the monarchy, and others, e.g., 137, belong to the time of the Exile. Some are even later,[10] and others have their origins in worship long before the time of Israel.[11] Psalms continued to be written as long as the Temple stood, and psalms later than the *Testament* are to be found in the Dead Sea Scrolls. Moreover, individual psalms did not remain static. They grew and were added to as the life of the community developed. Psalm 19, for instance, is apparently a combination of an earlier hymn (vv. 1–6) with a later meditation in the wisdom tradition (7–14), but C. S. Lewis can speak of it as "one of the greatest lyrics in the world."[12] This vitality, in more than one sense of the word, is evidence again of the truth that praise and life are inseparable.

The Speaking of Man to God

Heinrich Ott has written of being told once by Martin Buber, "I met our former Prime Minister, David Ben Gurion, at a reception. He asked me, 'Professor Buber, why do you really believe in God?' I answered him, 'If one could speak only *about* God then I would not believe either. But I believe in God because one can speak *to* him . . . .' "[13] It is this speaking to YHWH, and being spoken to by him, which is the whole essence of the Psalms, and brings most vividly to the fore the utterly personal quality of YHWH as he appears in the pages of the *Testament*.

Speaking to YHWH in the Psalms takes the form of praise and supplication:[14] (*a*) praise in terms of what YHWH has shown himself to be,

9. It is useful to compare the Song of Miriam, a very brief and ancient cry of praise in Exod. 15:21, with its developed form in the preceding psalm (Exod. 15:1–18).

10. E.g., the elaborate liturgical psalms, 105-106, 136.

11. See additional notes.

12. C. S. Lewis, *Reflections on the Psalms* (London: Collins, 1958), p. 56. See also additional notes.

13. Heinrich Ott, *God*, trans. Iain and Ute Nicol (Edinburgh: The Saint Andrew's Press, 1974), p. 79.

14. We are adopting here Westermann's terms (*Praise of God*, pp. 31–35) rather than the more usual hymn, thanksgiving, lament, etc.

> Praise YHWH, all nations!
> Extol him, all peoples!
> For great is his steadfast love towards us;
>   and the faithfulness of YHWH endures for ever.
>
> Psalm 117:1–2

more frequently, (*b*) praise in terms of what he has done,[15]

> Blessed be YHWH,
>   who has not given us
>   as prey to their teeth!
> We have escaped as a bird
>   from the snare of the fowlers;
> the snare is broken
>   and we have escaped!
>
> Psalm 124:6–7

(*c*) supplication for help in a critical situation,

> Have mercy upon us, YHWH, have mercy upon us,
>   for we have had more than enough of contempt.
> Too long our soul has been sated
>   with the scorn of those who are at ease,
>   the contempt of the proud.
>
> Psalm 123:3–4[16]

These praises and supplications are expressed both on behalf of the whole community, as in the examples given above, and in individual terms, as in some of the examples listed in the footnote. All the forms, however, merge into each other, "I" into "We," and sorrow into joy,

> Thou art my King and my God,
>   who ordainest victories for Jacob.
> Through thee we push down our foes;
>   through thy name we tread down our assailants.
> For not in my bow do I trust,
>   nor can my sword save me.
> But thou hast saved us from our foes,
>   and has put to confusion those who hate us.
>
> Psalm 44:4–7

> Give ear to my words, YHWH;
>   give heed to my groaning.
> Hearken to the sound of my cry,

15. "It can be safely said that without the Psalms much of the effect and meaning of the Old Testament would be absent from its revelation. They show us, in intense and profound, yet in simple and universal expression, what revelation is by what revelation does" (Robinson, *Inspiration and Revelation*, p. 265).

16. For further examples see, e.g., (*a*) Pss. 121; 147:1–11; 149; 150; (*b*) Pss. 40:1–3; 46:8–10; 66:5–7; 85:1–3; (*c*) Pss. 12:1–2; 54:1–3; 55:1–15; 60:1–3. However, this is but a small selection from the whole.

> my King and my God,
>   for to thee do I pray.
>
> .   .   .   .
>
> Let all who take refuge in thee rejoice,
>   let them ever sing for joy;
>
> .   .   .   .
>
> For thou dost bless the righteous, YHWH,
>   thou dost cover him with favor as with a shield.
>
>   Psalm 5:1–2, 11–12

There is indeed no sorrow too desolate for praise, nor any that can
sunder the solitary from the community,

> These things I remember,
>   as I pour out my soul:
> how I went with the throng,
>   and led them in procession to the house of God,
> with glad shouts and songs of thanksgiving,
>   a multitude keeping festival.
> Why are you cast down, O my soul,
>   and why are you disquieted within me?
> Hope in God; for I shall again praise him,
>   my help and my God.
>
>   Psalm 42:4–5[17]

> Out of the depths I cry to thee, YHWH!
>   YHWH, hear my voice!
> Let thy ears be attentive
>   to the voice of my supplications!
>
> .   .   .   .
>
> O Israel, hope in YHWH!
>   for with YHWH there is steadfast love,
>   and with him is plenteous redemption.
>
>   Psalm 130:1–2, 7–8

> My God, my God, why has thou forsaken me?
>   Why art thou so far from helping me,
>   from the words of my groaning?
> O my God, I cry by day, but thou dost not answer;
>   and by night, but find no rest.
>
> .   .   .   .
>
> I am a worm, and no man;
>   scorned by men, and despised by the people.
> All who see me mock at me.
>
> .   .   .   .
>
> I will tell of thy name to my brethren;
>   in the midst of the congregation I will praise thee:

17. The whole of Pss. 42–43, which are really one psalm, should be read in this
context.

> You who fear YHWH, praise him!
> all you sons of Jacob, glorify him,
> and stand in awe of him, all you sons of Israel!
>
> Psalm 22:1–2, 6–7, 22–23

This binding together of lament and thanksgiving into one whole is one of the chief features which distinguish the Hebrew psalms from those of the surrounding nations, and there is in the whole Psalter almost no lamentation which does not breathe forth confidence or explode into praise.[18] Living as they did at the crossroads of the world, the people were well acquainted with grief, but in the Temple all cried, "Glory!"[19]

The Disclosure of YHWH in the Psalms

We have already seen in the two previous chapters how the worship of Israel was built upon the understanding of Creation and covenant,

> YHWH, thou hast been our dwelling place
> in all generations.
> Before the mountains were brought forth,
> or ever thou hadst formed the earth and the world,
> from everlasting to everlasting thou art God.
>
> Psalm 90:1–2

> Gather to me my faithful ones,
> who made a covenant with me by sacrifice!
>
> Psalm 50:5

> Thou hast said, "I have made a covenant with my chosen one,
> I have sworn to David, my servant:
> 'I will establish your descendants for ever,
> I will build your throne for all generations.' "
>
> Psalm 89:3–4[20]

Creation and covenant were the basis of their abiding confidence in YHWH. In the Psalter no place is allowed to other gods, and vain was the help of man.

---

18. The "laments" among the Psalms include 3, 4, 5, 6, 7, 12, 13, 17, 22, 25, 26, 27, 28, 30, 31, 32, 35, 38, 39, 40, 41, 42–43, 44, 51, 54, 55, 56, 57, 59, 60, 61, 63, 64, 69, 70, 71, 74, 77, 79, 80, 83, 85, 86, 88, 90, 94, 102, 109, 123, 125, 126, 130, 140, 141, 142, 143. Ps. 88 comes, it is true, closest to complete desolation.

19. Ps. 29:9.

20. Covenant included both the covenant at Sinai and the covenant with the house of David, e.g., Pss. 25:14; 44:17; 74:20–21; 103:18; 105:7–11; 111:5; 132:11–12. But the concept is more pervasive in the Psalter than this list would suggest. Every mention of *hesed* (translated "steadfast love" in RSV and "loving kindness" in KJV) presupposes the covenant, for it means unshakable loyalty to the agreement. See Pss. 17:7; 25:6; 26:3; 36:7, 10; 40:10, 11; 42:8; 48:9; 51:1; 63:3; 69:16; 88:11; 89:33, 49; 92:2; 103:4; 107:43; 119:88, 149, 159; 138:2; 143:8.

> Put not your trust in princes,
>> in a son of man, in whom there is no help.
>>>> Psalm 146:3

> Yet thou art holy,
>> enthroned on the praises of Israel.
> In thee our fathers trusted;
>> they trusted, and thou didst deliver them.
> To thee they cried, and were saved.
>>>> Psalm 22:3–5

YHWH alone was king, the absolute ruler of the universe.

> Sing praises to God, sing praises!
>> sing praises to our king, sing praises!
> For God is the king of all the earth;
>> sing praises with a psalm!
> God reigns over the nations;
>> God sits upon his holy throne.
>>>> Psalm 47:6–8

> YHWH reigns; he is robed in majesty;
>> YHWH is robed, he is girded with strength.
> Yea, the world is established; it shall never be moved;
>> thy throne is established from of old;
>> thou art from everlasting.
>>>> Psalm 93:1–2

To praise YHWH as king meant to acclaim him as defender of his people and the supreme judge, for that is what the word "king" meant in those days. In the time of Samuel the people had demanded a king so that he "may govern us and go out before us and fight our battles,"[21] and Solomon, upon becoming king, prayed for an "understanding mind to govern thy people, that I may discern between good and evil."[22] So much the more did YHWH defend and govern, for the earthly king was but his vassal.

> Contend, YHWH, with those who contend with me;
>> fight against those who fight against me!
> Take hold of shield and buckler,
>> and rise for my help!
>>>> Psalm 35:1–2

> If it had not been YHWH who was on our side,
>> when men rose up against us,
> then they would have swallowed us up alive,
>> when their anger was kindled against us.
>>>> Psalm 124:2–3

21. I Sam. 8:19.   22. I Kings 3:9.

YHWH sits enthroned for ever,
   he has established his throne for judgment;
and he judges the world with righteousness,
   he judges the peoples with equity.

Psalm 9:7–8

YHWH's throne is in heaven:
   his eyes behold, his eyelids test, the children of men.
YHWH tests the righteous and the wicked,
   and his soul hates him that loves violence.

Psalm 11:4–66[23]

In ancient Israel the king, if he was fulfilling his true function, represented the hope of all those who had suffered injustice, and who were unable to get a fair trial.[24] All who had been wronged could go to him, knowing both that he had full power to act and that ideally his position and wealth set him above any temptation of bribery. He had the authority to right all wrongs and to cherish and maintain law and order in the land in the true sense of the term.[25] But clearly, not all the kings of Israel and Judah did in fact fulfill this function, and of only some is it written that the people did them great honor at their death, or that the minstrels continued long after to make lamentation for them.[26] YHWH alone was held to perform this function with complete faithfulness, and to be actively concerned for "the comfortless troubles' sake of the needy" and "the deep sighing of the poor."[27]

The ordinary people knew themselves to live in a manifestly unjust world. They were at the mercy of the wealthy merchants and landowners, and even more seriously at the mercy of the great international powers, from whom not even the king could normally protect them. Therefore, all creation should rejoice at the presence of YHWH,

   for he comes to judge the earth;
  he will judge the world with righteousness,
   and the peoples with his truth.

Psalm 96:13

Come, behold the works of YHWH,
   how he wrought desolations in the earth.
He makes wars to cease to the end of the earth;
   he breaks the bow and shatters the spear,

---

23. See also Pss. 7:8, 12; 14:2; 50:6; 75:6–7; 76:8–9; 99:4.
24. This function is set out clearly in 72:1–4, a psalm for the enthronement of a new king.
25. See additional notes.
26. This was said of Hezekiah and Josiah (II Chron. 32:33; 35:25).
27. From Miles Coverdale's translation of Ps. 12:5 in the "Great Bible" (1638 C.E.).

> he burns the chariots with fire!
> "Be still, and know that I am God.
> I am exalted among the nations,
> I am exalted in the earth."
>
> Psalm 46:8–10

Of the greatest importance is the dynamic activity of YHWH, so continually insisted upon in the *Testament,* combined with overwhelming passion for righteousness.

> God is a righteous judge,
> and a God who has indignation every day.
>
> Psalm 7:11

YHWH is not in the *Testament* an absentee ruler, a *deus otiosus,* remote and indifferent,

> Have they no knowledge, all the evildoers,
> who eat up my people as they eat bread,
> and do not call upon YHWH?
>
> Psalm 14:4, cf. 53:1–5

> Why does the wicked renounce God,
> and say in his heart, "Thou wilt not call to account"?
> Thou dost see; yea, thou dost note trouble and vexation,
> that thou mayest take it into thy hands.
>
> Psalm 10:13–14

> "Because the poor are despoiled, because the needy groan,
> I will now arise" says YHWH,
> "I will place him in the safety for which he longs."
>
> Psalm 12:5

> YHWH sets the prisoners free;
> YHWH opens the eyes of the blind.
> YHWH lifts up those who are bowed down;
> YHWH loves the righteous.
> YHWH watches over the sojourners,
> he upholds the widow and the fatherless;
> but the way of the wicked he brings to ruin.
>
> Psalm 146:7–9[28]

The absolute righteousness and integrity of YHWH are to be taken seriously, and those who close their hearts to pity, speaking arrogantly with their mouths,[29] should beware of his judgment, for

---

28. For other passages describing YHWH as the protector of the helpless, see Pss. 9:9–10, 12, 18; 10:14, 17–18; 68:5–6; 69:33; 103:6; 113:5–9; 140:12.
29. Ps. 17:10.

> To the wicked God says:
> "What right have you to recite my statutes,[30]
>   or take my covenant on your lips?
> For you hate discipline,
>   and you cast my words behind you.
> If you see a thief, you are a friend of his;
>   and you keep company with adulterers.
> You give your mouth free rein for evil,
>   and your tongue frames deceit.
> You sit and speak against your brother;
>   you slander your own mother's son.
> These things you have done and I have been silent;
>   you thought that I was one like yourself.
> But now I rebuke you, and lay the charge before you."
>
> Psalm 50:16-21

Yet never to be forgotten is the mercy of YHWH, who is "good and forgiving, abounding in steadfast love to all who call upon thee."[31] One of the most constant refrains of Israelite worship was the proclamation:

> Thou, YHWH, art a God merciful and gracious,
>   slow to anger and abounding in steadfast love and mercy.
>
> Psalms 86:15; 103:8; 145:8[32]

In the *Testament,* the absolutely just judge is the one who sees that the whole purpose of justice is the reestablishment of the sinner. To those who say, "Our transgressions and our sins are upon us, and we waste away because of them; how then can we live?" the prophetic answer is emphatic: "As I live, says YHWH, I do not enjoy myself when a wicked person dies. What I want is that the wicked should turn back from his way and live. Turn back, turn back from your evil ways, for why will you die?"[33]

> Let the wicked forsake his way,
>   and the unrighteous man his thoughts;
> let him return to YHWH, that he may have mercy on him,
>   and to our God, for he will abundantly pardon.
>
> Isaiah 55:7

These oracles were both spoken in the dark days of the Exile, but the ideas were not new, for they were embedded already in Israelite worship,

30. This psalm probably belongs to a covenant renewal festival when the statutes were recited publicly. The prophet proclaimed this oracle of YHWH to the people in the course of the ceremony.
31. Ps. 86:5.
32. This refrain is not confined to the Psalms. See also Exod. 34:6; Deut. 4:31; II Chron. 30:9; Neh. 9:17, 31; Joel 2:13; Jonah 4:2.
33. Ezek. 33:10-11 (trans. D. B.).

When our transgressions prevail over us,
    thou dost forgive them.

Psalm 65:3

YHWH, thou wast favorable to thy land;
    thou didst restore the fortunes of Jacob.
Thou didst forgive the iniquity of thy people;
    thou didst pardon all their sin.

Psalm 85:1–2

Bless YHWH, O my soul,
    and forget not all his benefits,
who forgives all your iniquity,
    and heals all your disease.

.   .   .   .

He will not always chide,
    nor will he keep his anger for ever.
He does not deal with us according to our sins,
    nor requite us according to our iniquities.

.   .   .   .

As far as the east is from the west,
    so far does he remove our transgressions from us.
As a father pities his children,
    So YHWH pities those who fear him.
For he knows our frame;
    he remembers that we are dust.

Psalm 103:2–14[34]

The Psalms and the People

In the language of the Psalms we come closest to the thinking of the ordinary Israelites. Certainly such superb poetry can hardly have been composed by mere peasants, and the entire Psalter has been purged of the corruptions of popular Israelite and Judean worship, so vividly portrayed in Ezekiel 8. Nevertheless, as we have seen, the first development of the psalms began, not in the formal worship of the sanctuary, but in the actual life of the people: in the rejoicing at harvest time, or at deliverance from some enemy, and in the tragedies of sickness and injustice. Moreover, all male members of the community participated fully in the worship at the great festivals, if not at other times.[35] The words of the worship were *their*

34. Some have argued on linguistic grounds that this psalm, one of the un-doubted glories of the Psalter, is postexilic, e.g., Deissler, *Le Livre des Psaumes,* Vol. II, p. 129. Not all scholars, however, agree and it seems best to ascribe it tentatively to the time of the monarchy.

35. The three great feasts were unleavened bread (Passover), wheat harvest (Weeks) and the vintage (Booths). This last, concluding the old year and preparing

words, and the blessing of the priests as well as the injunctions of the prophets were addressed to the multitude.[36]

We must beware, of course, of thinking that in the Psalter the whole of Israelite worship is portrayed. For instance, from the relatively small number of references to sacrifice, some of them favorable, but some also critical, it would be difficult to grasp how large a part sacrifices played in the activity of the sanctuary right up to the destruction of the Temple in 70 C.E.[37] Yet what is manifested beyond all doubt is the glory, majesty, authority, integrity, and faithfulness of YHWH, together with his constant activity, his mighty acts, both now and in the past, his demands for justice, and his mercy and forgiveness.

These are the basis of the prophetic teaching.[38] The Word of YHWH through the prophets was proclaimed in the sanctuary as well as in the market place, and the words in which the great prophets of the *Testament* interpreted the Word were, more often than not, the words of Israelite worship. Before we study the Prophets, therefore, we need to have first an intimate knowledge of the Psalms.

Yet such is the willfulness of man, and his readiness to make himself the criterion of worth, that even the exalted language of true adoration can become for him a delusion and a deceit. In celebrating, as they were right to do, the justice and the mighty acts of YHWH, the people slipped only too easily into claiming for themselves the mercy, and leaving the condemnation to those outside.[39] We must not exaggerate this, for confession of sin is an integral part of the Psalms.[40] Nevertheless, it did happen, and the people were, not unnaturally, wont to think of military glory, "the pride of Jacob" as something which YHWH loved.[41]

But the Word of YHWH, though interpreted in the words of Israelite

---

for the new, was apparently the occasion also of the renewal of the covenant, either annually or every seven years. Many of the psalms, e.g., 50, 65, 78, seem to belong originally to this festival. This is discussed by Arthur Weiser (*The Psalms: A Commentary*, trans. Herbert Hartwell, Philadelphia: The Westminster Press, 1962, pp. 35–52), though he has been criticized for attempting to fit all the psalms into this category. For the three feasts see Exod. 23:14–17; 34:22–23; Deut. 16:1–17.

36. For summons to the people to join in the recital of the mighty acts of YHWH, see Pss. 124:1; 129:1. In Ps. 136 the second half of each verse is the congregational response.

37. See Pss. 4:5; 5:3; 20:3; 40:6–7; 50:5, 8; 51:16–19; 54:6; 56:12; 66: 13–15; 76:11; 116:17; 141:2. The paying of vows also refers to the making of an offering, or sacrifice (Pss. 22:25; 50:14; 56:12; 61:5, 8; 66:13; 76:11; 116:14, 18).

38. Hos. 6:6.

39. This was not, of course, an error peculiar to Israelites. It is a human failing, and some of us believe that today it colors much of what we call "liturgical revival."

40. Pss. 19:12ff.; 25:7, 11; 32:1–5; 38:18; 51:1–9; 106:6; 139:23–24; 141: 3–5; 143:2.

41. Ps. 47:4.

worship, was not constrained by those words, and could wholly reverse them:

> YHWH, God, has sworn by himself:
> I abhor the pride of Jacob.
>
> Amos 6:8[42]

It is not surprising that Amos was told to leave the sanctuary, and indeed, to get out of the country altogether.[43] His oracles seemed to those in power dangerously close to "cursing God and the king,"[44] and they told him to go. They were sure that they had the authority of Scripture for saying so, but they did not speak the Word of God.

ADDITIONAL NOTES TO CHAPTER 11

11. Ps. 29 is generally agreed to be a Canaanite (probably Phoenician) hymn, transformed to the worship of YHWH, whose name is insisted upon. The places mentioned are Phoenician and Syrian, Kadesh being the famous Syrian town of that name. In Israelite thinking, of course, it became the Kadesh of the Exodus experience. Ps. 104 has already been mentioned in Chap. 9 as having been based upon a much earlier Egyptian hymn to the Sun. Fifty years ago it was common to think of most of the psalms as being postexilic and to speak of the Psalter as "the hymn book of the Second Temple." Evidence from parallels in the surrounding nations has caused modern scholars to retreat from this position and recent commentaries have tended to ascribe the great majority of the psalms to the period of the Israelite monarchy.

12. Most scholars consider that the psalm has an earlier and a later section, but not all would agree. J. H. Eaton and Alphonse Deissler both regard it as a unity, though Eaton says that the first section contains ancient material (Eaton, *Psalms: An Introduction and Commentary*, London: SCM Press, 1967, p. 65; Deissler, *Le Livre des Psaumes*, Paris: Beauchesne, 1966, Vol. I, p. 95). There can be no doubt, however, that Ps. 108 is composed of parts of two other psalms (57:1–11; 60:5–12).

25. When I first went to Jordan (then Transjordan) forty years ago, the Emir Abdullah still held open court every Friday after attending the prayers in the mosque. Anyone in the country could go to him for help, and he viewed this direct access to the ruler as an essential of good government.

42. The word translated "pride" is *gaon*, which means "swelling, exaltation." It is used, for example, for the jungle area each side of the river Jordan, where the river regularly overflowed its banks in spring (Josh. 3:15; Jer. 12:5; 49:19; 50:44; Zech. 11:2). From Ps. 46:3 and from the other passages in the oracles collected in Amos 6 (vv. 1–2, 13) the sense of military expansion seems here unavoidable. At this period the Israelite empire had reached its greatest extent since the time of David (II Kings 14:25). Curiously enough, hardly any commentator has noticed that Amos is directly contradicting the psalm.

42. See additional notes.
43. Amos 7:10–13.
44. Exod. 22:28; see also I Kings 21:13.

12. The Words of the Wise

BACKGROUND READING: Proverbs 10–29.

> To understand a proverb and a figure,
> the words of the wise and their riddles.
>
> Proverbs 1:6

Wisdom and Wise Men

As we have already seen, wise men formed, together with the prophets and priests, a recognizable class or group in ancient Israel. They had their own distinctive body of teaching, and their words are to be found in what today we call the Wisdom literature, that is to say the books of Proverbs, Job, Ecclesiastes (or Qoheleth), and in some of the Psalms.[1] Ecclesiastes is one of the very latest books in the *Testament,* but some of the material, especially in Proverbs, is very ancient, having first taken shape in the earliest days of the community. We are therefore concerned here, as we were in the Psalms, with a pattern of thought extending over the whole period of the *Testament* and continuing indeed well beyond it.

This literature has two roots, one local and one foreign. Within Israel itself there had always been men and women who were accounted "wise." They included a wide variety of people, talented craftsmen of various kinds,[2] women trained in the laments to sing at funerals,[3] knowledgeable pilots and shipbuilders,[4] and even those who squandered their skill in making graven images.[5] The wise were "the skilled and experienced, the workmen with technical knowledge, those learned in the ancient arts and lore, the elders, the fathers and mothers, the teachers in the schools for wisdom, the writers of songs and fables and allegories, the makers of

---

1. E.g. Pss. 1, 37, 73, 91, 119, 127, 128, 133, 139.
2. Exod. 28:3; 31:2–6; 35:10, 25–26; 35:30–36:8; I Kings 7:14; I Chron. 22:15; etc. N.B. The word translated in RSV as "ability" or "skill" is in Hebrew *hochmah,* or "wisdom."
3. Jer. 9:17.
4. Ezek. 27:8–9.　　5. Isa. 40:20; Jer. 10:9.

riddles and proverbs, the judges, the philosophers."[6] All these were understood to have been given wisdom and discernment by God, so that they might perceive the structure of things and use this knowledge for the benefit of the whole community. In course of time, however, when people spoke of the "wise men" they meant a more specialized group: those older and experienced persons, whose judgment was accepted in matters of dispute, and to whom the young and immature came for advice and teaching.

With the establishment of the monarchy, and especially during the reign of Solomon, another group of "wise men" had to be brought in from beyond the frontiers, since they did not yet exist in Israel. These were the trained scribes and administrators needed for the keeping of records, and the smooth running of the government, and particularly those learned men appointed to advise the king and to represent him in his dealings with foreign nations. In the early years of the administration there had been heavy reliance upon foreign models, and even when this was no longer needed, affairs of state sent the officials upon long journeys and kept them in constant contact with the outside world. In consequence, their "wisdom" was not localized, but international in character. This was thought entirely proper, for the wisdom of the great imperial powers and such nations as Phoenicia and Tyre, with their vast international trade, was proverbial in Israel.[7]

These two groups, the wise elders with their roots firmly in Israelite soil and the royal advisers gathering knowledge and understanding from all over the world, did not remain separate. Both were concerned with administration and education, and so their functions became merged. Disputes would be adjudicated both by local elders and by officially appointed judges, and in the last resort by the king himself, as the chief judge. Education involved not only the training of all young men to play their part in the community, but also the more specialized teaching of those who would carry on their fathers' work in government, and especially the preparation of the young heir to the throne.

With this intermingling of the two sources of wisdom there developed that distinct group of people who came to be known succinctly as "the Wise." Though they cannot have been confined to the capital, the main body of them were certainly to be found there, and their work was done in judgment at the gate, in teaching and discussion in the Temple courts, and in counsel and administration in the royal palace, immediately next

6. Sheldon Blank, "Wisdom," *ID*, IV, p. 856.
7. See e.g., Isa. 19:11–13; Jer. 49:7; Ezek. 28:3–5, 11, 17; Dan. 2:12; 5:7; Obad. 8. It is true that the prophets often condemn the wisdom of the other nations, but the fact that they think it necessary to do so shows that this wisdom was already famous.

door to the Temple. In general their accumulated wisdom was committed to memory, but from time to time during the monarchy collections of sayings of the wise were made in writing.[8] We find these in the *Testament* gathered together in Proverbs 10–29.[9]

With the destruction of Jerusalem and the beginning of the Exile an important change took place. Henceforward there would be no more royal government or great business of state, and the administrative function of the wise came, therefore, to have only a minor role. On the other hand, much importance was attached to educating the young in their duties as members of the Jewish community. The vast body of inherited Israelite wisdom was in future dedicated to this purpose. It took on also a more consciously literary character, such as we find in the poems in Job. Yet, though the whole thrust of this education was designed to maintain a community faithful to the God of Israel, and obedient to his laws, the thinking of the wise was still strongly influenced by foreign ideas, and maintained its definite international character. The Exile in Babylon, the tremendous impact of Persian, and subsequently Greek, thought, and constant communication with Jewish communities now widely scattered over the world—all contributed to ensure this. Finally, a new element entered into their thinking. This was the beginning of speculative thought, which could often be strongly critical of traditional wisdom teaching. This is illustrated by the book of Job, where the speeches of Elihu in chapters 32–37 were almost certainly added by a more orthodox writer to redress the balance of Job's criticism. It becomes even stronger in the third-century book of Ecclesiastes.

The book of Job has as its background the disaster of the Exile, a problem which was to exercise Jewish minds for years after it happened, and so we must postpone consideration of it until we come to that period.[10] Ecclesiastes belongs to the struggle to come to terms with Greek thought, but to discuss this struggle would mean examining also the later Wisdom literature which lies outside the *Testament*.[11] Therefore, in this chapter we must confine ourselves to Proverbs 10–29. Here we have the words of the Wise as they developed during the more than four centuries

8. The clearest indication of this is found in Prov. 25:1, which speaks of a collection made by the men of Hezekiah's court.

9. The first nine chapters of Proverbs contain ten discourses, added in the fourth or third century B.C.E. to provide an introduction to the older collection. Chapters 30 and 31 are made up of four short appendixes, also added at a later date.

10. See below, Chap. 15.

11. Especially the book of Wisdom and Ecclesiasticus (or Sirach). These belong to that group of books which do not form part of the Hebrew Bible, but are found in the ancient Greek version of the Hebrew Scriptures known as the Septuagint. In Catholic Bibles they are included as part of the Old Testament, but are described as "deutero-canonical," i.e., added later to the Canon.

of the monarchy. They parallel in time the words of the great prophets, but they were not addressed to the same problems.

Where Shall Wisdom Be Found?

> The beginning of wisdom is this: Get wisdom
> and whatever you get, get insight.

So said a later Wisdom teacher,[12] and this certainly was, from the very beginning, the purpose of those who studied to be wise, but the problem was how to attain it.

> Where shall wisdom be found?
> And where is the place of understanding?
> Man does not know the way to it.
>
> Job 28:12–13

Moreover, what were they looking for when they searched for wisdom, and studied the writings of other nations in order to discover it?[13]

They were trying to learn the secret of a harmonious society, of all that is comprised in the Hebrew word *shalom*. This means, as does also its Arabic equivalent *salaam,* wholeness, completeness, and therefore soundness, well-being, welfare, health, peace, friendship, and good relations of all members of the community with each other. The chief concern of the Wise, whether they were teachers, judges, or members of the royal council, was the building up, and the maintenance from age to age, of a society that was at unity in itself. They were well acquainted with the dangers of civil strife and rebellion, and they saw as good and wise everything which contributed to the harmony and well-being of the country, and as evil and foolish all those activities and attitudes of mind which made for strife and dissension.

"The good was experienced . . . quite simply as a force, as something which determined life, something experienced daily as effective, that is as something present, about which there need be as little discussion as about light and darkness, the good was therefore . . . something which was very definitely active. 'Good' is that which does good; 'evil' is that which causes harm. Both good and evil create social conditions; in a completely 'outward' sense they can build up or destroy the community, property, happiness, reputation, welfare of children and much more besides."[14]

---

12. Prov. 4:7.
13. Prov. 22:17–24:22 is quite evidently based upon the Egyptian *Instruction of Amen-em-opet.* See Pritchard, ANET, pp. 421–24.
14. Gerhard von Rad, *Wisdom in Israel,* trans. James D. Martin (Nashville: Abingdon Press, 1972), p. 77.

The Wise were well aware that poverty is a major cause of civil disorder, and so they sought to promote careful cultivation of the fields and
an equitable distribution of wealth, rebuking both the lazy and the
avaricious.

> I passed by the field of a sluggard,
>> by the vineyard of a man without sense;
> and lo, it was all overgrown with thorns;
>> and the ground was covered with nettles;
>> and its stone wall was broken down.
> Then I saw and considered it;
>> I looked and received instruction.
> A little sleep, a little slumber,
>> a little folding of the hands to rest,
> and poverty will come upon you like a robber,
>> and want like an armed man.
>>> Proverbs 24:30–34[15]

> All day long the wicked covets,
>> but the righteous gives and does not hold back.
>>> Proverbs 21:26[16]

They were concerned also to see that justice was done: first that the
causes of dispute and litigation be removed, and second that if a case
should come to court it should be judged fairly.

> Remove not the ancient landmark,
>> which your fathers have set.
>>> Proverbs 22:28[17]

> A false witness will not go unpunished,
>> and he who utters lies will perish.
>>> Proverbs 19:9

> A wicked man accepts a bribe from the bosom
>> to pervert the ways of justice.
>>> Proverbs 17:23[18]

Throughout the varied collection of sayings we find a deep concern for
good government, and especially for the role of the king, who sets the
standard which others follow, for

> if a ruler listens to falsehood,
>> all his officials will be wicked.
>>> Proverbs 29:12

15. Cf., Prov. 10:4–5, 26; 13:4; 14:23; 20:4; 26:16; etc.
16. Cf., Prov. 11:26; 22:9; etc.   17. Cf., Prov. 23:10.
18. Cf., Prov. 15:27; 16:8; 18:5; 19:9; etc.

In their terms a righteous man is one who "understands the rights of the poor,"[19] and

> if a king judges the poor with equity
>   his throne will be established for ever.
>
> Proverbs 29:14

To promote this wholeness and well-being of society the virtues they inculcated were the avoidance of all envy, slander, and pride,[20] and more positively generosity, tolerance, humility and that most difficult of all virtues, readiness to forgive one's enemies:

> If your enemy is hungry, give him bread to eat;
>   and if he is thirsty, give him water to drink.
>
> Proverbs 25:21

None of this wisdom was peculiarly Israelite, for the principles of justice and harmony in society are universal. Those who were responsible for administering and maintaining the patterns of society were therefore entirely right to learn from the experience of other nations, and to seek this kind of wisdom as widely as possible. Nevertheless, their presentation of it was thoroughly Israelite, for it had to be tested against their own experience, and interpreted in terms true to that experience.

This is evident from the marked down-playing of nature as a source of wisdom. The Wise shared with the prophets of YHWH a profound distrust of all attempts to use anything in nature as representing the ultimate Reality, from which all meaning is derived, and they give no evidence of any systematic study of the natural world. Both in Proverbs 10–29 and in the prophetic literature of the same period parallels drawn from nature are never more than general knowledge, such as comes from casual, day-to-day observation.

> As snow in summer or rain in harvest,
>   so honor is not fitting for a fool.
>
> Proverbs 26:1

> Like a roaring lion or a charging bear,
>   is a wicked ruler over a poor people.
>
> Proverbs 28:15[21]

In the prolonged struggle against seeing the natural world as "sacred," in the sense of revealing the *mysterium tremendum et fascinans*[22] which both

---

19. Prov. 29:7.

20. See e.g., Prov. 11:2, 9, 12–13; 12:17, 22; 14:5; 16:32; 18:12; 19:11; 21:1–4; 24:1; 27:2.

21. See also Prov. 19:12; 25:13; and in the prophets, Isa. 1:3; Jer. 2:24; 8:7.

22. "The terrifying and fascinating mystery," a term used by Rudolf Otto in his book *The Idea of the Holy* for what comes upon man when he encounters the divine.

appalls mankind and lures them with a siren song, the Wise in Israel were wholeheartedly Yahwist. In their teaching those powerful symbols of the tree of life, the sacred spring, and the divine bull, which commanded the awe and reverence of the surrounding nations, become no more than metaphors:

> The fruit of the righteous is a tree of life,
> but lawlessness takes away lives.
>
> Proverbs 11:30[23]

> The teaching of the wise is a fountain of life,
> that one may avoid the snares of death.
>
> Proverbs 13:14[24]

> Where there are no oxen, there is no grain:
> but abundant crops come by the strength of an ox.
>
> Proverbs 14:4

It is true that King Solomon, traditionally the founder of wisdom in Israel, is said to have spoken "of trees, from the cedar that is in Lebanon to the hyssop that grows out of the wall. He spoke also of beasts, and of birds, and of reptiles, and of fish."[25] But there is good reason to think that this is a much later description of him.[26] In the Wisdom teaching of the monarchy, men are not instructed to study nature, nor do we find there any systematic arrangement of natural phenomena. Where we do find it is in the postexilic teaching, by which time, of course, the Wise had been exposed to the methods of Babylonian scholars and the struggle with Baal worship had been brought to a decisive end.[27]

The Fear of YHWH

The concern of the Wise was not with nature but with men and women, and with the patterns of human behavior. Consequently, many of their sayings seem to speak only of man, as is evidenced by most of what has been quoted so far. But it would be wrong to think of them as secular humanists, for whom God was distant and unconcerned. They believed that "the fear of YHWH is instruction in wisdom,"[28] and YHWH is

23. Cf., Prov. 13:12; 15:4.
24. See also Prov. 14:27; 16:22; and Ps. 1.
25. I Kings 4:33.
26. R. B. Y. Scott, "Solomon and the Beginnings of Wisdom in Israel," in *Wisdom in Israel and in the Ancient Near East,* ed. M. Noth and D. Winton Thomas (Leiden: E. J. Brill, 1960), pp. 262–79.
27. We find this method in the material added later to the book of Proverbs (Chaps. 1–9; 30–31; see e.g., 5:6–11; 30:18–31), in the book of Job, especially in the speeches of Elihu, e.g., 37:14–17, as well as in Wisdom literature later than the time of the *Testament.*
28. Prov. 15:33.

spoken of in Proverbs 10–29 sixty-six times. Moreover, for them God was unquestionably YHWH. They mention no other, and the more general word *Elohim* occurs only once.[29]

The word "fear" is itself apt to alarm the modern reader, who is inclined to think that the true God should inspire love rather than fear. But we need to recollect how seriously the ancient Israelites took the concept of "God," and how for them the word meant absolute Reality and dynamic power, against which no protection was possible. Only the fool does not stand in awe, and feel the cold grip of fear, when he is confronted by Reality and power over which he can exercise no control. For the Israelites no other power than that of YHWH could defend them against the terrifying onslaughts of their enemies, but this meant saying also that the power of YHWH was such that men and women must be afraid before it. And how much the more when together with power goes awareness of judgment and absolute righteousness!

To fear YHWH meant, therefore, to take him with the utmost seriousness, and this for the wise men, no less than for the prophets and the priests, was the foundation of all true wisdom and understanding. But when the Wise spoke of taking YHWH with deep seriousness, i.e., "fearing" him, the idea of overwhelming power does not seem to have been uppermost in their minds. They thought, rather, of that proper humility of the created being before his Creator, of which the prophet Micah also spoke,

> He has showed you, O man, what is good;
> and what does YHWH require of you
> but to do justice, and to love kindness [*hesed*],
> and to walk humbly with your God?
>
> Micah 6:8

They thought of the absence of arrogance, and the sense of moderation and restraint, which hold men back from getting into evil, and consequently dangerous, ways. Three sayings which have been grouped together illustrate this well:

> The rich and the poor meet together;
> YHWH is the maker of them all.
> A prudent man sees danger and hides himself;
> but the simple go on, and suffer for it.
> The reward for humility and the fear of YHWH
> is riches and honor and life.
>
> Proverbs 22:2–4

29. Prov. 25:2.

"He who oppresses a poor man insults his Maker," it is said elsewhere,[30] and this oppression cannot be practiced with impunity, for "YHWH tears down the house of the proud, but maintains the widow's boundaries."[31] Any man of sense, therefore, will perceive this danger and humble himself, for only where this sense of restraint prevails can that prosperity and well-being which make for human happiness prevail also. The goal of the Wise, as has been said above, was always harmony, and the binding into a tranquil whole of that human society which so easily disintegrates into bitterness and strife. YHWH they saw to be the only author of peace and builder of concord, and they taught steadfastly that knowledge of his ways could alone promote that unity which they so earnestly desired. It is true that they taught individuals, but they were not concerned with the individual as such. They abhorred all private gain, and urged any who listened to live at peace with other men, which they knew well was exactly what they would not do if left to themselves. Without the fear of YHWH they could see no hope for peace or justice.

> Better is a little with the fear of YHWH
>   than great treasure and trouble with it.
> Better is a dinner of herbs where love is
>   than a fatted ox and hatred with it.
>
>   Proverbs 15:16–17

> Every one who is arrogant is an abomination to YHWH;
>   be assured, he will not go unpunished.
> By loyalty and faithfulness iniquity is atoned for,
>   and by the fear of YHWH a man avoids evil.
> When a man's ways please YHWH,
>   he makes even his enemies to be at peace with him.
>
>   Proverbs 16:5–7

The Activity of YHWH in the Book of Proverbs

These teachers of wisdom were "sons of Israel" born and bred, and they could not speak of YHWH except in terms of his activity, and as one whose "eyes are in every place, keeping watch on the evil and the good."[32] All their instruction was given with a sense of his ever watchful presence, for

> the eyes of YHWH keep watch over knowledge,
> but he overthrows the words of the faithless.
>
>   Proverbs 22:12[33]

30. Prov. 14:31.   31. Prov. 15:25.
32. Prov. 15:3.
33. Cf., Prov. 15:11; 17:3; 21:1–2. See also additional notes.

YHWH they believed to be indeed the Creator, and his work of creation to be rational and directed toward a goal. "YHWH," they said, "has made everything for its purpose."[34] It is idle, therefore, for men to set forward their own purposes and plans as if YHWH could be left out of account.

> Many are the plans in the mind of a man,
>> but it is the purpose of YHWH that will be established.
>>>> Proverbs 19:21

> No wisdom, no understanding, no counsel,
>> can avail against YHWH.
> The horse is made ready for the day of battle,
>> but the victory belongs to YHWH.
>>>> Proverbs 21:30–31[35]

His activity is seen especially in terms of his passion for justice and integrity at the gate, and the prohibition of false weights and balances is always ascribed to him, and never in terms only of man's relation to man.

> A just balance and scales belong to YHWH;
>> all the weights in the bag are his work.
>>>> Proverbs 16:11[36]

The administration of justice is frequently mentioned without bringing in the name of YHWH directly, but this does not mean that the work of the judges was thought of as anything less than the work of YHWH, which he had entrusted to men.

> Evil men do not understand justice,
>> but those who seek YHWH understand it completely.
>>>> Proverbs 28:5[37]

The Wise would have agreed with the prophets that the most important service of YHWH is done in the gate rather than the sanctuary, and that

> to do righteousness and justice
>> is more acceptable to YHWH than sacrifice.
>>>> Proverbs 21:3[38]

In Proverbs, as in the Psalms, YHWH is himself the searching and testing judge, and "as the crucible is for silver, and the furnace for gold," so with no less intensity does YHWH test the hearts of men.[39] His ap-

34. Prov. 16:4.
35. Cf., Prov. 16:9, 33; 19:21; 20:22, 24.
36. Cf., Prov. 11:1; 20:10, 23.
37. For justice without the mention of YHWH see, e.g., Prov. 15:27; 16:8; 17:23; 18:5; 19:8; etc.
38. Cf., Isa. 1:11–17; Hos. 6:4–6; Amos 5:21–24; Micah 6:1–8.
39. Prov. 17:3.

pointed representative on earth is the king, to whom it should be an abomination to do evil,[40] and who, as he "sits on the throne of judgment, winnows all evil with his eyes,"[41] doing therefore on earth what YHWH does from his throne in heaven.[42] Similarly the judges throughout the land, being appointed by the king, are entrusted with the work of YHWH, who is present with power at each trial.

> Do not rob the poor, because he is poor,
>> or crush the afflicted at the gate;
> for YHWH will plead their cause,
>> and despoil of life those who despoil them.
>
> Proverbs 22:22–23

YHWH is the protector of the poor and needy, and of all who put their trust in him,[43] and the punisher of the wicked.[44]

It may be argued that none of this is new, and indeed it is not. There is no new revelation of God in these sayings, nor should we expect it. The wise men were not set in opposition to the prophets and the priests, for they understood the work of the seer and the teacher of *Torah* to be essential to the well-being of the community.

> Where there is no prophecy the people cast off restraint,
>> but blessed is he who keeps *Torah*.
>
> Proverbs 29:18

It is true that it was not given to them to see visions and dream dreams, to consult the oracle or to offer sacrifice for sin. To have taken upon themselves responsibilities entrusted by YHWH to other members of the community would have been exactly that arrogant behavior which they so wholly deplored. It was not their role to stir men to passionate enthusiasm or to bring them in penitence to their knees, to proclaim their joy or find words for their grief. Their job was to promote and maintain the peace, reconciling the people to each other, and without their knowledge and understanding the community could not have lived.

Before we take up again our study of the great crises of Israelite history and the tremendous oracles of mercy and judgment uttered by YHWH through his prophets, it is fitting to dwell for a while upon this other disclosure of himself to his people. It lacks the splendor and tempestuous force of the prophetic word, but it is no less the divine gift.

> Though YHWH give you the bread of adversity and the water of affliction,
> yet your Teacher will not hide himself any more, but your eyes shall see

40. Prov. 16:12.
41. Prov. 20:8.   42. Ps. 11:4.
43. Prov. 10:3; 15:25; 16:7; 18:10; 23:10–11.
44. Prov. 10:3, 27, 29; 16:5.

your Teacher. And your ears shall hear a word behind you, saying, "This is the way, walk in it."

.　　　　　　　　　　　　Isaiah 30:20–21

The words of the Wise enabled the people of YHWH, not only to live, but to live anywhere and under any conditions. Their broad tolerance, their patience and restraint, their humility and their learning, and above all their readiness to enter into discussion with foreign peoples and learn wisdom also from them, while at the same time remaining faithful to YHWH and to him alone—all this made known to the faithful how to live in true harmony, both among themselves and with the Creator of the world. "Happy is the man who finds wisdom," said a teacher who followed in their steps,[45] for he finds something more precious than jewels. "Nothing you desire can compare with her. . . . Her ways are ways of pleasantness, and all her paths are peace."

ADDITIONAL NOTES TO CHAPTER 12

33. Since the Wise were concerned with permanent patterns of behavior rather than the confrontation with YHWH through historical events, they were less inclined to think of YHWH in terms of the Absolutely Other. It is important to remember that the "Other" is a model for understanding "God," parallel to the models of Person, King, Judge and Father. It must not be used as a complete explanation of "God," because then it also becomes an idol. At the same time we need to recollect that the "otherness" of YHWH in no way excludes his presence. It is probably inaccurate to speak of YHWH as "immanent," because that means literally "dwelling in," and throughout the *Testament* the idea of YHWH dwelling anywhere is resolutely rejected. His dwelling is in heaven, but even the heaven of heavens cannot contain him. Yet though YHWH is not thought of as immanent, he is unquestionably held to be present, demanding here and now an answer from men and women. Here the Wise and the prophets would have been in agreement, and indeed, as the Wisdom literature develops, this theme of encounter becomes more marked. See, for instance, the personification of Wisdom in Prov. 1–9.

45. Prov. 3:13, 15, 17.

THE CLIMAX OF
PROPHETIC THOUGHT

13. Reality against Reality

BACKGROUND READING: II Kings 14:23–20:21; II Chronicles 26:1–15;
Isaiah 1; 5; 7–8; 9:8–10:19; 22:1–8; 28:1–30:17; 31; Hosea;
Amos; Micah 1–3; 6:1–7:7.

The Assyrian Empire and the Destruction of Identity

We must now resume our consideration of the crises listed in the
second chapter. It will be recalled that these were not merely temporary
problems, but calamities of frightening magnitude, thrusting the Israelite
people into a strange and foreign world, governed, it seemed, by values
altogether different from their own. Each crisis presented something
wholly new to their experience, something so serious and menacing that
it threatened to overwhelm them, and raised the question of whether it
was still valid to trust in YHWH alone. Did that which had saved and
preserved them in the past have such strength that it could prevail against
the power that now confronted them?

We are in this chapter concerned with the fifth of these crises, which
first began to strike home to the mass of the people in 742 B.C.E., "the
year that king Uzziah died."[1] By this date it was becoming clear even to
the ordinary citizen that the forty golden years immediately preceding
were at an end. The long reigns of Jeroboam II in the northern kingdom
(786–746), and his contemporary Uzziah in Judah (783–742), had been
years of security. The boundaries had been pushed once again outward,
the land itself had been strongly fortified, and the "nations" held at a distance.[2] But when Uzziah died, Jeroboam II had been dead for four years,

1. Isa. 6:1. N.B. Uzziah is also called Azariah in II Kings. The dates of the kings
of Israel and Judah in this period are a matter of some dispute. We are adopting
here those of John Bright, *History of Israel,* which will probably be those most
familiar to the reader. For the reigns of Jeroboam II and Uzziah see II Kings
15:23–16:7; II Chron. 26:1–15. For the history of this period see Bright, *History,*
Chap. 7, and Noth, *History,* pp. 253–269.
2. II Kings 14:23–25; II Chron. 26:1–15.

and the rapid internal collapse of the northern kingdom was already evident. Moreover, the mighty Tiglath-pileser had been five years on the throne in distant Assyria, and had started his brutal policy of expansion. In 743 a coalition had been formed to resist his attacks on northern Syria, but it had failed. By 738 Tyre, Damascus and Samaria, as well as other northern states, were all being forced to pay tribute to the Great King.

Tribute, however, was only the beginning, and herein lay the newness of the situation. Other Assyrian kings had exacted heavy tribute from the peoples they vanquished, as did all conquering rulers of the day. There was nothing new about that, nor about the fact of expansionist warfare and its ghastly devastation. What was new was Tiglath-pileser's determination to eliminate the kingdoms which refused his rule, to make them Assyrian provinces, and by forcible transfers of population to wipe out forever their historic identity as a people, removing all possibility of rebellion. This purpose he pursued with ruthless consistency until his death in 727, and thereafter it was followed by his successors.

The Assyrians viewed the policy as eminently reasonable amidst the incessant warfare which plagued the ancient Middle Eastern world, and savaged the trade routes on which their cities depended for existence. They strove to impose order by sheer force upon the restless and unruly nations, welding together the known world of their day into one coherent whole within the structure of an imperial peace. Theirs was an extraordinary achievement, for it had no precedent, and many of the methods they initiated continued almost unchanged into the Persian, the Hellenistic, and even the Roman empires. Yet to most of the frightened people of Israel and Judah this seemed to promise nothing but a descent into *Sheol,* the dusty realm of death, their extermination as a people of the covenant, and the extinguishing of YHWH as the source of life and meaning. A new system of order seemed destined to prevail, based upon an alien interpretation of the world, and drawing its strength from quite another "god."[3]

There was full foundation for their anxiety and fears. The Assyrian progress southward along the great highway from the north which led to Egypt was as relentless as a lava flow. Damascus and Tyre were incorporated into the empire in 734; the kingdom of Israel in 722, and the Philistine city of Ashdod in 711. An inhabitant of Jerusalem could then set out at midday, and *walk* to the edge of the Judean hills, there to see the smoke rising from the towns the Assyrians were pillaging, and walk back to his home, reaching it before the gates were closed at sunset. The city was swollen by refugees from the now nonexistent kingdom of Israel, and Judah had become what in these days we would call a satellite state. It had a ruler and administration of its own, but existed only by permis-

3. See additional notes.

sion of the Assyrian king. It was required so completely to accept the imperial system that a great Assyrian altar was set up in the Temple area for public sacrifice and offerings, while the altar of YHWH was moved to a secondary place, to be used for the consulting of the oracle.[4] King Hezekiah rebelled against this domination. He insisted on a pure worship of YHWH in Jerusalem, to the exclusion of all foreign gods, itself an act of political rebellion in those days, and he took part in at least one coalition to resist Assyria.[5]

This provoked a furious response from Sennacherib, then the Assyrian king. In 701 he ravaged the whole land of Judah and besieged Jerusalem, shutting up Hezekiah, as he said, "like a bird in a cage." He withdrew at last after the payment of a back-breaking tribute, leaving Hezekiah to rule over the fragment of a state, completely at the mercy of Assyrian power.[6] Without any doubt this was a shattering defeat, and the next three quarters of a century is almost a complete blank in Judean history, so subservient had she become. Yet it was so much better than what the people had dreaded would happen to them, total extinction, and the scattering of the population throughout the Assyrian empire, that the withdrawal of the Assyrian army was ever afterward thought of as a victory.[7]

The Disclosure of God through the Prophets

These were the terrible events which the eighth-century prophets interpreted. Often there was panic and despair,

> When the house of David was told, "Syria is in league with Ephraim," his heart and the heart of his people shook as the trees of the forest shake before the wind.
>
> > Isaiah 7:2

> "This day is a day of distress, of rebuke and of disgrace; children have come to the birth, and there is no strength to bring them forth."
> > The comment of Hezekiah in 701 (Isaiah 37:3)

> They shall say to the mountains, Cover us,
>   and to the hills, Fall upon us.
>
> > Hosea 10:8

> Deep from the earth shall you speak,
>   from low in the dust your words shall come;
>   your voice shall come from the ground like the voice of a ghost,
>   and your speech shall whisper out of the dust.
>
> > Isaiah 29:4[8]

4. II Kings 16:10–18. See also additional notes.
5. II Kings 18:1–8.   6. See additional notes.
7. II Kings 19:32–36; Isa. 29:5–8. See also additional notes.
8. Although the verbs in these prophetic passages are future, they describe

In the face of this despair the Word is that there is no need for panic.

For YHWH spoke thus to me with his strong hand upon me, and warned me not to walk in the way of this people, saying: "Do not call conspiracy all that this people call conspiracy, and do not fear what they fear, nor be in dread. But YHWH of hosts, him you shall regard as holy; let him be your fear, and let him be your dread."

Isaiah 8:11–13

But no less false to the truth of the situation was the constant bolstering up of national morale upon illusory grounds, the argument so familiar to us today that the crisis is less serious than it seems, for there is nothing new here; we have won through in the past, and so we can win through again, as if all that was needed was optimism.[9] Repeatedly the people said

> in pride and in arrogance of heart:
> "The bricks have fallen,
>   but we will build with dressed stones;
> the sycamores have been cut down,
>   but we will put cedars in their place."

Isaiah 9:9–10

> Their preaching is, "Do not preach;
>   one should not preach of things like this.
> Disgrace will not overtake us."

Micah 2:6 (trans. D. B.)

> We have made a covenant with death,
>   and with Sheol we have an agreement;
> when the overwhelming scourge passes through
>   it will not come to us.

Isaiah 28:15

In face of this appalling complacency the prophet had no alternative but to reply:

> I will make justice the line,
>   and righteousness the plummet;
> and hail will sweep away the refuge of lies,
>   and waters will overwhelm the shelter.
> Then your covenant with death will be annulled,
>   and your agreement with Sheol will not stand;
> when the overwhelming scourge passes through
>   you will be beaten down by it.

Isaiah 28:17–18

---

something which we have every reason to believe actually happened. It is clear from Isa. 22:1–14 that the situation in Jerusalem during the siege was a desperate one.

9. See additional notes.

> As for me, I am filled with power,
>> with the spirit of YHWH,
>> and with justice and might,
> to declare to Jacob his transgression
> and to Israel his sin.

Micah 3:8

If we try to discover what is new in the proclamation of YHWH in the eighth-century prophets (Amos, Hosea, Micah and Isaiah), we shall find that they insist that in one sense they are saying nothing new. They take their stand resolutely upon the Exodus and the covenant,[10] and maintain that nothing here has been changed.

> When Israel was a child, I loved him,
>> and out of Egypt I called my son.
> [But] the more I called them,
>> the more they went from me;
> they kept sacrificing to the Baals,
>> and burning incense to idols.

Hosea 11:1–2

> O my people, what have I done to you?
> In what have I wearied you? Answer me!
> For I brought you up out of the land of Egypt,
>> and redeemed you from the house of bondage.

Micah 6:3–4

There is here no new God, but the same God who had delivered the people from Egypt and made an agreement with them, coming to demand that this agreement be kept. Unlike any other covenant or treaty made between a protected people and a Great King, this covenant imposed no regular payment of tribute. Sacrifices and burnt offerings, or any other form of recompense to YHWH for his protection, formed no part of the original agreement, as contained in the Ten Commandments. "Did you bring to me sacrifices and offerings the forty years in the wilderness, O house of Israel?" asked Amos, evidently expecting the answer "No."[11]

> I desire faithfulness to the covenant and not sacrifice,
>> the knowledge of God instead of burnt offerings.

Hosea 6:6[12]

10. In Amos, Hosea and Micah the covenant is the covenant with the people at Sinai; in Isaiah, who taught in Jerusalem, emphasis is laid on the covenant with David.

11. Amos 5:25.

12. Trans. D. B. The word *hesed*, translated in the RSV "steadfast love," means being absolutely faithful to the agreement made, as YHWH always is, and therefore showing unceasing love. The classic discussion of this word is found in Nelson Glueck, *Hesed in the Bible*, trans. Alfred Gottschalk (Cincinnati: The Hebrew Union College Press, 1967). "Knowledge" in Hebrew terms always meant a close personal relationship, rather than knowing something only with one's mind.

When the people asked:

> With what shall I come before YHWH,
>   and bow myself before God on high?
> Shall I come before him with burnt offerings,
>   with calves a year old?

the prophetic answer stated clearly that there was no new commandment:

> He has showed you, O man, what is good;
>   and what does YHWH require of you
> but to do justice, to be steadfast in your love[13]
> and to walk humbly with your God.
>
> Micah 6:8

In other words, what the people had promised to do as their side of the agreement with YHWH was to establish, cherish and maintain a just and harmonious society. This they had manifestly failed to do.

> For the vineyard of YHWH of hosts
>   is the house of Israel,
> and the men of Judah
>   are his pleasant planting;
> and he looked for justice,
>   but behold, bloodshed;
> for righteousness,
>   but behold a cry!
>
> Isaiah 5:7

The eighth-century prophets transferred, as it were, the entire question of covenant from the sanctuary to the gate, i.e., to the marketplace and the law court, and found there a blatant disregard of faithfulness and agreement:

> When will the new moon be over,
>   that we may sell grain?
> And the sabbath,
>   that we may offer wheat for sale,
> that we may charge a high price for a small measure,[14]
>   and deal deceitfully with false balances?
>
> Amos 8:5

> They covet fields, and seize them;
>   and houses, and take them away;
> they oppress a man and his house,
>   a man and his inheritance.
>
> Micah 2:2

---

13. Trans. D. B. Lit., "to love *hesed*." See additional notes.
14. Trans. D. B. RSV translates more literally, "that we may make the ephah small and the shekel great."

Woe to those who are heroes at drinking wine,
and valiant men in mixing strong drink,
who acquit the guilty for a bribe,
and deprive the innocent of his right!

Isaiah 5:22–23

YHWH the Only God, and Covenant the Only Basis of Society

Amos came from Judah to speak in the northern kingdom of Israel, which was then still enjoying prosperity under Jeroboam II. He was, it would seem, a government official with a considerable knowledge of administration and of international affairs,[15] fully conscious that the critical need of the day was universal order, to end the constant strife between rival nations. The Assyrians would shortly seek to impose order by force, but Amos proclaimed that what had been true for the people of Israel must be true for all people everywhere: that fundamental to the order of the world is the making of agreements and keeping them. This is the true knowledge of YHWH, for the maintenance of any honest agreement means that each side must keep faith with that which is "other." The crimes of which Amos accuses the nations in 1:3–2:3 are breaches of peace treaties made between them.[16] He saw also that just as covenant applies to all nations, so the Exodus was not peculiar to Israel alone:

"Are you not like the Ethiopians to me,
O people of Israel?" says YHWH.
"Did I not bring up Israel from the land of Egypt,
and the Philistines from Caphtor and the Syrians
from Kir?"

Amos 9:7

What was peculiar to the people of Israel was that YHWH had "known" only them,[17] which is to say that only with them had there been this close personal relationship, for "know" in Hebrew does not mean merely "to be acquainted with," or "to have intellectual knowledge of."[18]

The consequences of this recognition that all nations experience YHWH, but that Israel alone had known YHWH directly, are enormous. For the first time clear proclamation is made that there can be no escape

15. It is certainly attractive to think of Amos as a simple shepherd speaking out against the powerful, as most authorities tend to do. However, the evidence is against this interpretation. Arvid Kapelrud has shown persuasively that he must have been an important official in charge of the royal herds, intended probably for the Temple sacrifices, and of the sycamore forests. (*Central Ideas in Amos,* Oslo: Oslo University Press, 1956, pp. 5–10.)

16. This is explicit in Amos 1:9, but implicit in all the other accusations. The condemnation of Judah in Amos 2:4–5 is almost certainly a later addition.

17. Amos 3:2.   18. See note 12, above.

from YHWH, no place to hide where the word of YHWH is without
authority:

> Though they hide themselves in the top of Carmel,
> from there I will search out and take them;
> and though they hide from my sight at the bottom of the sea,
> there I will command the serpent and it shall bite them.
> And though they go into captivity before their enemies,
> there I will command the sword and it shall slay them.
>
> Amos 9:3–4

There can, in his thinking, be only one pattern of order throughout
the world and that is the order of YHWH, the order established by
covenant and agreement, and not that imposed by military might.

The people confidently expected a "Day of YHWH," when everything
amiss in the world would be put right, when, as they hoped, the foreign
nations would be suppressed and taught to keep their place. But if it is
true that the Judge of all the earth must do what is right,[19] then the
severest judgment must fall on those to whom had been entrusted the
full understanding of covenant, and who had so tragically failed to keep
it. According to the word of YHWH made known through Amos, and
in the teaching of all the prophets who followed him, the greater the
gift bestowed upon any people, the greater the responsibility, and the
more serious and searching the judgment:

> Woe to you that desire the day of YHWH!
> Why would you have the day of YHWH?
> It is darkness, and not light.
>
> Amos 5:18

> YHWH of hosts has a day
> against all that is proud and lofty,
> against all that is lifted up and high;
> against all the cedars of Lebanon,
> lofty and lifted up;
> and against all the oaks of Bashan;
> against all the high mountains,
> and against all the lofty hills;
> against every high tower,
> and against every fortified wall.
>
> Isaiah 2:12–15[20]

The Enduring Quality of the Covenant

It was given to the prophet Hosea to take yet a stage further this
recognition that covenant is inescapable. Amos had seen, as it were,

19. Gen. 18:25.
20. See additional notes.

that there is no limit to its breadth, to its extension throughout the world. Hosea saw that there is no limit to its depth, for its roots go so deep that it cannot be eradicated. Into whatever chaotic abyss man is plunged, he cannot arrive at a situation in which the covenant and the *hesed,* the steadfast love, of YHWH does not prevail.

This was the message that he proclaimed in a world that was falling to pieces around him. Once the strong hand of Jeroboam II had been removed by death, the kingdom of Israel collapsed, as Amos had seen that it would, into anarchy and civil strife.

> Gilead is a city of evildoers,
>   tracked with blood.
> As robbers lie in wait for a man,
>   so the priests are banded together;
> they murder on the way to Shechem,
>   yea, they commit villainy.
>
> Hosea 6:8–9

Despite desperate efforts to gain protection by political maneuvers,[21] the country was in no state to resist the fury of an invader and in less than twenty-five years the capital city of Samaria, from which Jeroboam II had governed an empire, was laid in ruins, and the "pride of Jacob" was extinguished forever.

> You have plowed iniquity,
>   you have reaped injustice,
>   you have eaten the fruit of lies.
> Because you trusted in your chariots
>   and in the multitude of your warriors,
> therefore the tumult of war shall arise among your people,
>   and all your fortresses shall be destroyed.
>
> Hosea 10:13–14

Not only was the country disintegrating, so also was Hosea's own family life, for his wife, Gomer, whom he seems to have married in good faith, had turned out to be faithless by nature.[22] In chapters 1–3 of his book the analogy between the two is drawn, the marriage contract and the subsequent divorce being seen as parallel to the covenant with YHWH and its rupture brought about by the people's own faithlessness. Hosea saw that every security that society provided would disappear, for it was happening even as he spoke.

21. II Kings 16:5 records an Israelite and Syrian effort to force Judah to join in a coalition against Assyria. Hos. 5:13; 7:11 reflect attempts to get either Assyrian or Egyptian protection. See also additional notes.

22. The commentators, as might be expected, have had a field day with the problem of Gomer and her harlotry, and their interpretations are many and various. The position adopted here is that to which the majority of American scholars seem to subscribe.

The children of Israel shall dwell many days without king or prince, without sacrifice or pillar, without ephod or teraphim.

Hosea 3:4[23]

> I will bring to an end all her mirth,
>   feast, new moon, and sabbath,
>   and every appointed festival.
> I will lay waste her vines and fig trees,
>   of which she said,
> "These are my wages,
>   which my lovers gave me."
> I will make them a scrubland,
>   fodder for wild beasts.
>
> Hosea 2:11–12 (Hebrew 13–14)[24]

But it was in the trackless, patternless wasteland, desolate and lifeless, that YHWH had first encountered the people, and there again he would confront them, when every other apparent source of life and meaning had withered and died:

> Behold, I will coax her,
>   and take her into the wasteland,
>   and speak to her very heart.
> It is from there that I will give her her vineyards,
>   and make the Valley of Trouble a gateway of hope.
>
> Hosea 2:14–15 (Hebrew 16–17)[25]

Reality against Reality

The understanding of YHWH as the only God is further developed in the first half of the book of Isaiah. This contains oracles centering around the developing Assyrian threat to Judah, the terrifying nearness

23. All the things listed here were things which symbolized security for the ancient Israelites. Hosea meant that there would be no proper government, no chance of offering sacrifices in the hope of pleasing God, no opportunity of consulting the oracle for help in a crisis (the ephod was used for this purpose— I Sam. 14:3, 18–19; 23:9; I Kings 2:26). Rulers, priests and prophets, to whom the people usually turned for help, would all be scattered.

24. Trans. D. B. *Ya'ar,* as so often, is here not forest, but is wild scrubland. See the parallel picture in Isa. 7:23–25. N.B. The numbering of the verses in Hos. 1–2 differs in the Hebrew from the English translations.

25. Trans. D. B. This is an exceedingly rich passage which really defies translation. To "speak to the heart" means both speak with utmost tenderness and also to speak to the innermost being. Isa. 40:2 said later that this moment had now come. The Valley of Achor, or Trouble, was the scene of the first disaster at the original entry into Canaan (Josh. 7:20–26), and had become proverbial in Israelite thought (see Isa. 65:10).

of the imperial armies, the plundering of all the villages and towns,
and the dread siege of the capital itself in the year 701 B.C.E.

> Your country lies desolate,
>   your cities are burned with fire;
> in your very presence
>   aliens devour your land;
>   it is desolate, as overthrown by aliens.
> And the daughter of Zion is left
>   like a booth in a vineyard,
>   like a lodge in a cucumber field,
>   like a besieged city.
> If YHWH of hosts
>   had not left us a few survivors,
> we should have been like Sodom,
>   and become like Gomorrah.
>
> Isaiah 1:7–9

The oracles of this period bind together into one the irrevocable judgment
that "the end has come upon my people"[26] and the assurance that the
covenant of YHWH must survive every desolation. On the one hand,
Isaiah warned of coming disaster:

> I will tell you
>   what I will do to my vineyard.
> I will remove its hedge,
>   and it shall be devoured;
> I will break down its wall,
>   and it shall be trampled down.
>
> Isaiah 5:5

And on the other hand, he promised deliverance:

> Behold, I am laying in Zion for a foundation
> a stone, a tested stone,
> a precious cornerstone, of a sure foundation:
>   "He who believes will not be in haste."
>
> Isaiah 28:16

"Hail will sweep away the refuge of lies, and waters overwhelm the
shelter," until it is "sheer terror to understand the message,"[27] but

> like birds hovering, so YHWH of hosts
>   will protect Jerusalem;
> he will protect it and deliver it,
>   he will spare and rescue it.
>
> Isaiah 31:5

26. Amos 8:2.   27. Isa. 28:17, 19.

How much all of this was spoken by Isaiah himself is a matter of much argument, since many oracles of YHWH later than his day have gathered round his name and are included in chapters 1–39 of the book. Some scholars have argued that to be consistent we should ascribe only the judgments and warnings of disaster to Isaiah himself, whom they regard as a prophet of doom, and that all the assurances and promises must be later additions.[28] This is too great a simplification. The majority of oracles concerning the Assyrian invasion must belong to the time of crisis itself, though such a passage as 29:5–8 may be a reflection soon after the preservation of the city. The oracles may be rightly called "Isaianic," in that they belong to the disclosure of God through the events of the Assyrian crisis and come from the community of Isaiah. It is too easily forgotten that the authenticity of an oracle does not rest on whether it was spoken by Isaiah, but on whether it was spoken by YHWH. The experience of the people of Judah was emphatically that in this sense the oracles under consideration are indeed words of truth.[29]

The double thrust of the oracles is clearly displayed in Chapter 10:

> Ah, Assyria, the rod of my anger,
>> the staff of my fury!
> Against a godless nation I send him,
>> and against the people of my wrath I command him,
> to take spoil and seize plunder,
>> and to tread them down like the mire of the streets.
> But he does not so intend,
>> and his mind does not so think;
> but it is in his mind to destroy,
>> and to cut off nations not a few;
> for he says:
> "Are not my commanders all kings?"
>
> .   .   .   .   .   .
>
> Shall the ax vaunt itself over him who hews with it,
>> or the saw magnify itself against him who wields it?
>
> .   .   .   .   .   .
>
> Therefore YHWH, YHWH of hosts,
>> will send wasting sickness among his stout warriors,
> and under his glory a burning will be kindled,
>> like the burning of fire.
>
> Isaiah 10:5–8, 15–16[30]

28. See additional notes.
29. Certainly the question of authorship is one of great scholarly and literary importance. This is not an attempt to downgrade it. All that is being said here is that it must not be allowed to obscure the question of the truth of the oracle.
30. The whole passage of Isa. 10:5–19 should be read to see how one oracle is set over against another.

At one and the same time it is said that this appalling invader, overwhelming in power and with relentless appetite, is being brought against the people by YHWH, and yet also that his proud heart and arrogant boasting must be punished, for despite all his efforts Jerusalem will endure. Among the people of Jerusalem the prophet, as it were, points to the might and dominion of Assyria, and says, "There you are confronted by God. That great empire is in this day and age the Reality with which you must come to terms. You cannot now go on living as you have lived before. You must repent, which is to rethink the whole pattern of your life as a nation and the assumptions upon which it is based. By no kind of political device, no alliance or treaty, can you avoid this necessity. You may toss and turn as much as you like, but you cannot have a quiet night's rest, if you will not face this fact."

> The bed is too short to stretch oneself on it,
> and the covering too narrow to wrap oneself in it.
>
> Isaiah 28:20

> Woe to the rebellious children, says YHWH,
> who carry out their plans apart from me,
> and sign agreements without my spirit,
> that they may add sin to sin.
> They set out to go down to Egypt,
> without seeking a Word from me,
> to take refuge in the strength of Pharaoh,
> and shelter in the shadow of Egypt.
> Therefore the strength of Pharaoh shall turn to your shame.
>
> Isaiah 30:1-3[31]

But no less are the Assyrians told about Jerusalem, "Here also is Reality, absolute and indestructible. You cannot sweep it aside from your path, or crush it into oblivion. It is 'of sure foundation.' "[32]

To both the message is the same, for in all this teaching there is but one God, one absolute Reality, against which every human pretension to glory is shattered:

> The haughty looks of man shall be brought low,
> and the pride of men shall be humbled;
> and YHWH alone shall be exalted in that day.
>
> Isaiah 2:11[33]

We come now to a disturbing question, for the words of the prophets were never meant to be confined within the pages of a book, there to

31. Trans. D. B. The phrase translated here "sign agreements" means literally "weave a web." It could perhaps mean "make plots."
32. Isa. 28:16.
33. See additional notes.

be safely studied at a distance. It is incumbent on us, therefore, at the very least to ask in what manner all this might apply to our own time and our own country. We can do no more here than suggest how this should be done, but surely it would be a great mistake to imagine that we can identify ourselves completely with those who worshiped YHWH in Jerusalem. Judah was a weak and tiny country. America is not. The power and might that once belonged to Assyria has now become our heritage, and we use this power continually to bend the world to our will, and ensure that events shall turn to our own advantage.[34] If we take the argument of the eighth-century prophets seriously, we shall find that God is not only on our side; he is just as much set over against us. In every political encounter truth is set against truth, right against right, Reality against Reality.

Other nations, said Amos, have had an Exodus. Every nation has had a history. Every lasting society, however great the evils it has done, is founded upon Reality, upon experience of the Absolute, and not, as we are often tempted to believe, merely upon delusion and falsehood. They must, of course, do their own rethinking, but that is not our concern. We cannot do it for them, since we do not stand in their position. Our concern is to discover what demands YHWH is making upon us through them, as we encounter them and find that they stand in our way. But of one thing we may be certain: we should beware of any political party which demands our *whole* allegiance, any policy which we are told we may not question, all moral absolutes which argue that right and justice are confined to one side in a conflict. We must beware especially of any kind of suggestion that the enemy is devilish and must be destroyed. We cannot destroy the enemy, for the enemy is always the other; the enemy is God.[35]

ADDITIONAL NOTES TO CHAPTER 13

3. In order to understand their predicament one must remember how very closely the "god" and the society were bound up with each other, and also how intensely the individual person felt himself to be a part of his community, so much so, in fact, that his identity depended upon its continuance. The structure of the society and its whole way of life were built upon the solid basis of the "god," i.e., the fundamental reality, in whom the people believed and whom they worshiped. They could not conceive of the society and the "god" apart from each other. Therefore, if the society and its way of life should be eliminated, it seemed to the people that the "god" would crumble also. In fact, this is exactly what the

34. This, of course, is the function of any country's foreign policy, and we are by no manner of means alone in this. We do no more than share the constant arrogance of mankind.

35. See additional notes.

Assyrian officer said had happened to the gods of the conquered cities (II Kings 18:34). The understanding of "God" as altogether transcending the society is a later concept and begins with the eighth-century prophets.

The alliances with foreign powers by which Israel tried to protect herself (Hos. 8:9–10; 12:1) meant always adopting to some extent the foreign country's way of life and consequently, in the thinking of the time, a moving away from YHWH, the foundation of the Israelite way of life.

4. This verse is difficult to translate, and the English versions do not all agree upon the purpose for the moving of the altar.

6. See the Assyrian account of this coalition and the siege of Jerusalem in Pritchard, ANET, pp. 287–88. The biblical record of the siege of Jerusalem is complicated, since it seems to include more than one account. II Kings 18:13–16 is apparently contemporary, and 18:17–19:37 a combination of two accounts written some time later, using contemporary material, but embellished by later tradition. See Brevard S. Childs, *Isaiah and the Assyrian Crisis* (London: SCM Press Ltd., 1967). See also Bright, *History*, pp. 277–308.

7. II Kings 19:32–36; Isa. 29:5–8. Some authorities have been scornful of the biblical record for glorifying what was an undoubted defeat, but this is quite unjust. An interesting parallel would be the escape of the British army from the Nazis at Dunkirk in 1940. By any objective reckoning this was a catastrophic defeat. Yet it was so much better than the complete annihilation of the army, which had been fully expected, that it has taken on for the British the quality of a victory, and even something of a legendary character.

9. It is not intended here to suggest that optimism is somehow a bad thing. A sturdy optimism in the face of frightening portents is a very necessary part of courage. However, what the prophets were attacking was that superficial optimism which is made a substitute for much needed reform, and which soothes people's fears without calling upon them to examine seriously the situation in which they find themselves.

13. It is very difficult to know exactly what the attitude of the biblical prophets to the cult actually was. In the light of so much polemic against the cult in the prophetic books, it is tempting to see them as unutterably opposed to it. But the problem is more complex. They were certainly diametrically opposed to the popular understanding of Temple sacrifices as a means of placating YHWH and a substitute for social justice, an understanding which doubtless many priests and prophets also shared. But they do not appear to have separated themselves from the worship of the sanctuary, and the evidence is strong that some of them at least may have acted as sanctuary prophets. On this subject see, e.g., Fohrer, *History of Israelite Religion,* Chaps. 18–20; Ringgren, *Israelite Religion,* Part II, Chap. 12; Rowley, *Worship in Ancient Israel,* Chap. 5; Vriezen, *The Religion of Ancient Israel,* Chap. VIII.

20. Isaiah is here speaking of the Day of YHWH as a day when every kind of arrogance will be laid low, and he quotes as symbols of such arrogance things which in the Israelite world were famous for their height and majesty. But there must have been more in his mind than symbolism, because in those days great trees and high mountains were considered sacred (Hos. 4:13). He was therefore saying that their sanctity would be destroyed. The high towers and walls were the defenses which people trusted would protect them from their enemies.

21. One Contributor commented here: There seem to be two periods when there is great temptation to worship other gods. First is a period of prosperity, such as during the time of Amos. Another time is during a period of total decay

and helplessness, when God is believed to have "died." The first period is present society, where wealth and social status become "ultimate concerns" of a demonic faith. In such a society there is no need for God—so the people believe. At the end of World War II literary atheistic existentialism became very popular on the grounds that God would not have allowed man to destroy himself. The war was man's responsibility. However, Hosea believed that there was a covenant between God and man, and that despite man's failure to keep this covenant, God, by reason of his *hesed,* would lead man back into the wilderness and restore order.

28. So, for instance, Sheldon H. Blank, *Prophetic Faith in Isaiah* (New York: Harper & Row, 1958). Otto Kaiser's argument that the oracles against Assyria belong to a very much later period seems to create quite as many difficulties as it attempts to solve. (*Isaiah 1–12* and *Isaiah 13–39,* trans. R. A. Wilson, Philadelphia: The Westminster Press, 1972, 1974).

33. Many of us would suggest that those who divide the judgments from the promises, and ascribe only the first to Isaiah, do not give sufficient weight to his passionate conviction that the Holy One of Israel is absolute. The very evident Assyrian arrogance could not, therefore, go without punishment. Though certainly much of Isa. 1–39 is later than his day, one must regard his understanding of YHWH as richer and more complex than some authorities would have us believe.

35. It must not be thought that because the enemy is God, our enemies are consequently "godly." It would be folly to suggest that the methods and purposes of the Nazis were anything but bestial and evil. Yet, the evil of Nazism has behind it, among other things, the arrogance of the Allies after World War I, their determination to punish Germany, and the bitter hatred of everything that was German (hatred which as a child I was brought up to think of as "right"). Although it was necessary to oppose Nazism to the utmost of our power, the very magnitude of its evil confronted us with an enormous question about the nature of man, and also about the foundations of our own society.

One Contributor disagreed firmly with the point of view put forward at the end of this chapter, and argued that Communism is a movement "devoid of love, truth, right and Reality." He added: "Surely there are devilish moments in history. We are right, I think, in looking upon the North Vietnamese as evil (or at least their leaders). We are wrong, not in opposing them, but in attempting to provide the only alternative to them, and in failing to see the cause of their success."

14. A Future and a Hope

BACKGROUND READING: II Kings 21–25; Psalm 137; Jeremiah 1–45; (especially 1–2; 5; 7–9; 17:1–18; 18; 23; 30–31); Lamentations; Ezekiel 1–24; 33–37 (especially 1–11; 18; 33–37); Nahum; Habakkuk 1–2; Zephaniah.

Terror on Every Side

The dark days of Assyrian rule over Judah persisted till the death of the last great king, Asshurbanipal, in 627 B.C.E. In Jerusalem, Manasseh, who had succeeded Hezekiah (687–642), was forced to submit without question to Assyrian power and direction, if he was to save the tattered fragments of Judean independence. Assyrian customs and Assyrian religion took hold in Judah. The sun and moon and stars were admitted to the council of YHWH, and worship was offered to them as if they were gods.[1] Manasseh

> built altars for all the host of heaven in the two courts of the house of YHWH. And he burned his son as an offering, and practised soothsaying and augury, and dealt with mediums and with wizards.
>
> II Kings 21:5–6

All opposition to this policy was ruthlessly suppressed, and it was said of Manasseh that he "shed very much innocent blood, till he had filled Jerusalem from one end to another."[2] The voices of those prophets who spoke for YHWH as the only true God were silenced, and no more than a vestige of their protest has come down to us:

> Behold, I am bringing upon Jerusalem and Judah such evil that the ears of every one who hears of it will tingle. . . . I will wipe Jerusalem as one wipes a dish, wiping it and turning it upside down.
>
> II Kings 21:12–13

---

1. Bright, *History,* pp. 311–12; George Ernest Wright, *The Old Testament against Its Environment* (London: SCM Press Ltd., 1950), pp. 30–41.
2. II Kings 21:16.

Nevertheless, though driven underground for these forty-five years of Manasseh's reign, and forbidden utterance in either sanctuary or gate, the Word of YHWH was still powerfully at work.[3] Some of the refugees from the shattered northern kingdom—prophets, priests and wise men—had begun to debate the meaning of their subjugation, and what must be done to keep the covenant of YHWH in this new and terrible period. Younger men who succeeded them continued their work in secret, and in due course the Word was given written form in what we know today as the book of Deuteronomy. But the days were still evil, and the scroll was hidden in one of the Temple buildings, not to be found there until after Manasseh's death.[4]

With the death of Asshurbanipal the distress of the conquered peoples seemed to lighten, for those who came after him were weaklings. Already in Jerusalem the tyranny had eased. In 640, after a brief revolution and counter-revolution,[5] the young King Josiah had come to the throne of Judah at the age of only eight years. At first a council of regents continued the pro-Assyrian policy, but without the absolutism of Manasseh, and the stern oracle of YHWH could once more be openly proclaimed by the prophet Zephaniah. However, in about 628, when Josiah himself took over the kingship, he seized the opportunity provided by Assyria's increasing weakness to establish Judah's independence, and to bring, as far as he could, all the old kingdom of Israel and the territory of the Philistines within his realm.[6] He initiated also a cleansing and restoration of the Temple, in the course of which the hidden scroll was found. On this authority religious reforms were carried the length and breadth of the country, a transformation without parallel in its history.[7] Josiah seems quite deliberately to have rejected the covenant, or treaty, with the Assyrian king and replaced it by a formal covenant with YHWH. This is also the intent of Deuteronomy.[8]

The decline of Assyria, and the fall of their capital, Nineveh, to the Babylonians and Medes in 612 B.C.E. caused much rejoicing in Judah, and the savage oracles of Nahum reflect the people's sense of liberation and excitement:

---

3. See additional notes.   4. See additional notes.
5. II Kings 21:19–24.
6. Bright, *History*, p. 316; Noth, *History*, pp. 272–74.
7. II Kings 22–23. See also additional notes.
8. The book of Deuteronomy is written in quite deliberate covenant terms. Chap. 27 provides for a covenant ceremony at Shechem (see Josh. 24), and the elaborate language of Chap. 28 imitates similar language in Assyrian treaties. (Mendenhall, "Covenant Forms in Israelite Tradition," *Biblical Archaeologist Reader* 3, 25–53; Hillers, *Covenant*, Chap. 11.)

Woe to the bloody city,
   all full of lies and booty!

. . . . . .

I will throw filth at you,
   and treat you with contempt,
   and make you a gazingstock.
And all who look on you will shrink from you and say,
Wasted is Nineveh; who will bemoan her?

Nahum 3:1, 6–7

But this rejoicing was short-lived, for disaster once more closed in upon them. In 609 Josiah was killed at Megiddo, as he tried to prevent the Egyptian army from going to the support of Assyria against the Babylonians. The brief spurt of independence came at once to an end, and Judah passed again under the domination of foreigners. For a year or two she was subservient to Egypt, but Nebuchadnezzar of Babylon, once secure upon his throne, made King Jehoiakim his vassal. Under this new vassalage Judah was restive, and did not hesitate to seek occasions of revolt. Twice in his fury Nebuchadnezzar besieged and captured Jerusalem. In 597 he exacted a crushing tribute, and carried away many of the royal family and leading citizens into exile, including among them the new young king, Jehoiachin. Ten years later, in 587, he put an end to all rebellion in Judah. The capital city, with its defensive walls, the great Temple of YHWH, and the royal palace, was smashed into ruins; the state was abolished; many officials were executed, and a large number of people was dragged away to join the other exiles in Babylon.

The magnitude of this tragedy can hardly be exaggerated. Some Western scholars have argued that the Exile was not so bad after all.[9] Certainly the people were not slaves in Babylon, and indeed the government seems to have treated them with tolerance. But in the last thirty years we have come to know much more about refugees and other victims of forced exile, and we have learned that material considerations are not enough. "Man does not live by bread alone."[10] Dislocation, disorientation, degradation—these are the things which come nigh to destroying a person. They take away his identity. They humiliate and confuse him. The land, the community, and the patterns of worship meant so much to men and women in those days that to be suddenly bereft of them cast the people into disarray. To be forced to trudge on foot day after day, and even month after month, toward a distant and

9. E.g., James Muilenburg, "Isaiah, Chapters 40–66," *Interpreter's Bible*, Vol. 5, pp. 396–97.
10. Deut. 8:3.

alien environment, and there to find oneself obedient to a people who worshiped other gods, spoke another language, and lived by quite another system—this was desolation indeed.

> By the waters of Babylon we sat down and wept
>
> .   .   .   .   .   .
>
> for there those who carried us off
>   demanded music and singing,
> and our captors called on us to be merry:
>   "Sing us one of the songs of Zion."
> How could we sing the song of YHWH
>   in a foreign land?
>
> Psalm 137:1–4[11]

> Is it nothing to you, all you who pass by?
>   Look and see
> if there is any sorrow like my sorrow.
>
> .   .   .   .   .   .
>
> My soul is bereft of peace,
>   I have forgotten what happiness is.
>
> Lamentations 1:12; 3:17

YHWH Has Become like an Enemy

Josiah had come to the throne in 640 B.C.E.; Jerusalem was destroyed more than fifty years later, in 587. The crisis we are now considering was therefore prolonged and complex. The encounter with YHWH, and the Word by which the people were confronted, was no less rich and varied. It was indeed so immense and overwhelming that most of the people could not bring themselves to accept it, for, as we shall see, it condemned not only their hopes but also their grief. Their day-to-day, down-to-earth, experience on each occasion seemed to be telling them one thing, and those lonely prophets, Zephaniah, Jeremiah, Habakkuk and Ezekiel, to be saying something altogether different. There were doubtless many other prophets of the time who said more or less what the people expected them to say,[12] but these prophets spoke of YHWH as the "Absolutely Other," as standing over against all that constituted the "world" of the people of Judah, the whole pattern of experience as they discerned it. The Word of YHWH thus proclaimed demanded that the people abandon this "world" of theirs, reject their own interpretations, and learn to look at events quite differently. While the Temple still stood

---

11. NEB, with two modifications: "the song of YHWH" for "the LORD'S song," and "waters" for "rivers." *Naharoth* meant the river Euphrates and the multitude of irrigation channels.

12. These were the many "false prophets" about whom Jeremiah speaks so bitterly (2:8; 4:9–10; 5:30–31; 14:11–16; 23:1–40).

and there yet seemed to be light in the world, these prophets spoke only of disaster; when the whole city was laid in ruins and the exiles were sunk in despair, these same prophets spoke of triumph and hope.

The effort of mind demanded of the people was so massive that it is little wonder that they did not immediately respond to the word, and even refused it completely. They were ready to hear those many other prophets whose oracles confirmed their hopes and fears, but against Zephaniah, Jeremiah and Ezekiel they turned in fury and derision. "Woe is me, my mother," said Jeremiah, "that you bore me, a man of strife and contention to the whole land! I have not lent, nor have I borrowed, yet all of them curse me" (Jer. 15:10).

> I will search Jerusalem with a lantern
> and punish all who sit in stupor over the dregs of their wine,
> who say to themselves,
> "YHWH will do nothing, good or bad."
>
> Zephaniah 1:12 (NEB)

> Behold, their ears are closed,
>   they cannot listen:
> Behold, the word of YHWH is to them an object of scorn.
>
> Jeremiah 6:10

> You are not sent to a people of foreign speech and a hard language, . . . whose words you cannot understand. Surely, if I sent you to such, they would listen to you. But the house of Israel will not listen to you, for they are not willing to listen to me.
>
> Ezekiel 3:5–7

Even when the Word of YHWH was that they were to be delivered from their misery, they could not be persuaded it was true.

> You are to them like one who sings love songs with a beautiful voice and plays well on an instrument, for they hear what you say, but they will not do it. When this comes—and come it will—then they will know that a prophet has been among them.
>
> Ezekiel 33:32–33

While the kingdom still stood the judgments pronounced by the eighth-century prophets were repeated with even greater emphasis, and the "Day of YHWH" yet more ominously proclaimed.

> A day of wrath is that day,
>   a day of distress and anguish,
> a day of ruin and devastation,
>   a day of darkness and gloom,
> a day of clouds and thick darkness,
>   a day of trumpet blast and battle cry

> against the fortified cities
>   and against the lofty battlements.
>
> Zephaniah 1:15–16

> O that my head were waters,
>   and my eyes a fountain of tears,
> that I might weep day and night
>   for the slain of the daughter of my people.
>
> Jeremiah 9:1

As in the days of Isaiah, so now also, the Word was that the terrible enemy was being brought against them by YHWH himself:

> Look, you treacherous people, look:
>   here is what will astonish and stun you,
> for there is work afoot in your days
> which you will not believe when it is told you.
> It is this: I am raising up the Chaldeans,
> that savage and impetuous nation,
>   who cross wide tracks of the earth
> to take possession of homes not theirs.
> Terror and awe go with them;
>
> .　　.　　.　　.　　.　　.　　.
>
> and dismayed are all those whose strength was their god.
>
> Habakkuk 1:5–7, 11 (NEB)

> Behold, I am bringing upon you
>   a nation from afar, O house of Israel,
>   says YHWH.
>
> .　　.　　.　　.　　.　　.
>
> a nation whose language you do not know,
>   nor can you understand what they say.
>
> .　　.　　.　　.　　.　　.
>
> They shall eat up your harvest and your food;
>   they shall eat up your sons and your daughters.
>
> Jeremiah 5:15–17

The reason given was that the country of Judah was no longer worth saving, for both leaders and people were wholly deceived, imprisoned in a fallacious and dishonest structure of thought.[13] They were convinced that YHWH must somehow step in and save Jerusalem from destruction, for if the great Temple of his worship were to be destroyed, he would surely himself suffer extinction.[14] It was the age-old human deception: the belief that ultimate Truth and Reality are to be identified with material forms, or with the social and political systems, which men and women

---

13. Jer. 5:1–5, 30–31; 6:13–21; 14:13–16; 23:16–40; Ezek. 11:1ff.; etc.
14. Jer. 7:1–20.

have constructed to represent them. But to say that the forms of society
have themselves the quality of Reality and Truth, and that they are
therefore indestructible and stand in no need of drastic reform, is in the
prophetic thinking a flat denial of Truth itself, and bound to bring disaster
upon those who maintain the fallacy.

> Be appalled, O heavens, at this,
>   be shocked, be utterly desolate . . .
> for my people have committed two evils:
>   they have forsaken me,
> the fountain of living waters,
>   and hewed out cisterns for themselves,
> broken cisterns,
>   that can hold no water.
>
> Jeremiah 2:12–13

> How can you say, "We are wise,
>   and the law of YHWH is with us"?
> But, behold, the false pen of the scribes
>   has made it into a lie.
>
> .   .   .   .   .   .
>
> From prophet to priest
>   every one deals falsely.
> They have healed the wound of my people lightly,
>   saying, "Peace, peace,"
>   when there is no peace.
>
> Jeremiah 8:8–11

Those who refuse the searching inquiry of Truth, and in the days
of their prosperity say, "I will not listen," make an enemy of YHWH,
who, though he may appear to remain silent, is "of purer eyes than to
behold evil, and cannot look on wrong."[15] So in 587 it proved to be:

> YHWH has become like an enemy,
>   he has destroyed Israel.
>
> .   .   .   .   .   .
>
> YHWH has brought to an end in Zion
>   appointed feast and sabbath,
> and in his fierce indignation has spurned
>   king and priest.

15. Hab. 1:13. The answer to Habakkuk's question is to be found in 2:3ff.

> The vision still awaits its time;
>   it hastens to the end—it will not lie.
> If it seems slow, wait for it;
>   it will surely come, it will not delay.

For those who in their prosperity will not listen, see Jer. 22:21.

> YHWH has scorned his altar,
> disowned his sanctuary;
>
> .   .   .   .   .   .
>
> YHWH has done what he proposed,
> has carried out his threat;
> as he ordained long ago,
> he has demolished without pity;
> he has made the enemy rejoice over you,
> and exalted the might of your foes.

Lamentations 2:5–7, 17

The Days to Come

Throughout the Fertile Crescent this period seems to have been marked by something of a "failure of nerve," and a desire to find security in a return to the past. "The sun in the ancient Orient was commencing to set and its peoples could not help but be obscurely and unhappily conscious of the approaching darkness."[16] Everywhere men sought to rediscover in the past what in their nostalgia they thought of as a safe and untroubled society, and then reconstruct it in their own age and thereby contrive for themselves once more an unshakable pattern of life. Exhaustive and detailed research was undertaken in order to gain an exact knowledge of the ancient society they desired to renew.

From this turning to original sources the community of Judah was by no means exempt, and the composition of Deuteronomy, together with the reform it inspired, must be seen in this light. The return to the days of the Exodus is here both conscious and deliberate. But the effect of the research was not the same as it was elsewhere. In Judah study of a supposedly placid past could disclose only dynamic activity, forever propelling the people forward, and antiquity itself thrust them into the future.

In Deuteronomy this is made apparent in a number of ways. First, the time of the Exodus is shown to have been very different from the halcyon experience that nostalgia for the good old days might suggest. It had been instead a "great and terrible wasteland."[17] Second, there is the clear command to the people not to remain where they were, not even at the mountain of God.

> You have stayed long enough at this mountain;
> turn and take up your journey.

Deuteronomy 1:6–7[18]

16. William Foxwell Albright, *From the Stone Age to Christianity* (Garden City, N.Y.: Doubleday, 2nd ed., 1957), p. 316. For details of the antiquarianism of this period, see the whole section, pp. 314–19. Also Miloš Bič, *Trois Prophètes dans un Temps de Ténèbres* (Paris: Les Editions du Cerf, 1968), pp. 33ff.

17. Deut. 1:19; 8:15.   18. See also Deut. 2:3.

Third, the promised land is steadily presented as something still to be attained in the future.[19] Moreover, Moses himself is firmly relegated to the past, and the fact that he was not allowed to enter the promised land is emphasized.[20] By all these means is it demonstrated that the past does not provide a safe refuge from the troubled present, and it is not something which can be merely dug up and reestablished.

But if the past is not to be reconstructed, nor is it to be rejected as if it were irrelevant, for the truth made known in the past confronts man in the present also. No less than sixty-eight times do the writers of Deuteronomy use the phrase "this day" in order to bring the past forward into the present, not as a reconstituted society, but as an existential question demanding an answer:

> Not with our fathers did YHWH make this covenant, but with us, who are all of us here alive this day.
>
> Deuteronomy 5:3

> Nor is it with you only that I make this sworn covenant, but with him who is not here with us this day as well as with him who stands here with us this day before YHWH our God.
>
> Deuteronomy 29:14–15

> See, I have set before you this day life and good, death and evil. . . . I call heaven and earth to witness against you this day, that I have set before you life and death, blessing and curse; therefore choose life, that you and your descendants may live.
>
> Deuteronomy 30:15, 19

> Lay to heart all the words that I enjoin upon you this day that you may command them to your children, that they may be careful to do all the works of this law. For it is no trifle for you, but it is your life.
>
> Deuteronomy 32:46–47[21]

Finally, the establishing of a covenant—and we have seen above that Deuteronomy was written in these terms—itself presupposes a future, during which the terms of the covenant are to be carried out. Covenants of necessity take the fact of the future for granted, and this in itself is a matter of great importance. As the terror closed in upon Judah from every side, and all defenses were laid in the dust, there were many who could not perceive a future at all:

19. There are no less than fifty references in Deuteronomy to the future possession of the land: see, e.g., 1:8; 4:1; 8:1, 7; 23:20.

20. Deut. 1:37–39; 3:23–28; 31:14ff.; 32:48–52; 34:1–8.

21. Occasionally the phrase "this day" in Deuteronomy refers to some historical situation which still prevailed in the seventh century, e.g., 3:14, but overwhelmingly the phrase is used for the commandments and statutes given "this day."

> Our fathers sinned, and are no more;
>   and we bear their iniquities.
> Slaves rule over us;
>   there is none to deliver us from their hand.
>
> Lamentations 5:7–8

However, at the very time that the Babylonian army was besieging Jerusalem, and about to capture and destroy it, a fact of which he was well aware, Jeremiah signed a contract for purchase of a piece of land, and ordered it to be preserved for a long time.[22] By this he demonstrated his complete confidence that there would be a future for the country, and the terms of this contract would some day be carried out.

The Gateway of Hope

The yearning for the past, which prevailed in the Middle East at that time, should come as no surprise. The ancient world did not in the least incline toward expecting a rosy future, nor did it think of hope as profitable to mankind. "Hope deferred makes the heart sick" said the ancient Hebrew proverb,[23] and the popular mind usually thought of hope as deceptive. "Against this background the mythical tale of Pandora's box, with which Hesiod begins his *Works and Days,* can be understood in its original meaning. *Elpis* [hope] always remains for man a treacherous expectancy. 'Hope and danger are similar so far as man is concerned. Both are evil demons,' says Theognis. . . . Hope is blind— so says the chained Prometheus of Aeschylus with complete candor."[24]

In Israelite thought, it is true, as we have already seen, that the forward-looking tendency did engender in the minds of many a facile optimism, which looked for a happy issue out of distress, and saw the "Day of YHWH" as one of reward for the Hebrew people. This kind of wishful thinking persisted throughout the last fifty years of Judah's history, and was even encouraged by many prophets, who said to the people in the name of YHWH, "You shall not see the sword, nor shall

22. Jer. 32:1–15.
23. Prov. 13:12. The verse as we have it today has a more positive ending, but this comes from the teaching of the Wise. The original form of these "two-limbed sayings" in the book of Proverbs was a popular "one-limbed saying," similar to our own proverbs, e.g., "Don't count your chickens before they are hatched." See William McKane, *Proverbs: A New Approach* (Philadelphia: The Westminster Press, 1970), pp. 1–2.
24. Walter Zimmerli, *Man and His Hope in the Old Testament* (Naperville, Ill.: Alec R. Allenson, 1968), p. 2. The whole book is a most valuable study of the subject. C. F. D. Moule, *The Meaning of Hope* (Philadelphia: Fortress Press, 1963), although mainly concerned with the New Testament, has a helpful concordance of all the biblical passages in which the word "hope" appears, indicating in each case the word in the original language.

you have famine, but I will give you assured peace in this place."[25] But those among the prophets who had truly stood in the council of YHWH[26] condemned this attitude, as raising only false hopes. For them the true basis of hope lay, not in the misguided belief that disaster would be deflected, but in the disaster itself and in its terrible completeness. In the grisly days of the siege, when the victims of the sword were called happier than those who wasted away from hunger, and "the hands of compassionate women boiled their own children," so that at least some of the family might live,[27] only one certain fact remained: the fact of YHWH, who had indeed "done what he purposed and carried out his threat."[28] Here alone was absolute Reality, for every other symbol of meaning and source of security had crumbled into dust.

> Her gates have sunk into the ground;
>   he has ruined and broken their bars;
> her kings and princes are among the Gentiles;[29]
>   the law is no more,
> and her prophets obtain
>   no vision from YHWH.
> The elders of the daughter of Zion
>   sit on the ground in silence;
> They have cast dust on their heads
>   and put on sackcloth.

Lamentations 2:9–10

A hundred and fifty years earlier the prophet Hosea had warned the northern kingdom that this would happen, and had promised that in the desolate wasteland YHWH would once again speak to the heart of his people.[30] So also in these days the prophet Ezekiel was condemned to silence, forbidden to utter anything but words of anguish and grief, until he heard from a fugitive that Jerusalem had finally fallen. Then, and only then, could he make known to the exiles wherein lay their true hope.[31]

We see the first stirrings of this hope in the book of Lamentations, and in the open acknowledgment there that "YHWH is in the right."[32]

> Who has commanded and it came to pass,
>   unless YHWH has ordained it?

25. Jer. 14:13ff.   26. Jer. 23:22.
27. For mention of the famine in Jerusalem at the time of its destruction and the resulting cannibalism, see Lam. 1:11; 2:11–12, 19–20; 4:4, 9–10.
28. Lam. 2:17.   29. RSV has "the nations" for "the Gentiles."
30. Hos. 2:2–25; 3:3–5. See above, Chap. 11.
31. Ezek. 3:24–27; 24:25–27; 33:21–22. "Dumb" cannot mean here that he was unable to speak at all, for the oracles of chaps. 4–24 certainly belong to this period.
32. Lam. 1:18.

Is it not from the mouth of the Most High
    that good and evil come?
Why should a living man complain,
    a man, about the punishment of his sins?

Lamentations 3:37–39

Remember my affliction and my bitterness,
    the wormwood and the gall!
My soul continually thinks of it
    and is bowed down within me.
But I call this to mind,
    and therefore I have hope:
The steadfast love of YHWH never ceases,
    his mercies never come to an end.

.   .   .   .

To crush under foot
    all the prisoners of the earth,
to turn aside the right of a man
    in the presence of the Most High,
to subvert a man in his cause,
    YHWH does not approve.

Lamentations 3:19–22, 34–36

The prophets of YHWH saw the root and cause of the disaster to have lain in the heart of man, which is "deceitful above all things, and desperately wicked."[33] They would have agreed with a very much later writer, who said that "God, when he made man, made him straightforward, but man invents endless subtleties of his own,"[34] for, as in the days of the flood, so now, "every imagination of the thoughts of his heart was only evil continually."[35] Therefore, Ezekiel called upon the exiles in Babylon to repent and turn from all their transgressions, saying, "Get yourselves a new heart and a new spirit! For why will you die, O house of Israel?"[36]

But it takes more than human resolution to bring about this change. YHWH himself must act, and this it is said he will certainly do, for he "takes no pleasure in the death of anyone."[37] Moreover, if the truth about YHWH is to be made known to the world, the people must be fitted to fulfill this function, a function which they had been incapable of performing in the corrupt society that had previously existed.

It is not for your sake, O house of Israel, that I am about to act, but for the sake of my holy name, which you have profaned among the nations to which you came. . . . The nations will know that I am YHWH . . .

---

33. Jer. 17:9 (KJV).   34. Eccl. 7:29 (NEB).
35. Gen. 6:5.   36. Ezek. 18:30–31.
37. Ezek. 18:32.

when through you I vindicate my holiness before their eyes. . . . I will
sprinkle clean water upon you . . . and from all your idols I will cleanse
you. A new heart I will give you, and a new spirit I will put within you;
and I will take out of your flesh the heart of stone and give you a heart of
flesh. And I will put my spirit within you, and cause you to walk in my
statutes and be careful to observe my ordinances.

Ezekiel 36:22–27

The old covenant had been shattered, said Jeremiah,[38] by the willful
failure of the people to think about it seriously and keep their side of it,
but this cannot mean the end of covenant relationship. Covenant is not
an added embellishment of society, but its very substance. There is no
coherent society where there is no agreement—agreement between all the
members of it, and agreement by the whole community to see that the
structures by which they live are in accord with Truth and Reality.
Without the assurance of covenant there can be no hope at all.

Behold, the days are coming, says YHWH, when I will make a new covenant with the house of Israel and the house of Judah, not like the covenant which I made with their fathers, when I took them by the hand to
bring them out of the land of Egypt, my covenant which they broke,
though I was their husband. . . . But this is the covenant which I will
make with the house of Israel after those days, says YHWH: I will put my
Torah within them and I will write it upon their hearts; and I will be their
God, and they shall be my people. And no longer shall each man teach his
neighbor and each his brother, saying, "Know YHWH," for they shall all
know me, from the least of them to the greatest.

Jeremiah 31:31–34

The message is one which looks toward healing, return and pardon.
It promises a most merciful new beginning. Yet the assurance is not
merely gentle consolation. It is a tremendous statement that he is making
here, for he is saying nothing else than that the words of Truth are to
be carved upon the hearts of men and women,[39] with all the terrible
demands they make. The requirements of covenant are absolute. It is
not going to be easier or more comfortable to be the people of YHWH
than it had been before—that is not the promise. The promise is that
it is going to be possible.[40]

In Israelite terms, the heart is understanding and the spirit is power.
The Word of YHWH is not changed. It is "like fire, . . . like a hammer
which breaks the rock in pieces,"[41] and the word of promise is no less
sure than the word of judgment. Because Jerusalem had been destroyed,
and the Word of YHWH had prevailed over "all the easy speeches that

38. The word he uses in Jer. 31:32 means "to break, shatter, render ineffectual."
39. Deut. 6:6–7.   40. See additional notes.   41. Jer. 23:29.

comfort cruel men,"[42] there should now be no room for doubt in the minds of any. Power and understanding should penetrate to their very being, purging every idol and false interpretation. Now the truth about creation, and mankind's tragic misuse of it, was clear for all to see. Now covenant could take on a new quality. Now, through the mouth of Jeremiah, the message of the Deuteronomists, meditating upon an earlier disaster, could be confirmed:

> This commandment which I command you this day is not too hard for you, neither is it far off. It is not in heaven, that you should say, "Who will go up for us to heaven and bring it to us, that we may hear it and do it?" Neither is it beyond the sea, that you should say, "Who will go over the sea for us, and bring it to us, that we may hear it and do it?" But the word is very near you; it is in your mouth and your heart, so that you can do it.
>
> Deuteronomy 30:11–14

ADDITIONAL NOTES TO CHAPTER 14

3. It is important to remember that *dabar* (word) in Hebrew is by no means confined to the spoken or written word, as the English translation tends to suggest. *Dabar* means "speech, discourse, judgment, command, message, advice," and also "thing, act, matter, affair, business, occupation." *Dabar* carries with it always the idea of speaking in order to achieve something, and of something new happening because a word has been uttered. A word once spoken is a thing actively at work, for good or for ill. It is always powerful. It can do good or it can do harm. Therefore, the phrase "the Word of YHWH" contains within it a whole variety of meanings and we must never try to confine it to only one. It must be thought of as thrusting power, compellingly at work in many different ways, charged with a definite purpose, and putting that purpose into effect. It creates, i.e., it brings into vivid existence something which did not exist before. The *dabar* (word) and the *ruach* (spirit) of YHWH are closely parallel to each other in meaning.

4. Some scholars believe that the scroll of Deuteronomy was written about the same time that it was found and was deliberately hidden by the writers in such a manner that it should be found by the builders and be brought to the attention of the king. There is, of course, no way of proving which interpretation is correct. In any case it is clear that Deuteronomy is the result of prolonged thought which must have been going on during the reign of Manasseh. The "statutes and ordinances" in Deuteronomy are found in chaps. 12–26. There is a complex introduction to these (see the "new beginnings" in 1:1; 4:1, and 5:1) and an even more complex conclusion (27–34). How much was included in the scroll found in the Temple is hard to say, probably less than the whole book, but more than just chaps. 12–26.

Gerhard von Rad has attributed the work to the country priests, or Levites (*Deuteronomy, A Commentary,* trans. Dorothea Barton, Philadelphia: The Westminster Press, 1966, p. 24; *Studies in Deuteronomy,* trans. David Stalker, London:

---

42. G. K. Chesterton, "O God of Earth and Altar," in *Collected Poems* (New York: Dodd, Mead, 1932), pp. 136–37.

SCM Press, Ltd. 1953, pp. 66–68). E. W. Nicholson claims that the prophetic party was responsible (*Deuteronomy and Tradition,* Oxford: Basil Blackwell, 1967, pp. 76ff.), and Moshe Weinfeld that it was the Wise Men ("Deuteronomy—The Present State of the Enquiry," JBL LXXXVI, 1967, pp. 249–62). Probably we must think of representatives of all three groups being involved. We need continually to remind ourselves that although these exponents of the Word of YHWH were clearly distinguished from each other, they were no more completely separate than are the administration, faculty and students of a college.

7. On the basis of the account of Josiah's youth in II Chron. 34:1–7 many scholars believe that the reforms were already being carried out in the country from before the time when the scroll was discovered in the Temple. The account in II Kings 22:1–23:20 says that the reforms were the result of the finding of the scroll. It is difficult to know which is the more correct account; though, since Chronicles was written well after Kings, it is possible that the picture of Josiah as virtuous from his youth up may be a later development.

40. One Contributor dissented from the argument put forward here on the grounds that this oracle belongs to a time later than that of Jeremiah and is eschatalogical in intent. He argued that it does not refer to the near future, but to a distant and idealized time, and so there is no question of whether or not it is "possible." He wrote: "The theme of salvation which runs through the *Testament* is probably the best way to think about Jer. 31:31–34. We must see how it fits into that scheme:

"1. Gathering of the people.

"2. Inward renewal (Jer. 32:37–40; Ezek. 11:19; 36:22–27).

"3. Complete unification (Ezek. 37:15–22) under King David (37:24), and dwelling in their own land.

"4. A new covenant, differing from the one in the Exodus from Egypt (Jer. 23:7) where sin had hindered the knowledge of God. He will forgive their iniquity and remember their sins no more (Jer. 31:31–34). . . . There will be a 'future and a hope' (Jer. 29:11).

"5. There will be a covenant of salvation (Ezek. 37:26ff.)."

This is undoubtedly a possible method of interpreting the passage, and has the support of some distinguished scholars. Over the theme of salvation he puts forward there is likely to be little dispute. The question is how much of the "Book of Consolation" (Jer. 30:1–31:40) belongs to Jeremiah's own time. Some of it certainly does, but probably not all of it, since there were doubtless additions. The argument advanced in this chapter is that the Jeremiah oracles, among which we would include Jer. 31:31–34, look forward to a return within a measurable time, although not immediately, and that they therefore envisage an actual community of men and women faced with the practical problems of carrying out the covenant. Nevertheless, it must be recognized that not all authorities would agree.

15. The Glory of YHWH Shall Be Revealed

BACKGROUND READING: Job 1–27; 29–31; 38–40:14; 42; Isaiah 40–55.

The Problem Posed by the Exile[1]

The fifty years following the destruction of Jerusalem in 587 B.C.E. were years of anguish of mind and near despair for the people of Judah, since what had happened seemed to most of them to have gone beyond the bounds of reason. The sheer magnitude of the disaster appalled them, and they did not know what to make of it. They were now divided into two groups: the leading citizens who had been removed to Babylon, and the ordinary people who had been left behind to carry on as best they might. They did, it is true, communicate with each other, but the journey could take as long as three months. The shape and structure of their society had been shattered and Jerusalem itself, the center of administration and of the worship of YHWH, lay in ruins. Their life, therefore, was bereft of all cohesion and coherence.

Moreover, most of them could see no possible alternative to this patternless life, since all political action was denied them. The Babylonians were not hard taskmasters, and both the exiles and those many Judeans who had remained behind were free to rebuild their economic livelihood. What they were certainly not free to do was to organize politically, for this would have been construed by the authorities as rebellion. But in the ancient Middle Eastern world religious and political activity were closely interwoven. As we have already seen, when people in those days spoke of their gods they were speaking of the fundamental Reality which endowed an otherwise chaotic world with order and meaning. Their society and the state were for them the practical

1. For the historical background to this period, see Peter R. Ackroyd, *Exile and Restoration* (Philadelphia: The Westminster Press, 1968), Chaps. I and II; Bright, *History*, Chap. 9; Noth, *History*, pp. 288–99.

consequence of this, for in their view the state was founded upon experience of Reality, and was designed to maintain the true order of things. "Freedom of religion," if they had used such a term, would have meant for them freedom to take political action in order to construct a coherent and orderly society as they understood it. Consequently, the prohibition of political action for the people of Judah severely limited their religious activity and gave to life in the Exilic period an irrational quality. There was a sharp cleavage between the order of the world as they had previously understood it to be and the situation in which they now found themselves.[2]

Yet another irrational element in their eyes was the gigantic disproportion between the punishment and the sin. The destruction of the nation seemed to them to be total, but they could not bring themselves to accept the argument that the national sinfulness had been commensurate with the destruction. On the one hand, the second generation of exiles began to say with some reason that it had not been they who had sinned and yet it was they who were suffering: "The fathers have eaten sour grapes, and the children's teeth are set on edge."[3] On the other hand, the older generation could remember Jerusalem as it had been before its ruin and all that the Temple worship had meant to them. Moreover, they could remember the tremendous efforts at reform made under King Josiah. They had been brought up on the stories of Abraham, and they knew that there had been more than ten righteous in the city, and yet it had become like Sodom and Gomorrah.[4] In face of this frustration many became cynical, and denied all possibility of change. "The days grow long," they said, "and every vision comes to nought."[5] Indeed they claimed that their right was disregarded by their God.[6]

We have already seen in the last chapter something of the disclosure of God through the prophets Jeremiah and Ezekiel in response to this sense of desolation. We must now turn to two other bodies of literature which speak to this crisis, the book of Job and chapters 40–55 of Isaiah.

The Revelation of God to Job

The book of Job is almost certainly later than Isaiah 40–55, but it is convenient to deal with it first, because we shall have rather less to say about it, important though it is. The structure of the book is far from

2. "The experience is to be seen in the reality of the situation, as distinct from mere theorizing about it. The reality of being in Exile, in the unclean land, produced a shattering reaction in Ezekiel—as no doubt in others who experienced it" (Ackroyd, *Exile and Restoration*, p. 108).

3. Jer. 31:29; Ezek. 18:2.   4. See Gen. 18:22–33.

5. Ezek. 12:21.   6. Isa. 40:27.

simple.[7] There is clearly an introduction and an epilogue in prose, enclosing between them an extended, and always magnificent, poetic section. This, however, is complex. The main poem is a debate between Job and his three friends, concluding with the appearance of God in a whirlwind and his address to Job, to which Job responds by complete submission and repentance "in dust and ashes" (42:1–6). There are two divine speeches at the end, but most scholars believe much of the second to be a later addition. Also added later were the speeches by Elihu, which interrupt the whole argument (chaps. 32–37) and the superb poem on Wisdom (chap. 28). We are therefore left with the main argument of the book, which is developed as follows:

A. A prologue written in prose (chaps. 1–2).
B. The poetic section:
    1. Job's lament (chap. 3).
    2. First cycle of speeches (chaps. 4–14).
    3. Second cycle of speeches (chaps. 15–21).
    4. A third cycle of speeches, which is unfortunately incomplete, and in the last section jumbled (chaps. 22–27).
    5. Job's final defense, consisting of three parts: "As I was" (chap. 29); "As I am now" (chap. 30); and a formal declaration of innocence (chap. 31).
    6. The appearance of God in the whirlwind, and Job's submission (chaps. 38–40:14 and 42:1–6).
C. Epilogue in prose (chap. 42:7–17).[8]

It seems probable that the date of the book in its original form is fairly soon after the return from Exile, somewhere toward the end of the sixth century or beginning of the fifth, and that the well-known legendary figure of Job is used to represent the exiled people of Judah, who had been overwhelmed by catastrophe, as drastic and complete as had been the disasters that happened to Job.[9] It is important that the events of the prologue and the whole poetic debate take place in Edom, traditionally famous for its wise men.[10] The prologue speaks freely of God as YHWH, and quite naturally because the writer himself belonged to the people of Judah, but Job and his friends, being Edomite, never use the name in their debate.[11] They use instead a variety of other words.[12] However, when God appears to Job in the whirlwind, he is quite specifically called YHWH.[13]

---

7. See additional notes.   8. See additional notes.
9. Job 1:13–19; 2:7–8. See also additional notes.
10. Jer. 49:7–16.
11. See additional notes.
12. In the debate *El* and *Eloah* are each used thirty-three times; *Shaddai* twenty-four times, and *Elohim* twice.
13. Job 38:1; 40:1, 3, 6; 42:1.

We have to recognize, therefore, that during the debate these Edomites do not speak with an understanding of YHWH at all, but talk throughout in terms of the static, or at best cyclical, understanding of the world, which characterized the nations among whom the people of Judah found themselves, and whose thinking they tended so often to adopt. Job opens the debate by asking, "Why is light given to a man whose way is hid?"[14] Why is man born at all, and into a world which he cannot comprehend or understand?

> For the thing that I fear comes upon me,
>   and what I dread befalls me.
> I am not at ease, nor am I quiet;
>   I have no rest; but trouble comes.
>
> Job 3:25–26

This is the question which the three friends attempt to answer. They all see "God" in terms of the natural world of observable phenomena, and all their illustrations are drawn from that world.[15]

> Can papyrus grow where there is no marsh?
>   Can reeds flourish where there is no water?
> While yet in flower and not cut down,
>   they wither before any other plant.
> Such are the paths of all who forget God.
>
> Job 8:11–13

Job himself uses similar examples:

> Ask the beasts, and they will teach you;
>   the birds of the air, and they will tell you;
> or the plants of the earth, and they will teach you;
>   and the fish of the sea will declare to you.
>
> Job 12:7–8

Not once do they discuss the problem of history. It is not surprising that in their discussion they make no progress, and that the debate itself is circular and repetitive. The form of the poem reflects its content.

The difference between Job and the friends is that they insist that the world conceived in this manner makes sense, while he is equally insistent that it no longer makes sense, because something has happened to him which in these terms is incomprehensible. He claims that it is quite insufficient to explain the suffering in terms of "sin," because the disaster has little relation to whatever sin there may have been.[16]

14. Job 3:23.
15. One Contributor objected that this was not true of Job 5:17ff. However, the things listed in this passage were thought of as the normal misfortunes of mankind.
16. This is the point of Chapters 29–31.

The₁ appears YHWH, whom they have never mentioned, and he appears as Creator. He praises Job for having spoken the truth about the event (42:7), but rebukes him severely for saying that the world is essentially meaningless (38:2). The argument of the book, therefore, is that the world cannot be explained in terms of permanence, and the rejection of all change, but must be understood in terms of creation, of the continual making of new things. The writer recalls his readers to the recognition that creation and salvation are closely allied to each other, and that the baffling tragedies of the present are to be given meaning by that which is still to be brought forth. Order and meaning, he claims, are created by the dynamic power of YHWH; they are not inherent in the nature of things.

Isaiah of Babylon

We come now to that prophet "whose mouth Yahweh filled with words of an unparalleled splendour,"[17] and who gathered together the whole Israelite knowledge of God into so rich a feast that we can do no more than taste of it. It is fitting that his name is unknown, for in all his teaching he directed the eyes and hearts of men to YHWH alone. For him this was the absolute, and the only, Reality. We must, however, give him some name, and since his poems have been preserved for us today in Isaiah 40–55 we call him the "Second Isaiah," or "Isaiah of Babylon," to distinguish him from that Isaiah who taught in Jerusalem in the time of the Assyrians. His teaching has as its background the meteoric rise to power of Cyrus the Great, who in hardly more than a decade raised Persia from a petty kingdom to master of the greatest empire the world had ever known. In 550 B.C.E. he captured Ecbatana, the capital of the Medes; in 546 Sardis and the kingdom of Croesus fell to him; and in 539 he conquered Babylon itself. The entire Middle Eastern world was never to be the same again.

We have no reason to believe that the exiles viewed this dramatic advance with enthusiasm, or regarded Cyrus as a possible savior. On the contrary, all the evidence suggests that they thought of themselves as helpless and forgotten people, who would gain nothing from the siege of Babylon but renewed suffering and who could expect no more of Cyrus than the exchange of one overlord for another. Indeed, when Isaiah used Israelite royal titles for Cyrus, calling him the Shepherd and the Anointed of YHWH[18] and said that he would be the one to rebuild Jerusalem, they

17. Gerhard von Rad, *The Message of the Prophets,* trans. D. M. G. Stalker (New York: Harper & Row, 1972), p. 206.
18. Isa. 44:28; 45:1.

greeted the statement with frank disbelief and brought upon themselves the prophet's sternest condemnation:

> Woe to him who strives with his maker,
>   an earthen vessel with the potter!
>
> .   .   .   .   .   .
>
> Will you question me about my children,
>   or command me concerning the work of my hands?
> I made the earth,
>   and created man upon it;
> it was my hands that stretched out the heavens,
>   and I commanded all their host.
> I have aroused him [i.e., Cyrus] in righteousness,
>   and I will make straight all his ways;
> he shall build my city,
>   and set my exiles free.
>
> Isaiah 45:9–13

From the beginning to end of these poems the sacred name of YHWH is insisted upon, to make clear that only in these terms can one speak at all of "God," of the ultimate and final Reality. To use other names, to attribute ultimate value to something other than YHWH, is here presented as a complete misunderstanding of the fundamental nature of things.

> I am YHWH, that is my name;
>   my glory I give to no other,
>   nor my praise to graven images.
>
> Isaiah 42:8[19]

Isaiah of Babylon says more emphatically than any other prophet had said before him that there is nothing at all in the world or in human experience which is not in some authentic sense the "work" of YHWH, that is to say, which does not derive its meaning and its value from YHWH.

> I am YHWH, and there is none else.
> I form light, and I create darkness;
>   I make good, and I create evil;
> I am YHWH, the doer of all these things.
>
> Isaiah 45:6–7[20]

If these words are taken seriously, they put an end to all human pretension, and forbid us to use our own values for words like "good" and "evil," for they speak of "such vast perspectives that we can only tremble

19. See also Isa. 41:25; 43:3, 13, 15; 44:6; 47:4; 48:2; etc.
20. Trans. D. B., reading "good," as in the Dead Sea Scrolls, in place of *shalom,* or "peace."

and fall silent."[21] They mean that when we look at foreign nations we must not see them as people to be treated as enemies or exploited for our advantage, but as men and women placed there by the direct intention of YHWH, for when he "formed the earth and made it . . . he did not create a chaos, he formed it to be inhabited."[22] We must know ourselves as but a very small part of the gigantic purposes of God.

But if this should be the truth about YHWH, then there is no reason to be afraid, or to dread the days that are to come, nor to seek solace for the menacing world that encloses us by studying the occult, or giving credence to pseudo-scientific interpretations,[23] for YHWH is he

> who frustrates the omens of babblers,
>   and makes fools of the diviners;
> who turns the wise men backward,
>   and makes their knowledge stupid.
>
> Isaiah 44:25[24]

If this is the truth, then are we delivered from any fear that there could come upon us any power which could obliterate YHWH,

> Fear not, nor be afraid;
>   have I not told you from of old and declared it?
>   And you are my witnesses!
> Is there any God besides me?
>   There is no rock; I know not any.
>
> Isaiah 44:8

Therefore, we have no need to cling to the past, but may go with boldness into the future.

> Remember not the former things,
>   nor consider the things of old.
> Behold I am doing a new thing;
>   now it springs forth, do you not perceive it?
>
> Isaiah 43:18–19

> Go forth from Babylon, flee from Chaldea,
>   declare this with a shout of joy, proclaim it,
> send it forth to the end of the earth;
>   say, "YHWH has redeemed his servant Jacob!"
>
> Isaiah 48:20

---

21. Claus Westermann, *Isaiah 40–66: A Commentary,* trans. D. M. G. Stalker (Philadelphia: The Westminster Press, 1969), p. 162.
22. Isa. 45:18.
23. For instance, the spate of books which has come out recently on the lines of Däniken's *Chariots of the Gods.*
24. Trans. D. B.

Isaiah of Babylon does not for one moment minimize the tragedy of the Exile, nor does he pretend that the people have not suffered.

> This is a people robbed and plundered,
>   they are all of them trapped in holes
>   and hidden in prisons;
> they have become a prey with none to rescue,
>   a spoil with none to say, "Restore!"
>
> Isaiah 42:22

He makes no claim that their captivity was not the result of their own wrongdoing and folly, nor does he build the morale of the people by suggesting that after all they were not so very guilty. He is no less insistent than the earlier prophets that the destruction of Jerusalem was a punishment from YHWH, and says that even now the people have not understood the significance of it.

> Who among you will give ear to this,
>   will attend and listen for the time to come?
> Who gave up Jacob to the spoiler,
>   and Israel to the robbers?
> Was it not YHWH, against whom we have sinned,
>   in whose ways they would not walk,
>   and whose law they would not obey?
> So he poured out upon him the heat of his anger,
>   and the might of battle;
> it set him on fire round about, but he did not understand;
>   it burned him, but he did not take it to heart.
>
> Isaiah 42:23–25

He agrees with Jeremiah and Ezekiel that the disaster itself is the foundation of confidence for the future. The very fact that the people of Judah are not in Jerusalem, but helpless and despondent exiles in Babylon, is abundant evidence of the validity of the Yahwist interpretation of the world. Stupid, ignorant, willful and even wicked they may well be, but if the question is raised of which interpretation of the world is valid, they can testify with absolute assurance that those who had stood in the council of YHWH[25] had indeed foreseen what was going to happen.

> Bring out the people who are blind, though they have eyes,
>   who are deaf, though they have ears!
> Let all the nations gather together,
>   and let the peoples assemble.
> Who among them can explain this,
>   and make us understand what happened in the past?

25. Jer. 23:22.

Let them bring witnesses in support of their case,
or let them listen and say, "That is the truth."
"You are *my* witnesses," says YHWH.

Isaiah 43:8–10[26]

Although these poems are uncompromisingly monotheist, the point at issue is not that of monotheism versus polytheism. The scathing denunciations of the gods of Babylon were not made because they were many, but because they were irrelevant. Earth-shaking events were taking place in the decade between 549 and 539, and the whole pattern of the world as men then understood it was dissolving around them. For centuries the Fertile Crescent had been largely self-contained, subject to the domination of either Egypt or Mesopotamia, but this familiar pattern was now to be no more. For more than a thousand years to come the dominant powers were to be Persian or European, and the management of the world was to be made on their terms.

Yet all the wisdom of the ancients had had no expectation of this devastating decade, nor could they explain it when it happened. They could not explain it, because their understanding of the world allowed them no recognition that anything of this kind could occur, and they could make no provision for a complete restructuring of the world. "Prediction was not confined to Israel; there were many forms of it in the Gentile world, including Babylon; it does not, however, stay the course, but comes to nothing. . . . Among the plethora of oracles addressed to Babylonian and Assyrian kings, not a single one has come down to us proclaiming the complete and final fall of the empire. They are almost entirely oracles of salvation, which were proved to be futile by the events which led to the fall of Assyria and later to the fall of Babylon."[27] Claiming to know the ultimate Reality of the world, in terms of which everything could be understood, and its meaning and pattern perceived, the learned found themselves confronted by something which they could not interpret, because it was entirely outside their experience.

The religion, culture and political structure of the Babylonian empire was neither idiotic nor merely superstitious. It was built upon a very careful and studious examination of the whole visible world of nature, including the heavenly bodies, about which they were well informed. Upon the basis of this accumulated knowledge they argued, very reasonably, that the structures of the world were not subject to change. In their understanding the alternative to the world as they knew it was not a new kind of world but chaos. The authorities in Babylon, who were responsible for administering the political structures of their day, could not conceive of their

26. Trans. D. B.
27. Westermann, *Isaiah 40–66*, pp. 156–57.

destruction. "Indeed, the belief that civilization must collapse unless one's own state or empire prevails in international affairs is probably common to all great political organisms."[28]

> Secure in your wicked ways you thought, "No one is looking."
> Your wisdom betrayed you, omniscient as you were,
>   and you said to your self,
> "I am, and who but I?"[29]
> Therefore evil shall come upon you,
>   and you will not know how to master it;
> disaster shall befall you,
>   and you will not be able to charm it away;
>   ruin all unforeseen
> shall come suddenly upon you.
> Persist in your spells and monstrous sorceries,
> maybe you can get help from them,
>   maybe you will yet inspire awe.
> But no! in spite of your many wiles you are powerless.
> Let your astrologers, your star-gazers
> who foretell your future month by month,
>   persist, and save you!
> But look, they are gone like chaff.
>
>   .   .   .   .
>
>   So much for your magicians
> with whom you have trafficked all your life:
> they have stumbled off, each to his own way,
>   and there is no one to save you.
>
> Isaiah 47:10–15 (NEB)

He accused the Babylonian gods of being no gods at all, because they could not, in his view, provide any meaning for the past, or explain the character of history and advise men about the kind of thing that could happen to them. Nor could they bring about any change.

> Set forth your case, says YHWH;
>   bring forth your proofs, says the King of Jacob.
> Let them bring them, and tell us
>   what is to happen.
> Tell us the former things, what they are,
>   that we may consider them,
> that we may know their outcome,
>   or declare to us the things that are to come.

---

28. Herbert Butterfield, *Man on His Past* (Boston: Beacon Press, 1960), p. 118.

29. This is a claim to have the quality of God, i.e., to provide the source of all meaning and authority.

> Tell us what is to come hereafter,
>   that we may know that you are gods;
> Do good, or do harm,
>   that we may be dismayed and terrified.
> Behold, you are nothing,
>   and your work is nought.
>
> Isaiah 41:21–24

The Maker of New Things

As made known through these poems, YHWH is indeed the "Absolutely Other." This is not to say that there is no contact or communication, for the entire universe is seen to be his handiwork, and there is nothing which is not given its existence and meaning by him. Yet, there is an absolute distinction. YHWH stands transcendent and alone. He alone *is*. Everything else has a derivative existence. He does not draw his significance from any other source, nor does anything else contribute to the order of the world which he has made.

> Who has directed the Spirit of YHWH,
>   or as his counsellor has instructed him?
> Whom did he consult for his enlightenment,
>   and who taught him the path of justice,
>   and taught him knowledge,
>   and showed him the way of understanding?
>
> Isaiah 40:13–14

He is *other,* because nothing at all can be compared to him.

> To what then will you compare me,
>   that I should be like him? says the Holy One.
>
> Isaiah 40:25

He is other than the gods, and in no way to be thought of in those terms. He is other than man, and not to be understood as a projection of human hopes and fears.[30] He is other than every civilization, culture and political achievement. Ultimate Reality is always other than what we think it is. We speak of establishing a "just and lasting peace," but if the words of Isaiah of Babylon are indeed the words of truth, then we must recognize that this is a "Babylonian" concept. With all our might, with all our political acumen, with all our deep concern for society, what we achieve is never truly peace, it is never wholly just, and it is certainly never lasting. It is none of these things because, despite our very best endeavors,

30. Isa. 55:8–9.

it takes no account of the "other," and by no manner of means can it provide for what is not yet part of our experience.

The "other" is always the absolute Reality by which every human system is judged. We are bound to strive for political solutions in the tense and troubled areas of the world, both abroad and in our own country, but no political decision can take into account every factor, or provide for all the peoples. These "others" are the test of the solution and of how long it will endure. No society can provide adequately for all its members, let alone making provision for all who are left outside, and it is these "others" who are the ultimate judges of the society, not those who are at home in it.

But it goes very much deeper than this. The experience of other people, even within our own country, is itself altogether other, and by no device can we ever make that experience our own, though of course we may study and learn about it. The white person cannot ever truly know what it is to be black, for he has already been shaped and given his identity by his experience of white culture; nor can the black person know what it is to be white. What confounds us all the time in our dealings with the Russians, the Chinese, the Indians, the Arabs, or any foreign people is that in them, in their culture and experience, we are confronted by Reality, fundamental and ineradicable. But we meet it always as the Other. It is not Reality *as we know it,* and we can neither encompass it nor incorporate it into our system. But otherness is not part of the *nature* of other people. The Russians, the Chinese, the Arabs, and the people of Southeast Asia are men and women just as we are, and we make a terrible mistake if we do not recognize this fact. What is "other" about them, and what demonstrates the Reality with which we must come to terms, is their *history.* It is their history that has made them what they are.

Isaiah of Babylon is able to assert that YHWH is indeed the right name for that ultimate Reality, in terms of which both the natural world and historical events can be understood, because YHWH had always been known as Creator. YHWH is for him not merely the one who made the world once upon a time, but the one who eternally makes the world, shaping and building it for a purpose. Therefore, to know YHWH is to perceive that basic to all understanding is the recognition of dynamic power continually at work, and constantly bringing into existence. He is not speaking of some inherent life force, but of purposeful creation, breaking down what is false, putting right what is wrong, overthrowing disorder and establishing order, and forever making new things, making indeed a new world flooded with light and glory. To know YHWH is for Isaiah of Babylon to know creation as an existential fact and as the primary condition of our existence.

> From this time forth I make you hear new things,
>   hidden things which you have not known.
> They are created now, not long ago;
>   before today you have never heard of them.
>
> Isaiah 48:6–7

Since the old patterns are destroyed and new structures brought into being, those who in the past had been misfits, in bondage to a system which allowed them no room, are brought out of the prison house into the light.[31] Nay more, they are to go home:

> Sing for joy, O heavens, and exult, O earth;
>   break forth, O mountains, into singing!
> For YHWH has comforted his people,
>   and will have compassion on his afflicted.
>
> Isaiah 49:13

> Comfort, comfort my people,
>   says your God.
> Speak tenderly to Jerusalem,
>   and cry to her
> that her warfare is ended,
>   and her iniquity is pardoned,
> that she has received at the hand of YHWH
>   double for all her sins.
>
> Isaiah 40:1–2

Creation and the Exodus are companion themes in these poems, but it is to be a new Exodus, and not merely a repetition of the old,

> for you shall not go out in haste,
>   and you shall not go in flight.
>
> Isaiah 52:12[32]

It is truly a new world that is being made.

Finally, this driving power of creation, this persistent making of new things, this refusal to tolerate a static and permanent world requires that everything comes to fruition in that which is other. Nothing exists for its own sake, and nothing is fulfilled in itself. The mind of man is here turned wholly away from himself toward the other in which he must find his fulfillment. This is declared to be the pattern of history. Cyrus is brought to Babylon in order that the exiles may go back to Jerusalem,[33] and the exiles return to Jerusalem in order that the *torah* and the *mishpat* of YHWH may go out to the entire world.

31. Isa. 49:9.
32. Contrast Exod. 12:11; Deut. 16:3.
33. Isa. 44:24–45:6, 19.

> It is too light a thing that you should be my servant
> to raise up the tribes of Jacob
> and to restore the preserved of Israel;
> I will give you as a light to the nations,
> that my salvation may reach to the end of the earth.
>
> Isaiah 49:6[34]

It is in this sense that we must understand the place of the "Servant," whose identity and function have so exercised the minds of the scholars.[35] Both prophet and people are included under this term, for, as we have seen in the Psalms, Israelite thought drew no sharp distinction between the individual and the community of which he was a part.[36] Although the language of political appointment is used of the Servant in 42:1, his function is not that of political authority, nor is he ever to exercise dominion over others. His role is to be the very opposite of self-assertive, for all power and authority belong to YHWH alone.

> He will not cry or lift up his voice,
> or make it heard in the street.
>
> Isaiah 42:2

> YHWH God has opened my ear,
> and I was not rebellious,
> I turned not backward.
> I gave my back to the smiters,
> and my cheeks to those who pulled out the beard;
> I hid not my face from shame and spitting.
>
> Isaiah 50:5–6

He is "despised and rejected by men,"[37] but it is the greatest mistake to imagine that he is therefore "smitten by God and afflicted,"[38] for the appalling tragedy of his suffering is given meaning by the fact that it is this which will bring all men and women face to face with the Reality first disclosed at Sinai, and deliver them thereby from bondage to all fallacious and purely human interpretations of the world.

> Kings shall shut their mouth because of him;
> for that which has not been told them they shall see,
> and that which they have not heard they shall understand.
>
> Isaiah 52:15

34. See additional notes.
35. The "Servant Songs" are usually said to be found in Isa. 42:1–4; 49:1–6; 50:4–11; and 52:13–53:12, but many scholars today would see these passages as an integral part of the main body of material, rather than as separate poems, and this is probably correct.
36. See above, Chap. 12.
37. Isa. 53:3.   38. Isa. 53:4.

He shall see the fruit of the travail of his soul and be satisfied;
by his knowledge shall the righteous one, my servant,
make many to be accounted righteous.

Isaiah 53:11

These words were written concerning the unhappy exiles in Babylon and also their prophet, who seems himself to have been rejected, but the meaning does not cease with them. Long ago Amos had shown that the history of Israel was not of a different kind from that of the surrounding nations, and that the activity of YHWH must extend throughout the whole world.[39] Therefore, when we observe the suffering of others, we should perceive, not that they have been duly punished for their sins, but always that they have been "wounded for *our* transgressions, and bruised for *our* iniquities."[40] The comfortless troubles of the needy are abundant in the world today, in the present Middle East, in Bangladesh, in Southeast Asia, in Africa, in Latin America and in our own country. It is easy to say of the multitude of refugees, of the starving and desolate, of the millions without work, of the underprivileged, and of all those whose hopelessness drives them to acts of violence, that the fault lies in themselves. It is easy to claim, as has often been said about such people, that they are shiftless by nature, lazy and not ready to work, that they are blind to their own follies, that they elect corrupt governments, and do nothing to help themselves. If Isaiah of Babylon is right, we must say instead that "the Lord has laid upon them the iniquities of us all," and that "by their stripes we are healed."[41]

Of course, they are not themselves pure and righteous, but at the very beginning Isaiah of Babylon had insisted that the suffering of his people far exceeded their sin.[42] This superabundance of suffering, he said, was the result of wanton exploitation by the most powerful nation of the time.[43] He argued that this "people robbed and plundered"[44] were the direct evidence of YHWH and his servant.[45] Therefore, those people whom we are so ready to despise and condemn may well prove to be our salvation, for they make known to us the truth about this world of time and history in which all our activities are conducted. They are the others[46] and through them and what has happened to them we are confronted

39. See above, Chap. 13.
40. Isa. 53:5. Although the kings, i.e., the rich and powerful, are said to have been reduced to horrified silence by the sight of the afflicted Servant, the comments that follow are their reaction. The "kings" and the "nations" were the mighty political forces of that time, and it would seem that if we are to apply this oracle to our own day, then we must ask whether the United States, at present the most powerful country in the world, does not stand in the place of those kings.
41. Isa. 53:6, 5   42. Isa. 40:2. See also additional notes.
43. Isa. 47:5–6.   44. Isa. 42:22.   45. Isa. 43:10.
46. See additional notes.

by the truly Other, absolute in judgment upon all human pretension and yet in mercy even now making that new world in which we can begin again.

ADDITIONAL NOTES TO CHAPTER 15

7. The date, the structure and the meaning of Job have all provoked the greatest possible discussion among scholars, and the interpretations have been very varied. For further information see among recent commentaries: Nahum N. Glatzer (ed.), *The Dimensions of Job: A Study and Selected Readings* (New York: Schocken Books, 1969). Robert Gordis, *The Book of God and Man* (Chicago: University of Chicago Press, 1965). Marvin H. Pope, *Job* (Garden City, N.Y.: Doubleday, 1965). H. H. Rowley, *Job* (New York: Thomas Nelson and Sons, 1970); also "The Book of Job and Its Meaning," *From Moses to Qumran* (New York: Association Press, 1963), pp. 141–86. Norman H. Snaith, *The Book of Job: Its Origin and Purpose* (London: SCM Press, 1968). Samuel Terrien, *Job: Poet of Existence* (Indianapolis: Bobbs-Merrill, 1957); "The Book of Job," in *Interpreter's Bible*, III, 1954.

8. Many scholars believe the prose sections to be by a different author, but the position adopted here is that although the prose tale of Job is much older, it has been adopted by, and owes its present written form to, the author of the main poem. Therefore, if we are to understand the argument, we must take both the poem and the prose sections together. It should be added that there is no suggestion here that the additional poetic material is unimportant. It is of great importance both theologically and for understanding the later Wisdom literature. All that is being said is that this material cannot be used as evidence for the meaning of the book of Job as originally written.

9. "Satan" in this story is not the devil of later thought, but rather "the satan," i.e., the adversary, who formed part of the "Council of YHWH."

A number of Contributors, with the support of many scholars, rejected this identification of Job with the Judean exiles (e.g., Pope, *Job*, pp. xxix, xxxiii-xxxiv). For the alternative view see, e.g., Terrien, *Job: Poet of Existence*, pp. 26–33; and "Job," *IB*, III, pp. 897ff. Admittedly, the interpretation put forward in this book is not that most commonly adopted, and there is not here sufficient room to develop it. We do suggest, however, that many scholars seem to be unduly influenced by modern ideas of the individual and by the concept of creation as something which happened once in the distant past. Second Isaiah certainly thought of creation as the constant activity of YHWH and the ancient Hebrew mind would have had no difficulty in seeing the individual as representing the community, without having been told to do so.

11. Job does speak of YHWH in 12:9, but this is generally thought to be a copyist's error, based upon a reminiscence of Isa. 41:20. He also uses it in his word of resignation in the prologue (1:21), but here the writer was probably quoting a well-known phrase, which he was not free to change. It would be false to assume that the four speakers were really talking about YHWH, even though they did not mention him, on the grounds that the writer knew quite well that there is only one God. One must remember that the specific name used for God played an emphatic part in ancient Hebrew thought, and consequently in their minds to use another name would be equivalent to speaking about another god.

34. This view has recently been challenged by Fredrick Holmgren in his book,

With Wings as Eagles (Chappaqua, N.Y.: Biblical Scholars Press, 1973), but he overstates his case. He insists upon Isaiah's "nationalism," and rejects any "missionary" role for the Servant. These, however, are modern concepts, which are out of place in a discussion of the Exilic period.

42. Here Isaiah seems, at least on the surface, to be in conflict with Ezek. 18, but Ezekiel was attacking the claim that "we haven't done anything wrong; it all happened before we were born." The usual translation of Isa. 40:2 has been kept here, but Ackroyd (*Exile and Restoration,* p. 122), following von Rad, translates the second line as "the equivalent for all her sins." It is well to be reminded of the problems of translation as we conclude our study, and of the importance of not being dogmatic in interpretation.

46. In Paraguay, "out of 500 people interviewed, 415 considered Indians to be inferior human beings; pressed further, 385 of them said the Indians were animals. Only Christian baptism, they said, could possibly give the Indians the right to be considered human beings!" (José Chipenda, "Indian Injustice," *One World,* Geneva, Switzerland, No. 4, 1975, p. 19). This kind of attitude is appallingly widespread. It was common in the 1950s to hear French people insist that the Algerians were "merely savages." The British term "wog" for people of the Middle East illustrates a similar contemptuous view. The extraordinary phrases, "body count" and "oriental human beings" (as distinct from "Americans" who were real people) used during the Vietnam war belong to the same category.

Chronological Table

1950–1800 Middle Bronze Age. Probable period of the Patriarchs.
1500–1300 Late Bronze Age. The Egyptian Empire, and the Hebrews under Egyptian domination.
1290–1224 Rameses II Pharaoh in Egypt. The Exodus probably occurred during his reign, perhaps round about 1280.
1250–1200 The Israelite "takeover" in Canaan.
1200–1020 The period of the Judges. In this same period the Philistines settled in the southern coastal area, and began to extend their control over much of Canaan.

THE UNITED MONARCHY

1220–1000 The reign of Saul.
1000– 961 The reign of David.
961– 922 The reign of Solomon.

THE DIVIDED MONARCHY

Judah, the Southern Kingdom	Israel, the Northern Kingdom
922–915 Rehoboam.	922–901 Jeroboam I.
913–873 Asa.	
873–849 Jehoshaphat.	876–869 Omri.
	869–850 Ahab.
837–800 Joash.	842–815 Jehu.
	815–801 Jehoahaz.
800–783 Amaziah.	801–786 Jehoash.
783–742 Uzziah (Azariah)	786–746 Jeroboam II.
735–715 Ahaz.	722 Fall of the Northern Kingdom.
715–687 Hezekiah.	
687–642 Manasseh.	
640–609 Josiah.	
609–598 Jehoiakim.	
597–587 Zedekiah.	
587 Destruction of Jerusalem.	

EXILE IN BABYLON

539 Conquest of Babylon by Cyrus the Great.

N.B. The early dates are only approximate, since we do not have the information to give them exactly. Also, in the lists of the kings of Judah and Israel those with only brief reigns have been omitted.

For Further Reading

In the course of preparing this book some three hundred books and articles were used. The Contributors were asked to submit every two weeks critical reports of all that they had read so that we might prepare a list of those books which might prove useful as additional reading, at both the introductory and the more advanced levels. It soon became clear, however, that not all people find the same book helpful and in some cases there was sharp disagreement, one person saying that a book was essential and another that it was of little value. The following lists are based upon the reports and upon our discussions, but it must be recognized that they are no more than a suggestion. Other people would certainly choose differently.

A. TEXTBOOKS

It was generally agreed that the beginner needs some kind of reference book to guide him or her through the confusing waters of the *Testament*. There are quite a number of good textbooks of this kind, the five listed here having been singled out by some of the Contributors for special praise.

Anderson, Bernhard W. *Understanding the Old Testament*. 3rd. ed. Englewood Cliffs, N.J.: Prentice-Hall, Inc., 1975. This emphasizes the covenant and is excellent for the history and the archaeological background.

Buck, Harry M. *People of the Lord: The History, Scriptures and Faith of Ancient Israel*. New York: Macmillan, 1966. This concentrates more upon the religion and its historical development. It is particularly helpful for its frequent commentaries upon specific biblical passages.

Gottwald, Norman K. *A Light to the Nations: An Introduction to the Old Testament*. New York: Harper & Brothers, 1959. This concentrates upon the theology within the framework of a literary history, but it is not as well illustrated as Anderson.

Kuntz, J. Kenneth. *The People of Ancient Israel: An Introduction to Old Testament Literature, History, and Thought*. New York: Harper & Row, 1974. This has the advantage of being the only one in paperback. It emphasizes biblical motifs and theology and of those listed here comes closest in its approach to the thinking behind this book.

Sandmel, Samuel. *The Hebrew Scriptures: An Introduction to the Literature and Religious Ideas*. New York: Alfred Knopf, 1963. An extremely

209

readable book, which begins with the Prophets, then studies the Writings, and concludes with the Narrative Books.

All these books have good bibliographies, those by Anderson and Kuntz being the most recent, and they should be consulted by anyone wishing to pursue his or her studies further.

B. FOR FURTHER READING

All the Contributors were asked to list the ten books which they had found most useful in helping them to understand the ideas discussed in *God and History in the Old Testament*. When these lists were compared with each other, it was found impossible to limit the number to ten, for all the following were recommended as particularly helpful.

Albright, W. F. *The Biblical Period from Abraham to Ezra: An Historical Survey.* Rev. ed. New York: Harper & Row, 1960. An excellent brief introduction to Israelite history by one of the greatest of American biblical scholars.

Anderson, Bernhard. *Out of the Depths: The Psalms Speak to Us Today.* Using the form-critical approach, this short book is a quite admirable introduction to the Psalter.

Anderson, G. W. *The History and Religion of Israel.* London: Oxford University Press, 1966. A good introductory review of the subject, which was strongly recommended by all who read it, though one or two were a little critical of the style.

Buber, Martin. *I and Thou.* 2nd ed., trans. R. Gregor Smith. New York: Scribner, 1958. This was the most widely read book, and the general opinion was that it is a difficult book, needing more than one reading, but immensely worthwhile. A fascinating study of the concept of "encounter," which is basic to understanding biblical thought. There is now a new translation by Walter Kaufmann (New York: Scribner, 1970).

Chesnut, J. Stanley. *The Old Testament Understanding of God.* Philadelphia: The Westminster Press, 1968. This is a helpful and readable book, which takes the reader through Israelite history to show the development of certain concepts and understanding of God, though not at a very profound level.

Dentan, Robert. *The Knowledge of God in Ancient Israel.* New York: Seabury Press, 1968. More than one person found this helpful in a number of ways as providing a guide to the development of the concept of God and of the cult in ancient Israel.

Eliade, Mircea. *The Sacred and the Profane: The Nature of Religion.* New York: Harvest Books, 1959. Strongly recommended as an introduction to religious man's understanding of myth and ritual.

Frankfort, Henri, Mrs. H. A. Frankfort, John A. Wilson, and Thorkild Jacobsen. *Before Philosophy: The Intellectual Adventure of Ancient Man.* Baltimore: Penguin Books, 1972. A quite admirable study of the religious thinking of ancient Egypt and Mesopotamia.

Goldman, Solomon. *The Ten Commandments*. Chicago: Chicago University Press, 1956. This won high praise for its insight and as providing an excellent introduction to the study of *torah*.

Guthrie, Harvey. *God and History in the Old Testament*. New York: Seabury Press, 1960. This book won a rather mixed reception. Some readers spoke of it as excellent, stimulating and impressive, but some others spoke of it as helpful, though not outstandingly so.

Harrelson, Walter. *From Fertility Cult to Worship*. Garden City: Doubleday, 1969. All agreed that this is easy to read and most called it helpful and informative. One Contributor, however, found it of little value.

Heaton, E. W. *The Old Testament Prophets*. Rev. ed. Baltimore: Penguin Books, 1961. This was generally agreed to be a valuable and readable introduction to prophetic thought, considered as a whole rather than individually.

Heschel, A. J. *The Prophets*. New York: Harper & Row, 1962. This is much longer than Heaton's book, but everyone who read it spoke of it as extremely readable and helpful as an introduction.

Hillers, Delbert R. *Covenant: The History of a Biblical Idea*. Baltimore: Johns Hopkins Press, 1970. An excellent brief introduction to the concept of "covenant" in the light of recent research. Strongly recommended.

Lys, Daniel. *The Meaning of the Old Testament: An Essay on Hermeneutics*. Nashville: Abingdon Press, 1967. Written from a decidedly Christian point of view, this is not a very easy book for the beginner, but all who read it agreed that it was extremely useful for its discussion of revelation through history.

Mackenzie, R. A. F. *Faith and History in the Old Testament*. Minneapolis: University of Minnesota Press, 1963. Paperback ed., Macmillan, New York. A very helpful introduction to the subject for the person without any previous knowledge.

Mellor, Enid B. (ed.). *The Making of the Old Testament*. Cambridge: Cambridge University Press, 1972. A good brief introduction, though concentrating entirely on the form-critical approach.

Ott, Heinrich. *God*. Tras. Iain and Ute Nicol. Edinburgh: The Saint Andrew Press, 1974. A short but excellent discussion of the understanding of God as person.

Otto, Rudolf. *The Idea of the Holy*. Trans. John W. Harvey. New York: Oxford University Press, 1923. The first ten chapters are particularly important. This is a classic work, and should be read by everyone, though the beginner may find it rather difficult the first time.

Otwell, John H. *I Will Be Your God: A Layman's Guide to Old Testament Study*. Nashville: Abingdon Press, 1967. (Published in Britain under the title, *A New Approach to the Old Testament*). This was generally agreed to be one of the best introductions to the writings of the *Testament* for the ordinary reader, with special emphasis upon form-criticism, though some readers commented that the first half was better than the second.

Ringgren, Helmer. *The Faith of the Psalmists*. Philadelphia: Fortress Press,

1963. An excellent book, balancing the scholarly study by a strong emphasis upon individual, personal religion.

Robinson, H. Wheeler. *Inspiration and Revelation in the Old Testament*. Oxford: Clarendon Press, 1967. This won high praise among those who read it. One reader commented, "To say that I thoroughly enjoyed this book would be an understatement; it is clear, concise and fascinating."

Rowley, H. H. *The Growth of the Old Testament*. New York: Harper & Row, 1963. A very clear and readable introduction to the formation of the books of the *Testament,* with special emphasis upon the development of the documents.

Scott, R. B. Y. *The Way of Wisdom*. New York: Macmillan, 1971. This is the best introduction to the Wisdom literature for the general reader, though some Contributors commented that while it is very easy to read, it sometimes lacks depth.

Von Rad, Gerhard. *The Message of the Prophets*. Trans. D. M. G. Stalker. New York: Harper & Row, 1972. This is a revision of the greater part of Vol. II of his *Old Testament Theology*. All those who read it agreed that it is a magnificent book and quite essential for anyone who wishes to understand the prophets, but some suggested that beginners might be well advised to begin first with either Heaton or Heschel.

Westermann, Claus. *Creation*. Trans. J. J. Sullivan. Philadelphia: Fortress Press, 1974. This little book was read by a large number of the Contributors and was strongly recommended by all of them as a quite excellent introduction to the first eleven chapters of Genesis.

————. *The Praise of God in the Psalms*. Trans. K. R. Crim. Richmond: John Knox Press, 1965. This also was very highly praised.

Wolff, Hans Walter. *The Old Testament: A Guide to its Writings*. Trans. Kenneth R. Crim. Philadelphia: Fortress Press, 1963. Very short, but good. Recommended for the complete beginner, but not for the more advanced student.

C. FOR MORE ADVANCED STUDY

1. *History:*

Bright, John. *A History of Israel*. 2nd ed. Philadelphia: The Westminster Press, 1972.

Bruce, F. F. *Israel and the Nations*. Exeter: Paternoster Publishers, 1969.

Herrmann, Siegfried. *A History of Israel in Old Testament Times*. Trans. John Bowden. London: SCM Press, 1975.

Noth, Martin. *The History of Israel*. Trans. Stanley Godman. New York: Harper & Row, 1960.

Robinson, Theodore H. *A History of Israel from the Exodus to the Fall of Jerusalem, 586 B.C.* Oxford: Clarendon Press, 1932.

Of these five it might be best to begin with any one of the first three. Bright represents the thinking of the majority of American scholars at the present time; Bruce is outstanding among the more conservative of the British scholars; and Herrmann binds together German and American thinking. All these books are straightforward and clear. Noth is somewhat more difficult, though extremely important. Robinson's book is now outdated, but still well worth reading.

2. *Religion (Israelite and general Middle Eastern):*

Albright, W. F. *Archaeology and the Religion of Israel.* Baltimore: Johns Hopkins Press, 1956.

————. *From the Stone Age to Christianity.* Baltimore: Doubleday, 2nd ed., 1957.

————. *Yahweh and the Gods of Canaan.* Garden City: Doubleday, 1968.

Alt, Albrecht. *Essays on Old Testament History and Religion.* Trans. R. A. Wilson. Oxford: Basil Blackwell, 1966.

De Vaux, Roland. *Ancient Israel:* Vol. I. *Social Institutions;* Vol. II, *Religious Institutions.* New York: McGraw-Hill, 1965.

Fohrer, Georg. *History of Israelite Religion.* Trans. David E. Green. Nashville: Abingdon Press, 1972.

Frankfort, Henri. *Ancient Egyptian Religion.* New York: Harper & Row, 1961.

Gray, John. *The Canaanites.* New York: Frederick A. Praeger, 1965.

Hooke, S. H. *Babylonian and Assyrian Religion.* Norman: University of Oklahoma Press, 1963.

James, E. O. *Myth and Ritual in the Ancient Near East.* London: Thames and Hudson, 1958.

Johnson, Aubrey R. *The One and the Many in the Israelite Conception of God.* Cardiff: University of Wales Press, 1961.

————. *Sacral Kingship in Ancient Israel.* Cardiff: University of Wales Press, 1955.

Kapelrud, Arvid S. *The Ras Shamra Discoveries and the Old Testament.* Trans. G. W. Anderson. Norman: University of Oklahoma Press, 1963.

Kaufmann, Yehezkiel. *The Religion of Israel.* Chicago: University of Chicago Press, 1960.

Oppenheim, Leo. *Ancient Mesopotamia.* Chicago: University of Chicago Press, 1970.

Pritchard, James B. *The Ancient Near East in Pictures relating to the Old Testament.* Princeton: Princeton University Press, 1954.

————. (ed.). *Ancient Near Eastern Texts relating to the Old Testament.* 2nd ed. corr. and rev. Princeton: Princeton University Press, 1955.

Ringgren, Helmer. *Israelite Religion.* Trans. David E. Green. Philadelphia: Fortress Press, 1966.

————. *Religions of the Ancient Near East.* Trans. John Sturdy. Philadelphia: The Westminster Press, 1973.

Robinson, H. Wheeler. *The Religious Ideas of the Old Testament.* London: Duckworth Press, 1964.

Rowley, H. H. *Worship in Ancient Israel.* London: S.P.C.K., 1967.

Saggs, H. W. F. *The Greatness that Was Babylon.* New York: New American Library, 1968.

Smith, W. Robertson. *Lectures on the Religion of the Semites.* New York: KTAV Publishing House, 1969.

Vriezen, Th. C. *The Religion of Ancient Israel.* Philadelphia: The Westminster Press, 1969.

Wright, George Ernest. *The Old Testament against Its Environment.* Naperville, Ill.: Alec R. Allenson, 1950.

All these are important books, but some are more difficult than others. Among those which might be suggested for "starters" are: Albright's *Archaeology and the Religion of Israel* and *Yahweh and the Gods of Canaan,* Frankfort's *Ancient Egyptian Religion,* Gray's *The Canaanites,* Hooke's *Babylonian and Assyrian Religion,* Robinson's *Religious Ideas of the Old Testament,* Vriezen's *Religion of Ancient Israel* and Wright's *Old Testament against Its Environment.* De Vaux's *Ancient Israel* and the two books by Pritchard are essential both for detailed study and for reference. A selection of the more important sections of the last two has been published in one volume under the title of *The Ancient Near East: An Anthology of Texts and Pictures,* edited by James B. Pritchard (Princeton University Press, 1958). Smith's *Religion of the Semites* was first published in 1889, but it still remains a classic work on primitive religion.

3. *Theology:*

Bright, John. *The Kingdom of God: The Biblical Concept and Its Meaning for the Church.* Nashville: Abingdon Press, 1953.

Eichrodt, Walther. *Theology of the Old Testament.* Trans. J. A. Baker. Philadelphia: The Westminster Press, Vol. I, 1961; Vol. II, 1967.

Heschel, A. J. *God in Search of Man.* New York: Farrar, Straus & Giroux, 1955.

Imschoot, Paul van. *The Theology of the Old Testament.* Trans. K. Sullivan and F. Buck. New York: Desclee, 1965.

Jacob, Edmond. *Theology of the Old Testament.* Trans. A. W. Heathcote and C. J. Allcock. New York: Harper & Row, 1958.

Koehler, Ludwig. *Old Testament Theology.* Trans. A. S. Todd. Philadelphia: The Westminster Press, 1957.

McKenzie. John L. *A Theology of the Old Testament.* Garden City: Doubleday, 1974.

North, C. R. *The Thought of the Old Testament.* London: Epworth Press, 1948.

Rowley, H. H. *The Faith of Israel: Aspects of Old Testament Thought.* Philadelphia: The Westminster Press, 1957.

Snaith, Norman. *The Distinctive Ideas of the Old Testament.* London: Epworth Press, 1947.

Von Rad, Gerhard. *Old Testament Theology.* Trans. D. M. G. Stalker. New York: Harper & Row, 1962–65.

Probably the easiest three books with which to begin are those by Bright, Heschel and North. Only the first part of Heschel's book is directly relevant to the *Testament,* but all those who read it spoke of it with deep appreciation. McKenzie has a useful section on the problems of writing a theology of the Old Testament. Anything by Rowley is worth reading, and *The Faith of Israel* is no exception. He has a straightforward style, a profound understanding of the *Testament* and a voluminous knowledge of the work of other scholars. Both Eichrodt and Von Rad are two-volume works of great importance, that by Von Rad being particularly valuable for its study of God as made known to ancient Israel in terms of its history.

4. *Archaeology:*

Albright, W. F. *The Archaeology of Palestine.* 4th ed. fully rev. Baltimore: Penguin Books, 1960.
Gray, John. *The Archaeology of the Old Testament.* New York: Harper & Row, 1965.
Kenyon, Kathleen M. *Archaeology in the Holy Land.* New York: Frederick A. Praeger, 1960.
Wright, George Ernest. *Biblical Archaeology,* 2nd ed. Philadelphia: The Westminster Press, 1962.

The books by Albright and Kenyon are rather more technical; it would be better to begin with Gray and Wright. All four are highly recommended.

For books on special aspects of Old Testament study the reader is advised to consult the bibliographies in Anderson, *Understanding the Old Testament* and Kuntz, *The People of Ancient Israel.*

INDEX

Index of Biblical References

APOCRYPHA

NEW TESTAMENT

Index of Authors

Index of Subject

Numbers in italics represent chapters in which the subject is dealt with passim.